T0349395

"A brilliant book . . . about remarkable women who loved, and needed, to walk—and why. . . . A great read."
—Lisa O'Kelly,
Associate Books Editor at
Guardian and Observer

"I read this book with hunger and it fed me well. . . . Abbs-Streets's perspective rivets for the richness of her inquiry, her persistence, her interaction with the works of her chosen women—and the fact that she walks their walks."
—**Ms. Magazine**

"Exhilarating."
—**Country Walking**

"Abbs-Streets is a witty and engaging guide, seamlessly weaving her own experience with those of her 'walking women,' all of whom discovered that the simple act of taking one step at a time can be the most powerful—and defiant—of all."
—Abbott Kahler,
New York Times bestselling author of
The Ghosts of Eden Park

"A triumph . . . I felt as though I were being lifted, carried up to peaks."
—Charlotte Peacock,
author of Into the Mountain:
A Life of Nan Shepherd

"I couldn't put it down. Quite extraordinary. . . . written in such a free flowing, readable style. I'm in awe."
—**Maggie Humm,**
author of *Talland House*

"I love how the act of walking connects the lives of these women—and how it transforms them. It makes me want to go for a hike just to see what happens. *Windswept* satisfies my endless appetite for untold stories of women's history, filling important gaps and bringing their stories into light."
—**Mia Kankimäki,**
author of *The Women I Think About at Night*

"Amazing. . . . lovely, haunting, inspiring and so well done."
—**Amy Von Lintel,**
author of *Georgia O'Keeffe's Wartime Texas Letters*

Windswept

Walking the Paths of Trailblazing Women

Annabel Abbs-Streets

 TIN HOUSE / Portland, Oregon

Copyright © 2021 by Annabel Abbs

First US Edition 2021
Printed in the United States of America
First paperback edition 2024

Manufacturing by Sheridan

Library of Congress Cataloging-in-Publication Data

Names: Abbs, Annabel, 1964– author.
Title: Windswept : walking the paths of trailblazing women / Annabel Abbs.
Description: Portland, Oregon : Tin House, 2021. |
Includes bibliographical references.
Identifiers: LCCN 2021019401 | ISBN 9781951142704 (hardcover) |
ISBN 9781951142780 (ebook)
Subjects: LCSH: Walking—Anecdotes. | Walking—Psychological aspects. |
Women hikers—Biography.
Classification: LCC GV199.5 .A23 2021 | DDC 796.51—dc23
LC record available at https://lccn.loc.gov/2021019401

Paperback ISBN 9781963108132

Tin House
2617 NW Thurman Street, Portland, OR 97210
www.tinhouse.com

Distributed by W. W. Norton & Company

1   2   3   4   5   6   7   8   9   0

To Saskia, the perfect walking companion

Contents

Walking Women

This book explores the walking lives of eight remarkable women, some well-known, some less known. For the sake of context and clarity, I have decided to introduce them here, at the very outset.

FRIEDA LAWRENCE NÉE VON RICHTHOFEN (1879–1956) was the German wife of D. H. Lawrence, but also the author of a memoir, *"Not I, but the Wind,"* and several essays. She was the model and inspiration for numerous characters in Lawrence's novels and stories, playing such a pivotal role in his work that she's often considered his collaborator.

GWEN JOHN (1876–1939) was a Welsh artist who lived and painted in France all her adult life. Now regarded as one of Britain's pre-eminent female artists, she spent most of her career in the shadow of her brother, Augustus, and her lover, Auguste Rodin. She is best known for her luminous portraits of women, one of which (*Dorelia by Lamplight, at Toulouse*) recently sold for over half a million dollars at auction in New York.

CLARA VYVYAN NÉE COLTMAN ROGERS (1885–1976) was an Australian-born writer who grew up in England, where she earned a first-class science degree and trained as a social worker, later working in the slums of east London. She nursed during World War I, then began a career of writing and market gardening from her home in Cornwall. An avid traveller and walker, she wrote over twenty books, all of which have now faded into obscurity.

NAN (ANNA) SHEPHERD (1893–1981) was a Scottish author, poet, essayist, and educator, whose memoir of hillwalking in the Cairngorms, *The Living Mountain*, is now justly recognised as one of the great pioneering pieces of nature writing.

SIMONE DE BEAUVOIR (1908–86) was a French writer, existentialist philosopher, and feminist theorist, now best known for her radical (at the time) feminist work *The Second Sex*. Her output was prolific: diaries, memoirs, essays, letters, and award-winning novels. Although she lived in Paris all her life, she escaped regularly to rural and remote landscapes.

GEORGIA O'KEEFFE (1887–1986) was an American artist, now considered one of the most significant artists of the twentieth century, and an icon in her own right. Famed for her flower and landscape paintings, she began her career in Texas but spent the latter half of her life in New Mexico. Both places inspired her until she died.

Also included, but without their own chapters, are:

DAPHNE DU MAURIER (1907–89) was a hugely popular English writer, best known for her novels *Rebecca*, *Frenchman's Creek*, *My Cousin Rachel*, and *Jamaica Inn* (all of which have been adapted for screen). She also wrote plays, short stories, biographies, and books about Cornwall, where she lived, not far from Clara Vyvyan. Much of her work reveals her deep love of wild landscapes.

EMMA GATEWOOD (1887–1973), better known as Grandma Gatewood, was an American pioneer of extreme hiking and the first woman to solo-walk the Appalachian Trail (2,050 miles), a hike she repeated three times, latterly aged seventy-five.

Careful readers will notice that some women are referred to by their surname and others by their first name. After much thought, I decided to use the name that felt right as I wrote. Frequently this was also the name that I imagined each subject would prefer. For example, I felt that Simone de Beauvoir would prefer to be known as Beauvoir rather than as Simone. Likewise O'Keeffe.

Frieda Lawrence (née von Richthofen) acquired four surnames during her lifetime but always thought of herself as simply Frieda. I suspect she would have laughed uproariously at my sleepless nights fretting over what to call the women in this book.

While a painter of Gwen John's stature should perhaps be referred to as John, the John name was appropriated early on by her artist brother, Augustus, leaving Gwen in a nominal vacuum later expressed through a disinclination to sign her paintings. For this reason she is Gwen here.

Clara Vyvyan published under both her maiden name (Coltman Rogers) and her married name. But because Vyvyan also resembles a first name (as does John), I felt the text read more clearly when I called her Clara. As Daphne du Maurier appears in the same chapter, she is Daphne.

Where I felt the choice of name made no difference, I deferred—in male literary tradition—to the surname.

For the purposes of this book, I have defined a *walking woman* as one who walked for pleasure, not drudgery, and who was able to make something of her walking rather than simply doing it of necessity. Sadly, this made it difficult to find historic women of colour or women who walked with their children or impoverished women. These women rarely had the opportunity to head off into the wilds for catharsis, adventure, or pleasure. However, they are unsurpassed when it comes to sheer mileage and endurance.

Finally, I have used the words *wild, remote, unpeopled,* and *rural* in their most general forms to indicate landscapes that are essentially non-urban and often unpopulated. The terms are not intended to denote specific topographies or geographies.

Introduction

Where Are the Women?

For once I felt truly free.

—MATHILDE BLIND (1841–96),
unpublished autobiographical fragment
on walking solo in the Alps, 1860

I'm walking the green crest of a hill, following my shadow which is long and blue and blurred. To my right lies the ocean, sequinned with sunlight. To my left the ridge falls away, turning to hedged squares of mustard, saffron, russet. The wind stirs in my hair and plucks at my shadow legs which are stretched surreally tall upon the grass. My brain trundles over and over, trying to locate the landscape: Where am I?

And then the image is gone and I'm elsewhere, crouched tight against the rocky flank of a mountain. Above me the sky is black and pitted. A vast orange moon lulls in the darkness. Someone is pulling my hand, urging me up. I stand and walk, step by steady step, along a narrow flinty path doused with moonlight. A stone pierces my boot, prodding the blistered sole of my foot. Again my mind churns, struggling to place my disconnected body. Where am I?

For hours I slip from one wilderness to another: from dazzling light to plunging dark; from air that is damp and sullen to air that flares with frost and ice; from oak forests to sandy moors to the ripening grass of . . . of where? Sounds come to me: the crunch of shingle beneath my feet; poplars soughing in the wind; the blunt teeth of sheep tearing at turf; the rawking of crows; the song of a thrush. I hold on to the sounds, storing them in the backs of my ears, hoping they'll reveal where I am, where I've been, where I'm going.

When I open my eyes, the room is blindingly white. A nurse in a blue dress is cranking up my bed. Tens of wires run from the back of my hand to a saline drip with a flashing red eye. The thrush sings dimly in my ears, but the drip is louder, bleeping urgently into my cubicle. I'm not marching over hills with a stiff breeze tugging at my hair. Nor am I sidling along the vertiginous lip of a mountain. I'm in a hospital bed. Slowly the wildernesses of my mind fade away. The electronic stutter of the drip amplifies, blotting out the hectoring crows, the chanting thrush. I remember where I am: London's Charing Cross Hospital. I've fallen and cracked my skull on the pavement, a fall so violent my neighbour will later say she thought it was the supermarket delivery man dropping a stack of palettes on the road.

There's nothing wrong with my legs, but I can't walk. Every movement is accompanied by rolling waves of giddiness. As if the earth tilts constantly beneath me. As if I'm drunker than I've ever been—or ever want to be.

"Your dinner's coming," says the nurse, pushing back the plastic curtains that surround my bed.

"When can I walk?" I don't want to eat, or drink. I want only one thing—to walk.

"Not long now," she says. But I'm not listening. Through the open door I see the corridor and the room opposite. I see people walking, balancing trays and carrying bags, a child dragging a plastic scooter, a man on a walker. Some are moving quickly, almost jogging. Others are strolling or limping or slowly scuffing their slippered feet along the linoleum.

I watch them, mesmerised by their movement. From somewhere I cannot locate—my feet? my gut? my head?—a deep inner ache swells. I try to place the ache, to attach it to my injury. But it's nothing like the hammer thud of my head. And it has none of the tenderness of a bruise or the sting of a cut. As I stare at the people walking past my cubicle, the ache spreads through me, pricking my eyes, catching in my throat, coiling in my stomach.

In that moment two thoughts strike me:

I have never fully appreciated what it is to walk, stride, shuffle, hobble, run. To be bipedal.

Without my legs I am captive. A prisoner.

My inner ache feels like a yearning, a longing to have the privilege of my legs returned to me. But it's a longing rimmed with regret—regret for all those years in which I walked without thinking. And for all those squandered years of sitting—in cars, in front of screens, at tables and desks and bars, in deckchairs and beds and baths.

The nurse peers into my eyes. "Oh dear . . . cheer up! Are your family visiting tonight?"

I blink and nod, even as I make a vow to myself: When I can walk again, I will do so at every opportunity. And I will nurture my legs as if they're the most precious possession I have.

"You'll be walking round this room in no time," says the nurse, as if she can read my thoughts.

Through my fuzzy-edged eyes I take in the plastic and concrete of my room, the cinder-block view through the window.

Everything is grey and white. It smells of . . . detergent? bleach? The heavy thrum of traffic drifts through the double glazing—sirens, horns, the screech of a motorbike. There is something not-right about walking here.

"I have to go back," I croak.

The nurse frowns, then smiles. "I'll bring your painkillers and refill your drip."

"I need to walk in the country . . . not cities or hospitals . . ." I slur to her departing back.

I close my eyes and make another pledge—all holidays, from this point forward, will be walking holidays. Our youngest child is seven. Our oldest is fourteen. No more lounging on a beach. No more lying by a pool. From now on, we're climbing stiles and mountains, walking over hills and through valleys, hiking along cliffs and ambling through forests . . . My wonderful, car-loving, speed-adoring, screen-gazing children will walk.

⌒

I grew up carless. My parents could not drive and steadfastly refused to take lessons. We walked because we had to. But we also walked, daily, for pleasure.

Much later, I fell in love with a mountaineer and my childhood ambles became mountainous treks through the remotest regions of the Himalayas, over the Alps, through the Peak District, the Lake District, the Brecon Beacons, and the Black Mountains of Wales. The mountaineer disappeared, eventually replaced by Matthew, who also loved walking and whom I married. Our weekends and holidays were spent hiking: Snowdonia, the South Downs, the Devon coastal path, Dartmoor, the Yorkshire moors, Mount Kilimanjaro.

The walking ceased abruptly with the birth of our first child. After our third child was born, I swapped a career I loved for the tyranny of domesticity. In an instant my world shrank.

⌒

Raising small children in a confined urban space left me hankering for greenery, for remoteness, for air. There were mornings when I craved trees so viscerally I thought my head would split, sending all remaining shreds of sanity into orbit.

I dragged my children to the local park. But this was a poor reconstruction of the supple, unenclosed spaces I was pining for. Instead I began reading about walking and nature, becoming adept at holding a book in one hand while using the other to load the washing machine, wipe noses, clean grazes, and build Lego. Every night I struggled through a few more paragraphs before sinking into exhausted, broken sleep.

For a while, reading was enough. I roamed imaginatively over mountains tipped white with snow, through ancient forests where light scattered from the high branches of trees, along vernal valleys fringed green with willow. In my mind's eye I rambled beside dashing streams and tumbling rivers, across moors and dales and waterlogged fens, while falcons and hawks wheeled above.

But something gnawed at me. Something I couldn't articulate. A vague, uneasy sense that these books were not really *for* me, that they were merely palliative. I tried to fend off this growing sense of disconnect, because without my vicarious reading I feared I might crack beneath the weight of domestic restraint.

⌣

One evening, as I turned off my lamp, my eye was caught by the books on my bedside table. I looked at the spines and noticed something I'd never noticed before: every book carried the name of a man. I felt a baffled surprise, because although I considered myself a feminist, I'd never paid much attention to the gender of an author when I bought or borrowed a book.

My book buying in those days involved a harried trip to the children's section of my local bookshop. As we rushed out—scooters, stuffed animals, stroller bulging and tipping with bags—I'd grab something from a passing table for myself, ideally with a bird or trees on the cover.

Seeing them stacked, spine by spine, a line of men, made me pause. I wondered if this was why I felt an odd disconnect, if this was why my reading felt more like medication than inspiration.

⌣

Eight days after my fall, I returned from the hospital to rest and let the plates of my fractured skull knit together. I was walking very slowly, on the arms of friends and family, but my brain was teeming with Big Ideas for Big Walks.

I looked through my books and noticed, again, the absence of women. As I tottered round my kitchen, my blundering brain turned over and over. I couldn't shake the image of rugged men striding out, sticks in hand, wind whisking through their hair, barely a domestic care upon their muscular, untroubled shoulders.

The juxtaposition between the compressed, constricted space of female domesticity and the vast vistas through which these unburdened men roved hung vividly and disruptively in my wide-awake mind. These "walking men" had mothers, wives, even children. But where were they? Why were they so rarely mentioned? Could it be that the absent women were creating the very homes that enabled these men to step out with such nonchalance and exuberance?

I wasn't angry with these men (most of whom were dead anyway), but I was angry at their unexamined dominance. And I was angry with myself for not expending more effort in seeking out books by women. For surely women had walked—and written about their experiences of walking?

I started exploring online, prowling around second-hand bookshops, investigating library catalogues. Women remained elusive. As Rebecca Solnit, one of the few female writers on the subject of walking, wrote: "Throughout the history of walking . . . the principal figures . . . have been men."[1]

Every now and then, Virginia Woolf's name appeared. I'd spent my teenage years in the shadow of the South Downs, where Woolf had lived and walked for much of her adult life. My parents were still there, so whenever I got the chance I plotted a Woolf route and began tracing her footsteps over the

South Downs. On these walks I felt my equilibrium return, my mood improve. I could breathe again.

I also felt exhilarated, walking as I imagined Woolf had walked—taking in the soft, sheep-nibbled curves of the Downs, the wrinkled silver sea in the distance, the larks springing from beneath my feet, the slack summer sun. I imagined Woolf's curious, disobedient mind drawing it all in, absorbing it, filtering it, transmuting it into art.

But the same old question kept nagging at me: Surely women, other than Virginia Woolf, had walked? Surely other women had written about the consolations of walking in rural places? A few names cropped up: Dorothy Wordsworth, the Brontës, Elizabeth Bennet in *Pride and Prejudice* . . . but none were accorded the celebrity and attention of the men piled up beside my bed.

⌒

My hunt for female walkers became more rigorous: although the wilderness has typically been the preserve of men and their yomping, touring, climbing, hunting, shooting, and fishing exploits, more and more accounts (often unpublished or out of print) of women walking long and remote distances were coming to light.

In the cool, modern interior of Munich's Alpine Museum, I found sepia photographs of women walking and climbing in tight corsets, trailing skirts, and wide-brimmed hats. And yet most had no recorded name. The men who appeared throughout the museum—alongside first editions of their books, examples of their paintings and photographs, sets of their original crampons—had named and dated plaques. But the women stared out from photographs, nameless and identity-less. I asked the museum assistant who they were.

She shrugged. "We do not know. Perhaps wives or sisters."

⌒

If walking in wildness is such a powerfully restorative and rejuvenating experience (and science increasingly bears this out), why has it been denied to women? Or has it? And if it hasn't, where are they? And why don't we know about them?

Many of the women who boldly embarked on hikes—and could have inspired later generations—have been carelessly lost in the fog of history. Some, like Nan Shepherd, are creeping back, their accounts rediscovered, reprinted, lauded. Others, like Simone de Beauvoir, are well-known, but not for their walking. Many more have disappeared, the casualties of a self-referencing male canon of walking and nature literature, of men-only hiking and climbing clubs, of publishing firms historically run by men, of misguided concerns for female safety.

And it's my fault too—for not seeking out these overlooked women earlier, for not promoting the small circle of women quietly walking and writing beyond the limelight. A circle, incidentally, that has grown enormously—and to great acclaim—in the last decade.

As I began researching—digging around in libraries and archives—I slowly amassed a collection of evidence suggesting that women, like men, have always walked. History is littered with invisible females for whom rural walking was a daily necessity, but in unpublished and out-of-print guidebooks, in letters, manuscripts, and paintings, I began finding women who also walked for inspiration, consolation, and liberation. Moreover, I had a growing sense that these women walked with infinitely more bravery, audacity, and complexity than their famous male counterparts. Unlike most male walkers, they hadn't served in the military or been educated in the ways of navigation or self-defence. To be seen alone in the wilds risked their social reputation as well as their physical safety, an outcome few men had cause to worry about. To hike as these women did required a level of courage—rashness, even—unimaginable to us now.

What sparked their sudden reckless urge to escape? What drove them to carry a rucksack for miles and miles, often alone, frequently in isolated and remote places? How did their experiences affect them?

I knew I didn't have enough space, either in my head or between the pages of a moderately sized book, to include all the remarkable women I'd discovered. So I chose a group of women for whom rural or wild walking had proved life-changing: Frieda Lawrence née von Richthofen; Gwen John; Clara Vyvyan née Coltman Rogers in partnership with Daphne du Maurier; Nan Shepherd; Simone de Beauvoir; Georgia O'Keeffe; and—in brief—Emma Gatewood.

What I discovered was often shocking, frequently dramatic, sometimes tragic, but always profoundly illuminating. These women walked not to "enjoy all the freedom a man is capable of having" (as the philosopher Jean-Jacques Rousseau did), nor for exercise, nor because the drudgery of circumstance necessitated it. These women walked in order to find minds of their own. They walked for emotional restitution. They walked to understand the capabilities of their own bodies. They walked to assert their independence. They walked to *become*.

Through the lens of these women and the landscapes in which they walked, I came to understand truths not only about them but about myself. Although I didn't know it at the time, my journey in their footsteps was also an attempt to walk and write myself free.

Because, like so many of the women I investigated, I too was walking away from something. As I walked in their footsteps—over deserts and plains, through valleys and mountain ranges, along canals, rivers, and the coast, imaginatively across maps—the *thing* I was escaping began to take shape. It wasn't quite as I expected. It was bigger, more unwieldy. And so this book became as much about tracks of thought as the tracks worn by female feet. And as much about how we walk as about how we become.

1

In the Beginning

I can only meditate when I am walking. When I stop I cease to think; my mind only works with my legs.

—JEAN-JACQUES ROUSSEAU, *Confessions*, 1782

As a child I walked, every day, through a verdant Welsh valley. We referred to this walk—along a wide, rutted track that ran beside a shallow stream—as "going up the *cwm*." *Cwm* is Welsh for valley. A Welsh person would say "*y cwm*." But we weren't Welsh. We were a self-exiled English family struggling to adopt the language and ways of the remote Welsh community my parents had chosen to live in. "The *cwm*" was neither wholly Welsh nor wholly English. Rather like us.

We were walking in the *cwm*, one damp, gusty day, when my father told me I was an experiment. I was almost ten, old enough to imagine glass pipettes and blue flames and showers of crimson sparks. In our house, science was never mentioned. So the word *experiment* thrilled me with its illicit connotations as well as seeming to confer upon me a magical status.

"What sort of experiment?" I asked, curiously.

"You've been raised to feel always at home," he replied. "Wherever you are and whoever you're with."

His words filled me with confusion. I couldn't imagine a time when I wouldn't *be* at home, let alone *feel* at home. The earlier images of pipettes, copper flames, and magical incantations slipped away, replaced by a vague feeling of unease. I understood then that one day I would be different, another person altogether. And I would be elsewhere. Presumably without my family. But— bafflingly and, I felt, a little disloyally—I would still feel *at home*.

"Is that why we don't go to school now?" I asked, wondering if my previous teacher, the enormous, black-clad Miss Jones, had realised I was an experiment. My little sister had also stopped going to school, which meant that perhaps she too was an experiment. I wasn't sure I wanted my sister to be an experiment.

My father lifted his gaze skywards and watched a buzzard rise and fall, one hand shading his eyes against the pared light. "You don't go to school because you can learn more out here, in this valley, than you'll ever learn in that hole of hell." He took his hand from his brow and swept it across the dripping green vista.

"But why am I an experiment?" I persisted.

"We've brought you up according to the principles of a genius called Rousseau," he replied.

I felt bewildered. I had never heard of Roo-so before. My father explained that Mr. Jean-Jacques Rousseau was a famous philosopher who wrote a book about a boy called Emile. Emile, it turned out, was the inspiration for my upbringing. Like him, I was being taught to "bear the buffets of fortune." Like him, I was learning "the keen sense of living" by planting seeds and watching butterflies. Mr. Roo-so (and his imagined Emile) also walked everywhere. Like us. "The book was banned and burnt," my father added with an extravagant flourish of his walking stick. "They made bonfires of it, just weeks after it was published. People danced around the flames." He shook his head, then paused and fixed his eyes on mine. "I'll recite you the opening line: 'Everything is good as it leaves the hands of the Author of things; everything degenerates in the hands of man.'"[1]

I cast an anxious glance at his walking stick. The end looked a little scuffed and scraped from where he'd used it to beat back brambles and nettles. Was that a sign of something *degenerating in the hands of a man*?

"Rousseau's ideas helped start the French Revolution," he added. "But *Emile* is his greatest book, and you're built on it. *Emile* is in your blood."

I didn't like the idea of having sprung from a boy. And I certainly didn't like the idea of having a boy in my blood. I would have preferred a princess. Preferably an adopted princess. But I liked the idea of "French." And I liked the idea of "revolution." Both words carried an indefinable whiff of something thrilling and exotic.

⌣

In those days, my parents were part of a revolution of their own making. My father, a poet, and my mother, an ex-journalist from *Vogue* magazine, had escaped to a small Welsh village to live a rustic, elemental life, growing fruit and vegetables and publishing obscure journals that they posted to their friends.

From this outpost on the bony coast of West Wales, we walked. We walked as a means of transport. We walked to forage for food. We walked to keep warm. We walked to protest. We walked because the landscape was beautiful and unspoilt. We walked because Jean-Jacques Rousseau prescribed it.

We did other things, of course: we learnt Welsh; we discovered how to live handsomely on a poet's pittance; we read (and read and read); we painted and crayoned; we cooked and gardened; we had chickens, cats, and a pig. But most of all, we walked.

⌒

There were absences in our Welsh life that may well have contributed to our fanatical walking. We had: no car; no central heating; no telephone; no television; no bicycles, scooters, roller skates—or anything with wheels; no holidays; no freezer, microwave, or washing machine; no radio, record player, or cassette deck; no money.

These are the things that were forbidden in our house: comics; anything written by Enid Blyton; dolls with ice-cream-cone breasts and names like Barbie or Sindy; sliced white bread in a plastic bag; sweets; pop music; platform shoes.

This was also the age of: no internet; no Amazon; no Uber; no fast-food restaurants; no low-cost airlines; no screens; no coffee machines . . . or any other twenty-first-century convenience for that matter.

But neither Mr. Rousseau nor the fictional Emile had had any of these things either.

⌒

Rousseau, the guardian angel of my childhood education, was the man who elevated the simple act of walking into something quasi-mystical, a supreme means of philosophical contemplation and self-reflection. He appears in almost every book on the subject of walking. His pithy quotes adorn book covers, websites, and walking blogs. For Rousseau, walking was an expression of freedom as well as the ideal means of collating his meandering thoughts. He began walking at the age of fifteen and spent much of his adult life walking and thinking, later writing: "Never did I think so much, exist so vividly, and experience so much, never have I been so much myself . . . as in the journeys I have taken alone and on foot."[2]

My induction began in the womb. While my mother was pregnant with me, my father read aloud to her from *Emile*. Every day, as she nursed her ballooning belly in their rented bed, his sonorous voice delivered Rousseau's views on the significance of breastfeeding, the evils of swaddling, the importance of outdoor play. Even now I wonder if Rousseau's urge to walk, his restlessness, his preoccupation with freedom, penetrated my foetal unconscious.

One day, much later, my father told me that Rousseau had abandoned all five of his children, leaving them as babies on the steps of an orphanage, against the wishes of his lifelong partner. I felt sickened and unsettled by this morsel of information. How had someone who couldn't raise his own children have had such sway over my childhood? Perhaps I should have worked my way through Rousseau's oeuvre, separated the man from his ideas. Instead, I tried to find out more about Thérèse Levasseur, the seamstress and hotel maid Rousseau lived with—but refused to marry—for thirty-three years. Although she is little more than a footnote in most Rousseau biographies, a bundle of her letters turned up in 1991, enabling scholars to read of her devastation and anguish when, after several weeks of nursing their first son, Rousseau insisted the tiny boy be given away. He made the same cruel demand after each of their babies was born. Utterly dependent on Rousseau, Thérèse unwillingly complied.[3]

For a while, Thérèse's life—its flattened, circumscribed space, her constant personal tragedy—haunted me. The only way I could shake myself free was by going out and walking. Because walking is nothing less than the bodily articulation of freedom. To walk is to know that we control our limbs and muscles, that we're able to move away, move on, *escape*.

And I wanted to escape the ghost of Thérèse. It seemed to me that it was she, not the fictional, hill-strolling Emile, who was circulating in my blood.

⌒

"Did the experiment work?" I asked my father, a few months after learning I was an experiment. My sister and I still hadn't returned to school. Our days were spent walking in search of wild flowers, then identifying them in our *Guide to Welsh Flora*, sketching them on silk-thin sheets of A4 paper, and writing poems about them. We hadn't added, divided, subtracted, or multiplied for months. Numbers, like science, weren't considered important in our home. I wondered if perhaps Mr. Jean-Jacques Rousseau and his Emile hadn't bothered with mathematics either.

"The experiment isn't over yet," my father replied enigmatically.

"But I walk everywhere," I said. I was tired of walking everywhere. I wanted to go somewhere in a car. Like Sian, who lived in the farm opposite our cottage. Sian rode in a car to school. Sian travelled by car to Aberystwyth. Sometimes Sian would wave a sticky pink hand from her wound-down window as her car slicked past. Sian had a life of motorised glamour and adventure. I was sick of being an experiment. Of not going anywhere except up the *cwm* or down to the pebble-grey beach with its reek of ocean rot. I wanted to be like Sian.

"Yes, you walk everywhere," repeated my father. "Rousseau would be very proud of you."

"But I thought he was dead," I said, confused. "Anyway, why can't we have a car like everyone else?" Or a TV, or a chest freezer, or a toaster, I added in my head. Sian had all of these in her house. She also had a pair of orange plastic platform shoes that I coveted, almost as much as I coveted her car.

"Perhaps we will." He rubbed at his beard, then added, "John the farmer is taking me out in his car tonight . . . for a driving lesson."

My heart skipped. A car! We would have a car and be like normal people! My father would be a normal father. Not a crazy, stick-wielding poet. And I would be a normal girl. Not an experiment. Not veined with the blood of a long-dead French boy.

Later that evening my father returned from his driving lesson subdued and sheepish. He had turned the car over in a ditch. He and John the farmer were unharmed but the car was a write-off. He never had another lesson. And I stopped dreaming of being *normal*.

⌒

Few women of the past who chose to walk long distances in unpeopled places were thought quite *normal.*

Simone de Beauvoir was considered strange because she chose to walk alone, wearing the wrong gear. Georgia O'Keeffe was deemed odd because she walked at night and hauled enormous bones across the desert. Gwen John was regarded as peculiar because she slept out beneath trees, often with her cats. Frieda Lawrence—perhaps the most transgressive of all—was thought outright *abnormal.* After all, what *normal* mother leaves her children in order to roam the world in unencumbered poverty?

⌒

Strange. Odd. Peculiar. Abnormal. Such confining words with their primal undertow of fear, of not-understanding, of not-belonging. But I'd been raised "to live at need among the snows of Iceland, or on the scorching rocks of Malta" (thank you, Mr. Roo-so). How could I resist the lure of these wild walking women with their bold, beguiling bravado? I couldn't. But could I ever be as brave?

2

In Search of Freedom

Frieda von Richthofen

Woods, Mountains, and Lakes. Germany and
Italy. Unfamiliar Space. Memory. Clothing.
Blood to the Brain. Wonder. Children.

*Something had gone down in her, something was broken
that would never be whole again. She accepted it all, the
suffering that had left her so raw, she accepted it.*

—FRIEDA VON RICHTHOFEN,
And the Fullness Thereof, 1964

On August 5, 1912, Frieda von Richthofen, a thirty-three-year-old German aristocrat and married mother of three, awoke to the sound of rain. It was 4:30 in the morning. Quivering strips of pearly light seeped through the sides of the shutters. She opened her eyes, dimly aware of her young lover strapping up their rucksacks and humming beneath his breath. At last she was about to embark on a real adventure, the sort of escapade she'd dreamt of for the last ten years. It had been a long, dry decade in which her emotionally restrained life in a comfortable suburban house on the edge of industrial Nottingham had almost driven her mad. A couple of illicit affairs and a deep love for her young children had (just about) preserved her sanity.

Her lover was the fledgling writer D. H. Lawrence, a penniless coal miner's son whom she'd met four months earlier. The pair of them had been poring over maps and guidebooks for days, plotting a route that would take them through "the Bavarian uplands and foothills," over the Austrian Tyrol, across the Jaufen Pass to Bolzano, and down to the vast lakes of Northern Italy. "The imperial road," Lawrence later called it, where "the great processions passed as the emperors went south . . . almost forgotten, the road has almost passed out of mind."[1]

It was an exercise in escape as much as it was an adventure. They were fleeing several things: Frieda's estranged husband, Professor Ernest Weekley; her parents, who objected to her lowly choice of lover; the postal service that brought Ernest's reams of letters sent care of Frieda's mother—missives that alternately forbade and begged her to come home, and increasingly sent Lawrence into paroxysms of fury and despair.

Later, this six-week walk would become much mythologised as their "elopement." But the evidence suggests this was less an elopement than a feverish bid for freedom and an inarticulate yearning for renewal. On the first misty, sodden step of that six-week walk, Frieda began the process of reinventing herself as a woman without children, scissoring herself free from the restrictions and responsibilities that accompanied being a mother in Edwardian England. Almost overnight she transformed herself from a fashionably dressed and hatted mother and manager of multiple household staff to someone else entirely: a woman who put comfort before fashion (rural hikes have a habit of doing this), who took responsibility for her own cooking and laundry, who swapped warm, soapy baths for ice-cold pools and the latest flushing lavatory for speedy squats among the bushes. More importantly, she became a woman without children, neighbours, or a network of local friends. All this she gave up in an attempt to reclaim and reassert her place in the world.

Frieda's isolation was exaggerated by her choice of paramour. Lawrence spoke with a Derbyshire accent. He dressed in cheap clothes and came from a rough mining village. He was also six years younger than she was, at a time when women were expected to marry older men. To leave children, a comfortable home, and a successful husband broke every taboo. To leave them for a man like this was unthinkable.

In 1912, this was not how women behaved. Least of all mothers.

⌣

Frieda and Lawrence put on their matching Burberry raincoats. Frieda donned a straw hat with a red velvet ribbon round the brim. Lawrence wore a battered panama. They squeezed a spirit stove into a canvas rucksack, planning to cook their supper at the side of the road. They had £23 between them, barely enough to reach Italy. Frieda suggested they sleep rough, in haylofts, to save money. But also because she had always yearned to sleep in a cocoon of hay. And on one occasion they did, resulting in a frozen, itchy night of sleeplessness.

I think about this as I pack, 106 years later to the day. Will I manage to show the same good grace and perseverance as Frieda? She was entirely unaccustomed to walking through snow, sleeping in iced haystacks, boiling eggs on a spirit stove. And yet she never suggested turning back, or taking the train on the newly opened railway line that crossed from Innsbruck to Bolzano and on to Verona.

I have the excuse of children-and-husband-in-tow. I glance at the four backpacks, the four pairs of walking boots, the four passports. This is our first family walk without all of our children. Our eldest daughters have decided, now they're eighteen, not to come with us. Like Frieda, I'm coming to terms with a life in which I'll no longer be defined as a mother. It's an un-settling feeling, reminding me that motherhood is a continuous accumulation of losses, a lengthy severing of the umbilical cord that once bound our children to us. The freedom I longed for, when they were hanging from my apron strings, now loiters on the horizon. But instead of feeling excitement, I feel a swift pang of sadness for a life that will never be the same again.

For a second I wonder if I'll ever fully understand Frieda von Richthofen, a woman so desperate for freedom, so de-termined to find herself, that she gave up the three children she adored. Retracing her steps is my attempt to climb inside her mind, to grasp how the topography of the Alps altered her emotional landscape during this tumultuous time. "We set out gaily," she wrote in her memoir, "*Not I, but the Wind*," penned twenty-four years later. "It was a great adventure for both (of us) . . . we were happy in our adventure, free." Later she wrote of how thrilling, how "very wonderful" this adventure was. And yet this momentous episode—in which both of them stepped into the unknown and which biographers agree was one of the great highlights of Lawrence's life—is given less than twenty-five lines in her memoir. This adventure turned out to be a reckless abandoning of her old self, a dramatic desertion of all that she was. A desertion in which Lawrence was not only complicit but the driving force. For isn't that the lot of the muse? To reinvent herself as her artist master requires?

But at this nascent stage, Frieda thought of herself as infinitely more than a muse. She hadn't abandoned her family merely to in-spire a man. She was to be a *collaborator*. And to do that she needed to be free. Lawrence wanted her free. She deserved to be free. But in fleeing her staid, professorial husband and inadvertently losing her children, did she really find freedom? I squeeze Frieda's memoir into my case, alongside a posthumously published medley of her reminiscences, written sporadically over her last decade and much of it semi-fictionalised. In a letter she had described these scraps of writing as "an interesting book of a woman's life" which she "would rather have published when . . . dead." She didn't live to complete or order these fragments of writing, but they were later edited and published as *And the Fullness Thereof.* I hope they'll contain the clues that have eluded me so far.

⌒

Packing complete, I shout at my children, who prefer screen scrolling to clambering over rocks with goats: "We're going on an adventure in the mountains. You'll need something warm in case we sleep in a haystack."

"No way I'm sleeping in a haystack," mutters Saskia.

"Do I have to come?" moans Hugo. "Why are we going to Germany, anyway? No one goes to Germany on holiday."

How ironic. I'm about to retrace the footsteps of a woman fleeing her husband and children . . . but with my own, stubbornly and complainingly, in tow.

"Yeah," agrees Saskia. "You've done your German book, so why are we going there again?"

She's right. I've written the story of Frieda. A few years ago I wrote a novel about the young Frieda Weekley (as she was then), which examined her predicament, her relationship with

Lawrence, and the collateral damage of her actions. Her escape from Nottingham is one of the big set pieces of the novel. I spent years researching it, reading every letter, every account left by friends and family. But I adroitly left out the six-week mountain hike. In a single line I skated over the experience Frieda described as her "great adventure," their almost-honeymoon. I tried to include it, of course. But I couldn't seem to make it work. It felt as though I was forcing the wrong piece of jigsaw into an almost-completed puzzle. Eventually I put it aside, twisted the plot around it. And that's the mystery. Why didn't I include Frieda's big adventure?

"I left out a crucial bit and I want to find out why," I say, cryptically.

Saskia yawns. "Yeah, whatever."

We arrive at our B&B, a red-brick block above a supermarket ringing with the metallic rattle of shopping carts. This is Schäftlarn, a nondescript suburb of Munich just north of the hamlet of Icking, where Frieda and Lawrence borrowed a flat belonging to her married sister's lover. Their five weeks here were mercurial—torrid and passionate one day, distraught the next. They barely knew each other, having met a mere eight weeks before when Ernest Weekley invited his old student, Lawrence, for lunch to discuss job prospects in Germany. Poor hapless Ernest was only trying to help Lawrence. But he was half an hour late for his own lunch. And in that half hour Lawrence and Frieda engaged in the sort of sparkling flirtatious conversation that both had yearned for but never found in Nottingham. Each was a revelation to the other. Lawrence walked eight miles back to Eastwood, the mining town where he grew up, and promptly sent Frieda a card telling her she was the most wonderful woman in all of England.

She lapped up his lavish words. For the last few years she'd devoted herself to her three young children, but she'd also indulged in discreet affairs to stave off the stifling boredom of being a Nottingham hausfrau, the wife of a workaholic etymologist who—she felt—had never understood her. It was a boredom thrown into sharp relief by the excesses of her elder and younger sisters, both of whom had remained in Germany and both of whom had thrilling lives that included greater wealth, extramarital lovers, and more highly developed senses of themselves. As their lives had expanded after marriage, Frieda's had diminished.

When all three sisters began having children, the rivalry fostered by their parents during their childhood reared its ugly head again, reaching a pinnacle in the summer of 1907 when Frieda made her way to Munich and snatched her older sister's lover from beneath her very nose. The seeds of all Frieda's later transgressions lay in this powerful but short-lived romance. The object of her passion was a pioneering psychoanalyst and exponent of free love called Otto Gross. A protégé of Freud and Jung, he repeatedly insisted on her need for liberty, telling her she was "born for freedom." By the time Lawrence walked into her life she was dangling like a ripe pear—primed to "be herself." She now saw this as her purpose on earth: to be, to exist, "like a trout in a stream or a daisy in the sun," she explained in her memoir.[2]

Small wonder she was enticed away so easily. Though naturally, the story's a little more complicated. For every biographer who thinks *he* lured *her* away, there's another who believes Frieda trapped him with her feminine wiles, that poor old Lawrence never had a chance. And then there's the third biographer—the one convinced they eloped in a rush of love and passion. There's a grain of truth in all of them, of course. Nothing is black and white. We are all shades of grey.

On Friday, May 3, 1912, Frieda packed a small bag and dressed her two young daughters in their travelling clothes before giving her son a goodbye embrace and then boarding a train for London. She was off to her father's military anniversary in Metz, the city where she'd grown up and where her baronial parents still lived. She took her daughters to her in-laws in Hampstead and then made her way to Charing Cross railway station. Here, outside the ladies' waiting room, she met Lawrence. Quite by chance he was also going to Germany to stay with relatives. It was a convenient opportunity for a few days alone together.

The night before leaving, Frieda had told Ernest that she hadn't been a faithful wife. When Ernest failed to respond to her bold confession, she fled the room in tears. But there was no mention of Lawrence, no mention of wanting a divorce. Certainly no suggestion that she was leaving for good. When she boarded the boat train to Metz, she had no idea this was to be the end of her life as a mother.

Within a few days, Frieda's aborted confession fell into place. Somehow, Ernest Weekley pieced the facts together and guessed she was in Metz with a lover. He cabled her, asking if she was alone and demanding a one-word answer, yes or no. She replied: "No."

Ernest was devastated, but it was her choice of lover that particularly riled him. As Frieda noted in her memoir, Lawrence was not considered worthy of a noblewoman like herself. Lawrence, Ernest complained, was "no gentleman." To him, being a gentleman—with its implications of duty, honour, and social standing—was of huge importance. Frieda's father, the Baron von Richthofen, agreed, describing Lawrence as "a penniless lout." To many onlookers, it was Frieda's choice of lover that was her greatest transgression. But to me it's Frieda's rash decision to assert her own freedom ahead of her family's well-being that is most radical. It was a decision that was to haunt her for the rest of her life.

⌒

Frieda and Lawrence had risen and dressed in the dark, then set out beneath beech and chestnut trees dripping with white mist. We are less ambitious, lingering to eat a meaty German breakfast, then deciding to cycle the ten miles Frieda and Lawrence walked down the Isar valley. Already I'm worrying over the way my family have compromised the authenticity of this trip. How can I fully understand Frieda when she walked and I'm cycling? Isn't that cheating? I tell myself that Frieda would have cycled if she could have afforded it, if rental bikes had been available, if fat-tyred mountain bikes had existed.

We cycle down to the River Isar, a wide dash of jade green with pebbly shores that merge into leafy banks, and then into beech forests that climb steeply before falling back to the river. Our bicycle wheels slurp through a mud-bound track running alongside the Isar. The air is warm, grainy with pollen and dust, and heavy with the smell of split wood and sawn trees. We cycle past the neatest log piles we've ever seen, arranged in order of length and girth and genus. It's the dog days of summer and the leaves are beginning to crisp and curl, but above the sky blazes blue.

The blue of the sky, the blue-green of the river on our left, the green of the beech forests, the smell of tree bark and sap and gently rotting leaves, the taste of earth and leaf on my tongue ... these are things touched on by Frieda in her scant, two-paragraph account: "the solid green of the valley ... the wind ... the mountains."[3] Things I've been reading about in studies of how nature affects our bodies, brains, and emotions. Blues and greens are thought to make us calmer, less anxious. One theory suggests that when we're surrounded by blue and green, we know that food and water are nearby and our bodies relax accordingly.[4]

Dozens of studies suggest that time in nature reduces blood pressure, boosts the immune system, lifts depression, improves energy, and lowers blood-sugar levels, as well as making us less inclined to brood over problems. In *The 3-Day Effect* and *The Nature Fix*, science journalist Florence Williams tests herself in and out of nature, finding repeatedly that, in it, her blood pressure falls, while her ability to problem-solve and think laterally improves. Frieda, a pantheist since childhood, would have turned her nose up at all this science: she knew intuitively that here, walking through forests, alongside rivers and streams, over mountains, they would find the resolution they needed. Later she wrote, "Those flowers . . . the fireflies at night and the glow-worms, the first beech leaves spreading on the trees like a delicate veil overhead, and our feet buried in last year's brown beech leaves, these were our time and our events."[5]

But Frieda wasn't aware of the science. And I am. I know forest air has a higher concentration of oxygen and is rich with phytoncides, the oils produced by trees to protect themselves from harmful insects and fungi. It's the phytoncides that scent the air, giving it that clean, pungent odour that feels instinctively calming. Studies show that phytoncides help lower stress hormones, blood pressure, and heart rate as well as helping us sleep better. Lawrence noticed this long before any knowledge of phytoncides, effusing, "The piny sweetness is rousing and defiant, like turpentine. . . . I am conscious that it helps to change me, vitally."[6] Frieda's love of trees—she slept in orchard trees as a child, even trying to take her lessons among the apple blossom—infected Lawrence, who developed a lifelong love of writing beneath them. In her foreword to his last novel, *The First Lady Chatterley*, Frieda described him sitting under an umbrella pine as he wrote the novel, among "thyme and mint tufts . . . purple anemones and wild gladioli and carpets of violets and myrtle. . . . There he would sit . . . so still that the lizards would run over him." Oddly enough, pine trees are the most prolific producers of phytoncides.

"The temperature's going to reach eighty-five degrees Fahrenheit today," I shout. "Which is good because that's when forests produce their highest concentrations of phytoncides."

No one answers. I stop my bike and scribble down names of wild flowers I've spotted: alpen roses with petals as thin and crumpled as tissue paper; edelweiss; purple harebells like silken bonnets; celandines; the rusty seeding stems of dock; spears of blue gentian. The laughter of Hugo and Saskia as their bikes jump and jolt over tree roots drifts towards me, along with Matthew's loud expressions of disbelief: "I had no idea Bavaria was so beautiful!" For a moment I feel euphoric. And I wonder if this was how Frieda felt as she walked these woodlands of beech and pine, if it was these very trees that helped assuage her grief and guilt.

We reach Icking, described by Lawrence and Frieda as the "little white village" but now a skein of houses surrounding a construction site and bisected by a busy road. There are no whiskery fields of wheat, no peasant women in dirndls stooping over their scythes, no bullock wagons laden with yellow wheels of mountain cheese. We find the house Frieda and Lawrence occupied, but it's covered in scaffolding and plastic sheeting. Between it and the green wooded horizon are a synthetic-orange crane, a building site, piles of newly made bricks, and row after row of roofs glistening with black solar panels. The village still has two churches, including one with a black onion dome sprouting from a burst of green foliage. But little else seems familiar from the accounts Lawrence and Frieda left.

It was in this village that Frieda lost "all ordinary sense of time and place." In her memoir, she described the view from their balcony with such striking immediacy it had hovered for months in my mind: "The Alps floated above us in palest blue. . . . The Isar rushed its glacier waters and hurried the rafts along in the valley below. The great beechwoods stretched for hours behind us."

I listen for the rush of water, the hurtle of river-borne rafts. All I can hear is the drone of a lawn mower and the never-ending whine of traffic. And no sighting of the Isar either. I strain desperately for a glimpse of the view she loved, the view that eased her vast weight of grief. Finally, I catch it—a few remaining beech trees rocking in the breeze behind the orange crane.

Never go back. Never go back. The disappointment of finding Frieda and Lawrence's first home beneath a rubble of plastic sheeting and scaffolding, their balcony gone, their view obliterated, reminds me of the only time I returned to my beloved childhood *cwm*.

Always a mistake to go back. And yet we do. We hope that returning to the places of our childhood will help us understand who we were and who we've become, a sort of joining of the dots. We hope a glimpse into our past will glue our diffusing memories of childhood joy. Psychologists now believe it's our most recent memory of an experience that endures, often blotting out all earlier memories, however lovingly we've preserved them. At the very least, those older memories are coloured and skewed by the later memory, altering them forever. I learnt this the hard way, before it was subject to the scrutiny of experts.

When I first met Matthew, I wanted to show him my Welsh valley, to share this place that was so deeply stamped inside me. It was twelve years since my family had left Wales for

England's South Downs, and it never occurred to me that my *cwm* might have changed. After a day of driving through drifting rain, we reached our B&B. The weather celebrated with us, a weak sun straining through the rain-lit clouds. We dumped our luggage and rushed out into the dying light, into the succulent smell of wet moss, unfurling bracken, crushed green grass.

I found my way back to the *cwm* with startling speed: up the muddy field, down the narrow path overhung with straggled trees, out onto the broad rutted track. It was as though the route had imprinted itself not upon my memory but upon the soles of my feet. We reached the valley a little too quickly, as if I'd misremembered the way, or perhaps my feet had taken a long-forgotten shortcut. I didn't give it a second thought because here was the stream, running pale and swift over pebbles as smooth and round as mushrooms. Here were the banks, rising steep and green, and sparkling with yellow celandines.

After a few strides, I knew something was wrong. I frowned and caught Matthew's eye. He'd sensed it too, as if thunder were rippling beyond the distant hills. Seconds later my ears began to fill with a hammering sound, as if my heart was trying to burst from my rib cage. Gradually I realised that the noise was coming not from inside my body but from the air around us. The valley was shaking with the strains of heavy metal, the bass bouncing off the water, the trees, the drystone wall that ran to our right. We walked on, stoically, saying nothing. Suddenly the screech of an electric guitar sliced through the air. The thudding bass grew louder. Wailing indecipherable vocals dropped from the sky. I wanted to turn around and go back but instead we went on, my hand gripping Matthew's.

To my surprise, we reached the end of the valley in fifteen minutes. The walk I remembered taking *hours* now took a mere *fifteen minutes*. The valley I'd thought of as a long, green ribbon, rolling mysteriously and infinitely into the secret heart of Wales, was a stunted track that ended with a square, whitewashed house, a crude full stop in the landscape. The house had been a mansion when I was a child, always empty, with a haunted, eerie air that had filled my head with witchy magical imaginings. Not any more. The house was surrounded by derelict cars and battered jags of metal, which alone seemed a travesty. Because no vehicles of any sort had ever gone up the *cwm*.

That night, I wept beneath the duvet. Not for the desecration of the valley but for the brutal desecration of a vast sweep of my childhood. Memories that had fed and sustained me for over a decade had been ripped from me, rewritten and re-bound. I knew that my valley would never mean the same.

Never go back. Never go back. Lawrence would have agreed entirely. He and Frieda spent the rest of their days pushing on, always somewhere new, always looking for "the new beginning,"[7] always taking that "leap from the known into the unknown."[8]

⌣

Frieda's fictionalised memoir (*And the Fullness Thereof*) and Lawrence's poems of this period show vividly her pain and grief, emotions she quickly learnt to hide, just as she'd learnt to hide her marital boredom and discontent from her first husband. Although Lawrence had enticed her away with promises of a "heaven on earth" home they would share with her children, he reneged on this in the face of Ernest's rage and bitterness. Worse still, he became racked with envy and gripped by a deep fear of losing Frieda. The more she expressed her anxiety over losing her children, the more enraged he became. Frieda masked her feelings by falling silent, gazing for hours in the direction of England, disappearing into herself.

In the weeks before they left to cross the Alps, Frieda couldn't decide whether to return to Ernest, whether to accept one of his offers (all conditional on her never seeing Lawrence again). In July she made her decision, writing to Ernest that she wouldn't be returning to Nottingham. It never occurred to her that she might lose access to her children. She believed in Ernest's innate, gentlemanly sense of fair play, and she didn't seem to grasp the intricacies of English law. But the law was clear—a woman found guilty of adultery forfeited all right to her progeny. Frieda stubbornly refused to countenance an outcome in which she'd be entirely deprived of her beloved children. Instead she harboured a misguided notion that Ernest would have them in term-time and she would have them in the long school holidays, a part-time mothering role that would give her ample time to become Lawrence's collaborator. Such a simple thing for intelligent adults to agree. Surely it was possible?

Frieda and Lawrence's decision to walk south, over the Alps to Italy, was both prescient and symbolic. When she agreed to this route, Frieda removed herself from the comfort of her homeland and mother tongue, from the brace of her parents and the support of her sisters. From this point on she would be without children, friends, family, language, or past. Thrown together in the wilds of a new land, Frieda and Lawrence would come face-to-face with their raw, unadorned selves. Their relationship would be tested and—all going well—cemented.

This is what happens when a familiar place is replaced by unfamiliar space: we can shed, find, renegotiate, reinvent ourselves with infinitely more ease. We can obliterate the past.

Say what you like, but Frieda was never going to achieve that in Nottingham.

⌣

The pair chose a punishing route that would fully occupy them with its steep climbs and its perilous twists and turns. Neither of them had walked or climbed in mountains before, neither was a skilled orienteer, and neither was particularly fit. Crossing mountain ranges still wearing a thick carapace of ice and walking through an untouched wilderness of scrub and rock was a metaphor for everything the couple had recently been through. Lawrence found the mountains bleak and terrifying, seeing there the eternal wrangle between life and death. Later, he made full use of his Alpine terror in *Women in Love*, sending Gerald Crich to a lonely death in the barren glaciers of the Alps. Frieda, however, thought it was "all very wonderful."

Their hike led them to an Italian village on the edge of Lake Garda, accessible only by steamer or on foot. Here they would be marooned, cut off from everyone who'd ever known them. Lawrence saw this severing of ties as vital: only by breaking with their pasts could they renew themselves, recreate themselves afresh. I suspect he also realised this was his best chance of keeping Frieda to himself, away from the lure of her children, away from the influence of her family, away from the sway of her old friends. Perhaps Frieda also recognised these benefits. Perhaps the ceaseless vacillation of the previous weeks (should she or shouldn't she return to Ernest?) had simply become too emotionally exhausting for her.

I credit her mountainous trek: it gave her the courage to seek out her own mind, and the space to make a profoundly difficult and complex decision. Philosophers and poets have long applauded the therapeutic powers of walking in nature. Now, science helps us understand how and why walking—wherever it takes place—is so effective.

New research shows that leg exercise—in particular weight-bearing leg exercise like walking—instructs the brain to produce the neurons needed to cope with stress and change.[9] The foot-to-ground impact of walking sends pressure waves surging through the arteries, dramatically increasing blood to the brain. I think about this as my own feet pound the pitted path beside the Isar. Did all that blood freely circulating through Frieda's brain, mixing and melding with a fresh rush of neurons, help her manage the inevitable stress of her situation? Did it help her organise and shape the emotional chaos of this volatile period?

On this walk, the pair averaged ten miles a day, much of it uphill and strenuous, much of it cold, always with their packs on their backs. On some days they walked farther still. Only when the weather was particularly hostile did they allow themselves the luxury of catching a train to the next town.

Imagine a different scenario: one in which Frieda had *sat* in her stuffy, airless parlour, exchanging anguished letters with Lawrence. Perhaps she would have followed advice to sleep on it. But how can sleep compare with walking? All that newly oxygenated blood powering through her brain, all those newly created neurons. All that Alpine air scouring her clean. Breathing new life into her. Would she have made the same decision with the same vigour and certainty from the confines of her Nottingham home? Somehow, I doubt it. Somehow, I think Lawrence knew this.

⌣

Before they reached the foothills of the Alps, Frieda and Lawrence had a few days of walking through the beech forests of Bavaria, plunging in and out of the Isar, and swimming in some of the smaller lakes along the way. Frieda vividly recounts losing him on the shores of the Kochelsee, panicking that Lawrence— who couldn't swim—had fallen into the lake and drowned.

On our second day in Germany we arrive at the Kochelsee, a lake whose rim is a curiously Caribbean turquoise. Its banks sprout thick fringes of grass and beds of dry, clattering reeds. Pale, fat fish with amber fins flick and flit beneath the glassy surface of the water. Saskia and Hugo peel off their clothes and plunge in. I lie down and close my eyes, the sunlight like warm velvet on my lids. The clanking of cowbells floats from the foothills, mingling with the children's splashing and shouting.

I try and make myself think about Frieda, but my brain instructs me otherwise. I don't want to give her another thought. I want only to lie here and listen to the cowbells and the excited shrieks of my children and the soft shooshing of the waves on the shore. I open my eyes and gaze across the lake to stands of silver birch, larch, pine. To the crenellated peaks of the Alps, jagged and ragged, their grey tips sheened rose pink from the ebbing sun. In their seams and crevices the gathered snow glints. Strips of mist, gauzy and tinged a pale violet, wind their way across the sky.

Frieda swoops back into my thoughts. And in that moment I feel quite certain it was this epiphanic trek over the Alps that determined her fate. On this walk she irrevocably broke the final threads that bound her to her three young children. On this walk she also came to terms with her loss while reinventing herself as the woman she believed she could be—the "free self" she had spent five years dreaming of.

Lawrence repeatedly impressed on Frieda her innate need for liberty. In the letter he sent to Ernest Weekley, in which he broke the news of their "elopement" and precipitated Frieda's crisis of motherhood, Lawrence wrote, "Mrs. Weekley is afraid of being stunted and not allowed to grow. . . . [She] must live largely and abundantly. It is her nature."

She couldn't simply *be* while married to Ernest in Nottingham. There she had played a role—the professor's wife and the good mother—mixing with the newly elevated middle classes for whom appearances were of the utmost importance. She later described her Nottingham self as "a hard bright shell," an outer self that had no connection with her inner self.

Away from the judgemental world of Edwardian England, walking through the wilds of Bavaria and over the Alps, with a man who wanted her only as she was, for who she was, must have felt exhilarating, regardless of the agony of losing her children.

I like the rhythm of walking. I like the way it produces Walking Thoughts, wisps of ideas that meander freely, spilling effortlessly into one another. Nietzsche famously said, "Only thoughts which come from walking have any value."[10] Obviously this isn't true: many brilliant ideas have come from people who were not walking at the time. But for me, walking allows new thoughts and ideas to swim to the surface, to take precedence over the detritus that preoccupies me for much of the time (incomplete school permission slips, light bulbs that need replacing, broken toasters, unwashed clothes, etc., etc.). Walking allows thoughts to connect more laterally with other reflections and impressions.

There's something about walking in green space that enables us to exist in the moment in a way nothing else does. Not even meditation. The combination of movement and landscape affects our brain in extraordinary ways. Not only do we become less anxious, less prone to brooding, less vulnerable to negative emotions, but we also gain an enhanced ability to focus on what's around us. Psychologists call this *attention*: we're less distracted, better able to exist in the here and now.

As we leave the Kochelsee behind and head into the mountains, an event that took place on Frieda and Lawrence's hike—and that has always confused me—suddenly and blindingly makes perfect sense. A few days after they walked round the Kochelsee, Bunny Garnett, the son of Lawrence's editor, and Bunny's friend Harold Hobson joined Frieda and Lawrence for the next leg of their journey, from Mayrhofen to Sterzing. While Lawrence and Bunny walked ahead looking for wild flowers, Frieda and the twenty-two-year-old Harold slipped into a hay hut and had sex.

For desk-bound weeks in a study the size of a shoebox, I'd tried to understand why Frieda indulged in such a casual, careless betrayal. Now it makes sense. Her betrayal was never *casual*. It was a means of claiming something for herself, making it clear to Lawrence that her body was her own, even if her children weren't. That to be truly free, she must have physical freedom over her body. Lawrence was deeply monogamous, believing in honesty at any price. But Frieda believed personal liberty and sexual freedom were inextricably linked. A few nights later, when Lawrence's map reading had gone horribly awry and the pair were lost in the mountains with darkness falling, she confessed. You have to admire her style. As Lawrence was at his least self-assured, as they were cold, hungry, and frightened, she tearfully delivered her bombshell. How could he not forgive her?

⌣

On our third day, I realise that I'm not dressed as Frieda would have been. I'm in state-of-the-art walking gear: lightweight moisture-munching black trousers, quick-drying black Lycra top, socks with cushioned heels of the latest technology. I flick through my Frieda notebook, scanning for the section headed "Clothing." My notes are legible for once: emerald-green woollen stockings, red pinafore or Bavarian dirndl, straw hat with red velvet ribbon. No mention of her footwear. It's too hot for wool stockings, but I put on a long dress. It's not red, but it's floral and multicoloured. Within thirty minutes my skirts have swished through knee-high grass and caught a bee in their flouncing hem. The panicked bee—trapped in the folds of my skirt—stings me. A stab of pain that starts to throb in rhythm with the tread of my feet. How on earth did women walk in long skirts?

I go to our B&B and change back into my lightweight trousers which can be tightened at the ankles and have lots of useful zipped pockets. Thank God for trousers and advanced fabric technology.

Later, I attempt nude sunbathing, all in the name of authenticity. Frieda had long enjoyed a spot of naked sunbathing, and on this walk she helped Lawrence overcome his hatred of the white, tubercular body he now possessed, encouraging him to join her as she disrobed in the sun or splashed naked in the ice-cold Isar. The rest of the time she escaped her body by dressing in sack-like clothes. Having cast aside the tightly corseted, demure dresses Ernest liked, she now dressed in shapeless pinafores, her hair caught in an unfashionable straggle at the nape of her neck. This radical change of style indicated that she was someone else now, someone with a new sense of herself and an invigorated sense of her own worth. But her style change also suggested that she had *become* someone who valued herself beyond appearance, someone for whom freedom meant being able to dress, or undress, exactly as she pleased. But while Frieda found liberty in sunbathing and swimming naked—a habit she continued for the rest of her life—I cannot. For me, being unclothed in the open air is a source of anxiety.

As I lie on a sun-warmed rock, fidgeting at my towel and shooting nervous glances here, there, and everywhere, all I want to do is cover up. The truth is, I feel far freer when trussed up in clothes. The more, the better. Perhaps I'm not as wild as I like to think.

We reach the *Gasthaus* where Lawrence and Frieda stayed, overlooking a small monastery. From here they wrote to friends describing their breakfasts of black bread and coffee beneath the
horse chestnut trees. The trees still exist. But the *Gasthaus* was
converted into a family home forty years ago. I wander round,
nonchalantly peering through windows and prodding at half-
open doors. In England this frequently results in generous invita-
tions and thrilling—to me—tours. But my German is too poor to
explain myself. So when the front door opens, unexpectedly, we
scurry away like naughty children. I feel disheartened at my lack
of linguistic ability, and it occurs to me that we are always trapped,
held back by something. Today, I'm constrained by my lack of
German. Tomorrow it'll be something else. Life is a constant navigation of restrictions, an endless series of negotiated constraints.

Even as Frieda and Lawrence celebrated their new-found
freedom—from their past lives and from the passionless pro-
vincialism of pious England—they were acutely aware of how
hemmed in they were. Frieda's presence had a profound effect
on Lawrence, sparking a creative surge that resulted in dozens
of short stories, poems, and essays, as well as his three acknowledged masterpieces: *Sons and Lovers*, *The Rainbow*, and *Women
in Love*. But as he led Frieda farther and farther away from
her previous life and from the children he feared above all, he
began to see how necessary she was to him. Not only for his
happiness but for the continued blooming of his genius. Many
of his poems are testimony to this feeling of necessity, a feeling
that occasionally tips into a terrified dependency:

The burden of self-accomplishment!

The charge of fulfilment!
And God, that she is *necessary*!
Necessary, and I have no choice!

⁓

He wrote several poems in the same vein, questioning whether he could live without her and expressing his horror of being "enfeebled" by her, claiming she had made him "a cripple." He believed love and freedom were incompatible, that to love meant to be possessed in some way—and that possession destroyed freedom.

Frieda discovered that her new-found liberty was similarly compromised. She left her husband, children, and friends to discover her own mind, to be freely herself. But freedom is infinitely more complicated than simply casting off the things we believe are constraining us. Hurting others in the pursuit of freedom and self-determination brought its own struts and bars, its own weight of guilt. Frieda never shared the great weight of her guilt. She couldn't. Lawrence wouldn't allow it. His friends joined forces with him, insisting that she put up or shut up, that her role was to foster his genius. At any price.

Meanwhile, he was feverishly ablaze with ideas, words streaming effortlessly from his pen. Was it any wonder that he was determined to have her, at any cost? Later he bragged that he had succeeded in "fastening Frieda's nose to my wagon."[11] She stayed with him for the rest of his life, travelling restlessly from country to country in his "savage pilgrimage." "We must keep moving on . . . round the world," he insisted. "I need change, novelty, to shock me out of complacence." Frieda, however, had other things on her mind: "I was like a cat without her kittens, and always in my mind was the care, 'Now if [my children] came where would I put them to sleep?'"[12]

But there was no chance of that happening. Ernest Weekley was so ashamed of his wife's conduct that he didn't tell his children a thing. For a year they had no idea where their mother was. Instead, he told them they had a "new Mama," their despised aunt Maude. All three children started new schools in a new city where no one knew them. They were forbidden from speaking German. Ernest used the full force of the law to punish his errant wife, ensuring she was denied all unsupervised access to her three children. Not until they reached the age of twenty-one were they free to see their mother.

A few nights back I'd been reading some scientific papers on the concept of awe, struggling through the ineffectual wording that denuded the idea even as it sought to explain it. Researchers consider awe to be one of the significant elements of being in wild places. Dramatic ravines, radiant sunsets, shimmering sweeps of water are a few of the things that inspire us with awe. One psychologist called it "the magic ingredient," while another used the quasi-mystical phrase "power in obscurity."[13] Whatever the term, the experience is the same: a melding of curiosity and humility in which we feel simultaneously diminished and exalted. Frieda had a great capacity for marvelling, for basking in awe. She and Lawrence called it "wonder," and her awkwardly Germanic writings reel with it: "sunrises over the Pacific"; "the wonder of newness"; "mountains . . . like tigers with their stripes of gold"; "snow [dripping] from the cedar trees that are alive with birds"; "blackberry hedges and mushroom fields and pale sunsets behind a filigree of trees"; "wonder before one's eyes."[14] She never lost her capacity for wonder, for marvelling at the sun, moon, stars, trees, clouds, and flowers.

The pair of them recognised *wonder* (which Lawrence also called "our sixth sense" and "the most precious element in life") long before today's scientists named and categorised it. They knew, even then, that the reductive process of analysing and naming it could rub away some of its shine: "The intrusion of the mental processes dims the brilliance, the magic. . . . Knowledge and wonder counteract one another. So that as knowledge increases wonder decreases," wrote Lawrence. I can imagine them fulminating and raging at our scientific attempts to understand it, to make it didactic and "as dead and boring as dogmatic religion."[15]

And while I sympathise with them, I don't entirely agree. For me, science still carries an illicit thrill, and so I find myself quoting from *The Lawrences* and then supporting it with *The Science*. Eventually, we agree: it's the dissolution of self, combined with feelings of elation, that is fundamental to the experience of awe or wonder, or magic, or power in obscurity, or whatever you want to call it.

Either way, to marvel is to understand the astonishing privilege of life.

Later that day, we experience wonder when we find our marshy path leaping with baby toads the size of thumbnails. We crouch down and let them jump into our palms and up our bare arms. We find fat, dead toads too, as big as our kneecaps with pink, oversized tongues lolling from their mouths. We flip them with sticks, marvelling at their plumpness, their intricate markings and huge back legs. We ponder what plague-of-toads has caused so many of them to die, leaving vulnerable orphan babies to leap into the hands of humans. We poke at the reed beds with long sticks to see if any adult toads have survived the pestilence. None appear.

One of the drawbacks of walking as a family is the noise we make: wildlife has plenty of time to slip silently away. But on this occasion we're lucky. Not only do the baby toads not yet know to jump away, but we come across a cattle grid containing an inch or so of murky water in its three-foot-deep concrete bunker. Here we spot fifteen captive toads, enormous squatting creatures for whom escape is impossible. We kneel down and bicker over which toad is the fattest. Hugo realises that "his" toad is, in fact, a mound of toads, four or five of them amassed in a dank, dark corner.

All these toads—imprisoned, orphaned, and abandoned—make me think of Frieda's lost children, of Rousseau and Thérèse's five deserted babies, of Thérèse locked into her menial hotel job and deprived of her progeny. I feel a flash of gratitude for being in this place and in this time. Here. Now. It's a lesson that those of us who live enthralled by history learn and relearn every day: never hanker after the past. For most of us, there is no better time than this.

⌒

After four days of following in Frieda's footsteps, we change direction. The Alpine route where Frieda walked "barefoot over icy stubble, laughing at wet and hunger and cold"[16] has been partially destroyed by the construction of a vast reservoir and a motorway whisking traffic to multiple ski resorts strung across the Alps. Besides, their route appears unnecessarily arduous and complicated. Perhaps if I didn't have my family in tow. Perhaps if we weren't squeezing a six-week journey into ten days of rushed holiday time. Already we've had to walk this route in three muddled chunks, in reverse order from that walked by Lawrence and Frieda. A year ago we arrived (six of us) in the Italian lakes ready to try the Gargnano-to-Riva-to-Bolzano leg of their journey, but a heatwave had made hiking impossible. We'd completed our version of the middle leg, over the Austrian Alps, two years before, in a week of drenching rain.

By the time we arrive in Germany for the Munich-to-Austria section we are a diminished family, four instead of six, and all of us feeling the absence. Like Frieda, I too begin this trek grieving for the past, for the irrevocable changes to come, for my old self as mother that is shrinking and fading. One day I'll be walking without any of my children, returning to an empty home. How will it feel? Who will I be?

During our walking and cycling beside the Isar and into the foothills of the Alps, I've learnt several things—just as my "science of nature" books said I would. Just as Frieda did. Before the walk, she was "steeped in misery . . . always missing the children," still thinking that "perhaps I will go to England and see

Ernest." Her see-sawing infuriated Lawrence, compelling him to withdraw all his earlier promises of making a home for her children. Their walk over the mountains ended her prevarications. By the time she arrived in Riva, on the northern shore of Lake Garda, she was ready to set up a permanent home with Lawrence. Although she hoped to have her children for holidays, the umbilical cord had been cleanly sliced. Her walk over the Alps, with its rhythms, distractions, and repeated moments of wonder, smoothed this process. Both Frieda and Lawrence were acutely sensitive to landscape. The wide-open spaces, the dizzying, dazzling grandeur of the mountains, helped give Frieda the oxygen and fortitude to make a shockingly daring decision.

There's another feeling induced by moving through an unfamiliar landscape that may have aided and abetted in the symbolic scissoring of Frieda's umbilical cord. When we walk, possessionless, in a landscape that is not our own, there comes over us a strange sense of being unattached, cut loose. At the same time we have a sense of being intimately bound to the land because there is nothing between it and ourselves. Nothing but a layer of clothing and the sole of a boot—unless we're barefoot, as Frieda often was. To feel simultaneously bound and unattached changes how we experience the world, giving us a rebellious sense of courage and optimism, a sense that things will be all right.

Meanwhile, we see the world not from the tight focal gaze employed for reading (or for working on screens) but through a gaze that sweeps widely and expansively, taking in the full panorama unfolding in front of us. Neuroscientists call this *panoramic vision*. They speculate that our brains work differently when we scan vistas and horizons. We relax; we are better able to process and store memories, to deal with uncertainty and anxiety. It's yet another element that helps me understand how Frieda might have accommodated the pain of parting from her children.

Something else occurs to me as I tread Frieda's footsteps. Would she have made the same decision if she had flown from London to Verona? Commercial air travel didn't exist then. But imagine if it had. Imagine if she'd jetted in on a charter flight, dropping from the sky a few hours after leaving Nottingham. Pulling her wheelie case behind her.

Walking uproots us, slowly and gently. We have time to acclimatise, to adapt, to reflect. Instead of being ripped from our homeland, we are *eased*. It's a different experience entirely.

So why did Frieda devote less than twenty-five lines of her memoir to this pivotal time in her life? As we climb through trackless forests of pines, towards the snow gleaming white and silver on the tips of the Alps, a line from her memoir wriggles into my head: "I wanted to keep it secret, all to myself."

Describing a memory in words alters it. When you put those words on paper, you capture it, master it, change it. A memory that once roamed freely through the mind, however blurry or grainy, ceases to roam. Instead it sets hard, crystallising from the edges in.

If those words are published—as her memoir was—the memory becomes not only set and confined but the property of others. You hand over the memory, clipped and shorn, to become what others make it. This journey was so vivid and intense, so personal, that neither Frieda nor Lawrence wanted to enclose it or share it. When Lawrence fictionalised a version of it in *Mr. Noon*, he never sought publication (unusually for him as they invariably needed the money). Instead, he consigned it to a drawer. Nor, after his death, did Frieda try and have *Mr. Noon* published—despite publishing other writings Lawrence had chosen to keep private. *Mr. Noon* stayed unpublished until 1984.

⌒

As the world recedes behind us, I pull together my scattered thoughts. Later, I think of these as Mountain Thoughts, ideas that need a little clearing or stringing together, thoughts that look different according to the light. Over the course of our walk I've reflected on the inevitable shrinking of our family and the prospect of a future which only sporadically includes children. The sadness I set off with has mutated into something else altogether, something flashing with promise and possibility. Easier here, of course, with the distractions of landscape and the infinite variety of each day. Not quite so easy when confronted with the empty bedrooms, the silence, the ghost of children departed.

Although Frieda and Thérèse Levasseur lost their children, they ultimately found some form of freedom. Helping Lawrence with his work and providing the emotional support and encounters he needed gave Frieda a strong feeling of purpose, blunting her deep sense of loss. Twenty months after their Alpine hike, and at his insistence, she married an increasingly restive and cantankerous Lawrence, arguably exchanging one form of entrapment for another. It wasn't until his death in 1930 that she became free to live as, and where, she wanted. In a bold attempt to finally assert her own identity she used the name "Frieda Lawrence geb. Freiin von Richthofen" on the opening page of her memoir. That, I suspect, was her definitive moment of freedom.

We know less of Thérèse, but we know that Rousseau eventually married her, even letting her accompany him on the odd walk. Of course, he obliterated her in public and for posterity, writing in his last great autobiographical work, *Reveries of the Solitary Walker*, "Here am I, then, alone upon the earth, having no brother, or neighbour, or friend or society but myself." What rubbish! Thérèse was loyal to him to the very end. In return, he left her all his worldly belongings when he died. She promptly remarried and lived another twenty years in the material comfort that had previously eluded her. We also know that two of her discarded children survived, producing descendants who became prosperous merchants and notaries. I like to think she was reunited with at least one of them. And perhaps she was. We'll never know.

I watch Hugo and Saskia clamber over the boulders that litter our path. It's not children or motherhood that constrains us, but the tyranny of their trappings—the merciless laundry, the grind of thrice-daily meals, the endless paperwork, the penury. It's also the workplace rules that dictate long hours, short holidays, the need to be constantly connected. Beyond this, our freedom is confined by a set of factors often within our control: our physical fitness, our disregard for social convention, our capacity for truculence.

⌣

The intimacy of family life is at its most intense while walking, often pivoting from gentle to savage in seconds. In a catalysing moment I realise that we argue (OK, fight) most frequently and at greatest volume when we're in urban areas: on roads, in towns and cities, anywhere faintly civilised. We also argue bitterly when we're lost. Hungry, tired, and lost in the concrete outskirts of a city is the worst predicament. We blame the map reader, the iPhone, the person who chose the route or the so-called holiday. We all blame each other. Only when we turn our united blame on someone else—the cartographer, the city architect, D. H. Lawrence—do we become harmonious again.

On the last of our ten days of walking we have the mother of all arguments. We arrive in an ugly suburb with instructions to catch a bus that we cannot find. We walk another mile to a *Bahnhof* to try and catch a train. The station is an empty platform, thirteen feet long, crushed between two mountains. We can't read the timetable; we can't work out which side of the platform to wait on. We have no idea where we are, or in which direction we need to go. Trains appear and disappear, confusingly travelling along the same track but in different directions. Some trains stutter along, while others race past. I shout the name of our destination, but no one understands me. Tempers flare—it's my fault now for speaking such terrible German—until we have no recriminations left. At last, a train stops and a ticket collector speaking perfect English invites us aboard and explains that we need the next station. Suddenly we're a happy family again. Just like that.

⌣

After six weeks, Frieda and Lawrence arrived in Riva, then an Austrian garrison town on Lake Garda. Vigorous ascents over steep mountain passes in snow and icy winds followed by nights in lice-ridden *Gasthäuser* had left them looking like "two tramps with rucksacks." Within days a trunk of cast-off clothes from Frieda's glamorous younger sister had arrived, swiftly followed by an advance of fifty pounds for *Sons and Lovers* from Lawrence's publisher. In a big feathered hat and a sequinned Paquin gown, an exuberantly overdressed Frieda and a shabbier Lawrence sauntered round the lake, celebrating their return to civilisation and rubbing shoulders with uniformed army officers and elegantly dressed women.

Because we're following their route in chunks, backwards, we return from our Alpine wilderness to the city of Munich. After ten days off-grid, the prospect of city life is enticing. Part of me loves cities—their frenetic energy, their press and rush, their intimacy and constant creativity. Cities reflect the splendid recklessness of the human spirit, and Munich promises to be a fine example of this, with some of the world's greatest art galleries, museums, and Jugendstil architecture. We too are looking forward to celebrating our return to civilisation, which we intend doing with a slap-up breakfast in a posh hotel.

This is the paradox of pitting the wilds against civilisation. We need both. And each enhances the other. The longer I'm away, the more I look forward to returning to civilisation. And the longer I'm in civilisation, the more I yearn for the wilderness.

As soon as we arrive, I feel a frisson at Munich's magnificence, and a sense of awe at humankind's urge and capacity to create, order, and build, as well as its ability to live so tightly together. Being in the mountains has heightened and intensified our sense of space, so that all these people living in close proximity suddenly feels both astonishing and oppressive.

It's a warm afternoon and the beerhouses spill crowds onto the sidewalks: talking, laughing, chinking beer steins, smoking, eating, arguing, gesticulating, kissing, hugging, backslapping, examining newly bought souvenirs, books, shoes. A group of bearded men carefully dressed in Tyrolean lederhosen and sleek women with coiffured hair and painted nails remind me of how I must look: as if I've come straight from the innards of a mountain. Which I have, more or less. My hair is overgrown, my fringe straddling my eyes so that I resemble a shaggy dog. And I'm still in my hiking gear, with the odd knot lurking in my hair. Not a smudge of make-up, naturally.

Over our celebratory breakfast, my first communication from the term-time world of school arrives, provoking a snort of laughter. The freshly installed headmaster at Hugo's school has sent an email that opens with the line, "You will be busy buying uniforms, sewing on name labels, refilling pencil cases, and organising school bags so all is ready for Day One." He continues, without any hint of irony, "I passionately believe that learning is life's greatest adventure." Well, I think, my son and I are busy learning and adventuring, so please forgive us when he arrives with unnamed uniform and a pencil case bereft of new pens.

Emails are a rude, jolting return to civilisation, a reminder that we cannot inhabit the wilderness forever. But emails while in a posh hotel in a thrilling new city are not the same as emails received after returning to the mundane but comforting demands of home. On the most challenging hikes (wet, cold, blistered, lost), it is home we long for: our own pillow, the mattress moulded uniquely to our curves. Frieda never went home. She returned to Nottingham only once, turning up at Ernest's rented bedsit and announcing herself to his new landlady as Mrs. Lawson. A furious Ernest turned her out, refusing to speak to her, telling her she was nothing more than a common prostitute. She pursued her children in the same vein, lying in wait outside their schools, crouching behind hedges in sleeting rain, scouring the streets of Chiswick until she spotted the red velvet curtains from her old Nottingham home. Always in tears.

In perhaps the most distressing of all her attempts to see her children, Frieda sneaked into the Chiswick house where Ernest had installed them alongside his elderly parents and siblings. She crept up the stairs to the nursery, where she could hear the sounds of talking and eating, the scrape of knife on plate, the rattle of spoon in bowl. She pushed open the door. Faces blanched, jaws dropped. And then her outraged sister-in-law leapt up, demanding Frieda leave at once. She refused. Ernest's elderly mother staggered furiously to her feet and pushed Frieda out of the nursery and down the hall, screaming, "Get out! Get out!" To Frieda's horror, her children joined in, shouting their own abuse at her. She fled, hurt and humiliated.

Later, her daughter recalled the severed bond, explaining that Frieda had become an "unreal woman to us by then . . . rather strange and even a little horrifying."[17]

Thinking of this episode prompts me to reread the email from my son's headmaster. The very words that, a few seconds ago, made me prickle with irritation and laugh with derision suddenly make me feel profoundly grateful. Uniform, pencil cases, name labels . . . the consolations of familiarity, of home. Anathema to Lawrence, of course. What he wanted was to be "tossed clean into the new . . . to the liberty of newness," unencumbered by material possessions.[18] But Frieda spent the rest of their days together trying to make a home in their relentless string of rented houses, sewing cushion covers and pinning her scarves to the wall.

After Lawrence died, she lived in the same ranch ("wild and far away from everything") in Taos, New Mexico, for much of her remaining twenty-six years. Here she cultivated a close group of friends, a surrogate for the family she'd sacrificed. And she walked. Her memoir is peppered with references to walking: "We were out of doors most of the day," she says, on "long walks." Her first outing with Lawrence, shortly after they met, had been "a long walk through the early spring woods and fields" of Derbyshire with her two young daughters. It was on this walk that she discovered she'd fallen in love with Lawrence. Later she wrote of "delicious female walks" with Katherine Mansfield, walks through Italian olive groves, walks into the jungles of Ceylon, walks along the Australian coast, walks through the canyons of New Mexico, or simply strolls among "the early almond blossoms pink and white, the asphodels, the wild narcissi and anemones."[19] Frieda walked in the country-side for the rest of her life.

But the pivotal walk of her life—the six-week walk she skirted in twenty-five lines—was the most significant. From here, Frieda emerged as *herself*, as the free woman she had always longed to be—dressing in scarlet pinafores and emerald stockings, swimming naked, making love *en plein air*, walking as she wished. She had also become the free woman Lawrence needed for his fiction. He made full use of her in his writing, continually remoulding her, most famously as Ursula in *Women in Love*, and Connie in *Lady Chatterley's Lover*. His novels shaped history, but Frieda was the catalyst.

⌒

"So why didn't you put the walk in your novel?" Saskia squeezes into her plane seat and snaps her seat belt shut.

"Superfluous to the plot," I say vaguely. The truth is a little more complex. I'd underestimated the walk's significance, and I hadn't been able to reconcile its joys with Frieda's painful decision to leave her children.

But I can't stop thinking about Thérèse. What if she had been accorded the same freedom to walk as Rousseau? What if she had left that Paris hotel, her belly as round and full as a harvest moon, and walked out of the city with Rousseau at her side? I have a dim sense that she might not have acquiesced so readily to having her future child plucked from her arms.

All conjecture, of course. But who knows?

And here's something else I didn't know, although I realised it much later. Walking the route of a woman renouncing her children, obsessing over another woman deprived of her children ... why the sudden preoccupation? It took me three years to see that Frieda's walk was also mine, an unbidden step in my own casting off.

But isn't that the way? As Shirley Toulson, one of my favourite unknown walker-writers, wrote, "The hardest thing of all to see is the thing that's really there."[20]

3

In Search of Self and Solitude

Gwen John

River Walking. France. Traffic. Solitude. Male Harassment.
Who Am I? What Am I? Vulnerability. The Sea.

I have been thinking of painting a good deal lately.
I think I shall do something good soon if I am left to myself
and not absolutely destroyed.

—GWEN JOHN, letter to Ursula Tyrwhitt, 1910

It was a hot, dry day in August 1903 when two young women clambered up the banks of the River Garonne, pushing their way through reeds and willow saplings, and shaking dead leaves from their hair. River mud caked their ankles. Their shoulders stooped beneath wooden easels, paint palettes, and portfolios of the cheapest art paper, which the women had bound with twine to their shoulder bags. Protruding from their belts and pockets were sable paintbrushes, sketching pencils, and tubes of paint. Their feet ached inside their button-up boots. The armpits of their dresses were salt-ringed with sweat.

Gwen John and Dorelia McNeil weren't old friends. They'd known each other a few months but Gwen had immediately fallen for Dorelia, smitten by her serenity, her composure, her ineluctable beauty. Dorelia had the face of an angel, the inner stillness of a saint. The only problem was that Gwen's younger brother, a married painter with a toddler and a new baby, also found Dorelia utterly irresistible. To make matters worse, Augustus John was married to one of Gwen's best friends, Ida. And Ida's heart was fracturing, her self-loathing swelling, as she watched Dorelia replace her as muse and model to the husband she adored, her "genius child," her Gus.

It was five years before "the age of Augustus John," Virginia Woolf's term for the epoch in which he was propelled, meteorically, to artistic stardom, ousting John Singer Sargent to become the world's most fashionable portrait painter. But in 1903 he was already feted, his celebrity predicted, his success assured. Today it is Gwen, the shy, timid sister, who is recognised as the greater painter, the true genius, one of the most celebrated female artists of the twentieth century. And Augustus, pitilessly dropped from the canon of twentieth-century art, languishes in her shadow. He saw it coming: in 1956, long after Gwen had died, he said, "Fifty years hence I shall be remembered only as the brother of Gwen John."[1]

Gwen's ambitious and bold plan to walk 620 miles from the coastal city of Bordeaux to the capital city of Rome, selling her sketches and paintings along the way, was to mark the end of her life in Britain forever. Although concocted on a whim, this walk signified the beginning of a new artistic journey for Gwen, dramatically altering the trajectory of her career and firmly exiling her from the age of Augustus John. Its little, unexpected events were to ripple into her future, bringing opportunities she couldn't possibly have foreseen as she trudged beside the Garonne, calf muscles aching, feet swollen, hair limp with perspiration.

Her trek denoted the end of family life as she knew it, the end of her dismal Welsh childhood. In the thirty-six years that followed, she never returned home. And she saw her father only twice: brief, unsatisfactory meetings that left her "tired out and unable to paint for days."[2]

Her walk also ended any childhood intimacy she'd shared
with Augustus—a decisive breaking of a bond that bloomed after being thrown together as bereaved children, but had since
become stifling and constraining for her. And in the ultimate
two-fingers to Augustus, Gwen had snatched Dorelia (whose
real name was Dorothy, but Augustus preferred the more exotic
Dorelia) from under his covetous nose. Naturally, he complained.
According to their artist friend Albert Rutherston, "Gwen and
Dorelia behaved like an eloping couple, flushed with excitement
and disapproved of by Augustus. The plan was impossible, he
insisted. It was also mad. But Gwen John brushed aside his ob-
jections and would not even listen to his arguments."[3] Augustus
insisted "the crazy walkers" travel with a pistol. They refused. A
knife beneath a makeshift pillow would have to do.

Years back, on the days when I was trapped at home, straitjack-
eted by several sick toddlers so that we couldn't tramp the fields
or get to the park, I would look at art books and point out birds,
fish, and seashells. On those bleak, confined days, it was looking
at paintings that preserved my sanity. There was one in particular
that I turned to time and time again. My children found it dull:
it contained no animals or shipwrecks, nothing I could weave
into a story. I found it compelling. Eventually I pinned it above
the washing machine in the subterranean cubicle where I spent
hours sorting, scrubbing, and soaking dirty laundry. Looking at
that painting was like lying in a warm, lavender-scented bath. It
should have amplified my feelings of swaddled suffocation, with

its single female figure in a bare, darkened room. But it didn't. In my cramped, windowless basement, I stared and stared at the woman I later discovered to be Dorelia. There was something about Gwen's painting of Dorelia that I couldn't put my finger on. It calmed me. But at the same time it seemed to reflect the emotional conflict in my life. Gwen's feelings of tenderness and affection for Dorelia radiated from her portrait, but there was an undercurrent of something else, something darker.

I began seeking out other Gwen John paintings, in books, in galleries, and online. They were always of women. Always alone. She never painted a man. She never painted a woman in company. They were always clothed (with one cold, unsparing exception: her portrait of Fenella Lovell). And they were always indoors. Some of her portraits felt sombre and tinged with sadness, but they all exuded a numinous serenity, so that looking at them was like gazing at the sea on a windless day, or breathing in geraniums with your eyes closed. Except that when I peered more closely, I felt a slight unease, a disquiet that kept me looking and looking, until a baby cried or the washing machine cycle ended or a toddler pulled at me with sticky, neglected fingers.

In Gwen's portraits, she shows us what an interior life looks like—its spiritual calm, its composure, its richness. My life at that point was bereft of solitude—and composure. I was fractious and often angry. Although I was always stupidly busy, I felt adrift and confused. I hadn't grasped how much I needed time alone. I'd recognised my feelings of suffocation, but I thought that leaving the house—children in tow—was all I needed. Gwen's paintings told me otherwise.

Her paintings showed not the painful, frightening experience of loneliness but the richly rewarding, dignified, and essential experience of solitude. Her women, comfortable in their own skin and in their own company, are testament to this. So why did they make me feel so unsettled?

I made copies of tens of her paintings and drawings and stuck them to the wall with Blu Tack, staring at them day after day. The women, I noticed, had no space around them. No air. What little physical space Gwen gave them was without distraction or detraction—austere walls that left the subject exposed and oddly vulnerable. Her brushwork and muted palette flattened the women so that they almost melted into the empty wall behind them. In her later portraits Gwen began to distort her models' bodies, giving them long arms, oversized, muscular, and often clasped hands, pyramidal bodies that pushed at the rim of the canvas. Somehow her paintings were both consoling *and* beguiling, soothing *and* unnerving, fragile *and* frightening. As if a tension lay at the heart of Gwen. As if she was desperately ordering herself within her portraits, trying to keep the conflicting parts of her personality together—but not quite managing it.

It was exactly how I felt. I'd thought that having lots of babies would create a family unit in which I would sit like some sort of earth mother, calm, whole, harmonious. I hadn't expected the intense emotional and physical confinement of motherhood, the continual sense that I had lost myself utterly, the visceral love, the paralysing guilt, the bewildering turmoil of it all. Gwen seemed to be painting my own troubled mind, with its aspirations of harmony and its reality of something altogether more complicated.

Of course, Gwen wasn't painting anything to do with me, or the mixed emotions of motherhood. She never had children. She couldn't understand the maternal calling and was scornful of women who chose children over their art, writing to Rodin, "Nobody ever erected a monument to anyone for having children."

⁓

When I set off in the footsteps of Gwen and Dorelia, it's many months after finishing Frieda's route with my family—and the first time in twenty-one years that I've been entirely alone for any length of time. I have ten days of being only with myself . . . of finally exploring the extended solitude that Gwen craved, that I'd snatched at with my hasty hilltop walks, that I'd often feared.

The prospect excites and terrifies me in equal measure. By the time I reach Bordeaux, the excitement has leached away. And the terror has expanded, so that I am palpably shaking. Although disgusted at my ludicrous fears, I can't seem to stop them whisking through my head. I keep recalling my unexplained collapse a few years ago, when a neighbour found me in an unconscious crumple and called an ambulance. In my mind's eye I see the same thing happening on an empty riverbank, my comatose body slipping silently into the river and drowning. I imagine being attacked or chased through black, compacted forests. The words of a friend toll in my head: Towpaths are the natural habitat of rapists and murderers. I check and recheck my (flimsy) walking poles, which Matthew has optimistically suggested could double as weapons.

Gwen and Dorelia weren't plagued by dark thoughts like these. Despite friends and family declaring their walk "impossible," "mad," "wild," "unprecedented," and "crazy," they remained unfazed. And yet their plan was both audacious and potentially dangerous. That Gwen chose to begin in Bordeaux, however, made perfect sense, for she was always drawn to water. And if any city has been made and shaped by the sea, by water, it is Bordeaux.

⌒

Bordeaux sits on the largest estuary in western Europe. For hundreds of years it was Europe's gateway to much of the world, from Lisbon to New York to Rio de Janeiro. The Bordeaux that greeted Gwen was built on the lucrative trading of coffee, sugar, cotton, and wine. Paintings show the old port fizzing with life: schooners unloading oranges from Spain and coffee from Africa, barges wobbling beneath barrels of wine and crates of dried figs, trawlers hauling nets of cod and baskets of oysters, warships spilling sailors, passenger boats disgorging ladies with parasols. Not to mention all the thin cats and hungry dogs, the well-fed merchants, the kohl-eyed prostitutes, the old ladies mending nets, and the barefoot boys fishing from rafts.

I find an empty river, a few rotting piers, and a Fred. Olsen cruise ship. The banks spin with hundreds of young Bordelais on bicycles, unicycles, skateboards, scooters, roller skates. They laugh into mobile phones, shiny hair streaming out behind them. Past Starbucks and McDonald's they fly, wheels spinning, spokes flashing silver in the sun. And yet the churning river—a gravy brown that the Bordelais call *café au lait*—is quiet and empty.

Fast-flowing water didn't intimidate Gwen in the least. Some
of her earliest walks followed a path known as "the frolic," which
ran beside the River Cleddau near her childhood home, and
where barges were tied to crumbling wharves. Another childhood
walk followed a millstream, while beach and clifftop walks were
also favourites. Her enduring love of water was shared with her
brothers and sister, two of whom made plans to follow the Mis-
sissippi from Minnesota to the Gulf of Mexico, and all of whom
spent much of their lives on rivers and lakes or beside the sea.

But the Garonne, with its width of 1,800 feet and its powerful current, bears little resemblance to the River Cleddau. The
stretch of river between Bordeaux and Toulouse is famously
perilous with rapids and shallows in summer, and floods and
high waters in winter. In full spate, the raging Garonne has
a history of sweeping away bridges, flooding and devastating
orchards, fields, ports, mills, and villages, obstinately re-carving
its furious meandering path.

Gwen knew nothing of this. Nor did she know about the
mascaret, a natural phenomenon of the silty Garonne, and at
its most powerful at the tail end of summer, exactly when the
women arrived. The mascaret throws up vast, roiling waves,
much sought-after by surfers and often reaching ten feet in
height. One such wave woke Gwen and Dorelia at 3:00 AM, as
they slept rough on one of the Garonne's many small islands. It
was an auspicious start, hinting at the adventures that were to
come. But it wasn't something I intended to emulate.

~

There's no record of the route taken by Gwen and Dorelia. A local historian tells me there was no riverside path in 1903, simply a series of ports, some linked by a cart track. All we know is that Gwen received her first letter at a post office in the small town of Langon. I step off the train at Langon and immediately find myself on the edge of a roundabout with tarmac roads curling in every direction, throbbing with early morning traffic. I look for a signpost. Or the tinsel glint of sunlight on water. Nothing. Everyone from the train has driven away. I'm all alone with no food, a map that doesn't cover Langon, and the tiniest bottle of water—in a no-man's-land of roads.

I walk along the edge of a road that *feels* as if it should be taking me to a river. "Castets?" I ask a passing cyclist. "The river route?"

"*Non.*" He points to a road with four lanes of thrumming traffic—trucks, trailers, tractors, mobile homes—haloed with a grey pall of exhaust fumes.

The only building nearby is a car rental shop, where I ask the same question and get the same reply: "*Non.*" The woman behind the counter offers to call me a taxi.

I think for a moment. Gwen and Dorelia often took lifts, in *charrettes* or wagons and once in a motor car. But to take a taxi on the first day? No, that feels like early-onset defeat. Or cheating. The woman tells me it's seven and a half miles, and looks aghast when I tell her, in halting French, that I will walk.

For two hours I walk, slowly and carefully, along a narrow strip of dead verge. Trucks whizz past with such speed that I and my *sac à dos* are repeatedly buffeted and I have to focus very hard on not tumbling from the verge. I'm jaywalking, I think with a mutinous thrill. I could be arrested. Or I could die here, struck by a swaying caravan or a speeding lorry. I know the figures: 1.25 million deaths on the road every year. One person killed every twenty-five seconds. The mutinous thrill evaporates. A motorbike zips past me, and I feel the hot breath of its engine on my bare arms.

With my face full of the taste and smell of diesel, and my ears pounding from the noise, I stop scanning the horizon for a river and screw my eyes tightly onto the traffic hurtling towards me. My muscles are stiff and tense with the effort of staying on the verge. An ache builds at the back of my unblinking eyes. This is not the romantic riverside walk I expected.

In 1903 the roads were shared: carts, wheelbarrows, the odd motor car and bicycle, horses, donkeys, herds of goats. But above all, walkers. Gwen and Dorelia shared a communal track that knitted together people, livestock, and communities. People exchanged passing pleasantries and critical pieces of information: the current state of the river, whether a bridge had been repaired, whether sheep were blocking the path ahead, whether rain was expected. Walking along roads was inherently social, and for Gwen and Dorelia it meant the offer of rides, food, and vital information on local people who might want their portraits painted.

How ironic. Even as I freely follow the open road, liberated from the chains of domesticity (and much else besides), I am constrained by a merciless stream of traffic compelling me to teeter on a verge the width of a tyre, picking my way through flattened cola cans, sweating plastic bottles, and discarded sweet wrappers. An isolated, disoriented, and faintly ridiculous figure.

Because in the country there are no pedestrian crossings, no traffic lights, no sidewalks, no community of fellow walkers. Just the odd flattened animal, its innards spewed presciently across the tarmac. And an endless, dizzying rush of traffic.

I wait, raging and impatient, to cross the road. Ten minutes of cursing, sweating, swallowing squalls of gasoline, every inch of me tightly coiled, ready to sprint.

It will be better when I reach Castets. Then, like Gwen and Dorelia, I can simply follow the call of the river. How hard can it be to follow a river?

⌒

My Welsh village was a mere fifty miles north of Gwen's childhood home. A road ran through it, cleaving the village in two. Crossing the road meant waiting for a gap in the traffic and then walking fast enough to miss oncoming cars but not so fast that we could fall and be crushed by a truck. My father didn't like waiting. Perpetually outraged at the precedence given to cars, he ignored every principle of road safety and strode into the highway, brandishing his stick in the air.

From here he would usher us across, like a hirsute lollipop lady, shouting, "Death to the motor car!" Trucks, trailers, motorbikes, motorhomes all stopped and waited, their drivers staring, slack-jawed, as we skipped across the road, grinning and waving while my father lurched and shouted, his hair gusting in the wind, his stick swiping through the air. "Death to the motor car! Death to the motor car!"

I have a sudden urge to raise my walking pole and walk into the traffic, as he did. But I don't. Instead, I translate his cry of rebellion into French and whisper it beneath my breath: "*Mort à la voiture! Mort à la voiture!*"

When I find the river, an immense grey heron whirls up from the reeds, unfolds its vast, pale wings, and skims low over the water. The motorway is instantly forgotten.

And there is nothing but heron.

⌇

The River Garonne is a hasty, capricious river. At her mouth she is thunderous, demanding. Later she shifts, still fickle, still maverick, but less attention-seeking, less hurried. She isn't pretty or elegant, like some of her more docile tributaries. She has none of the poise of the Thames, or the elegance of the Seine.

But where I meet her, at Castets, she has a ruthlessness that swims beneath her quiet surface, erupting every now and then where a fallen trunk or a clot of reeds blocks her path. Here the current whips up, eddying this way and that.

As I begin following her, muddling my way along sharply shifting banks, I realise that I'm *not* following her. She is shoving towards the sea. I am walking inland, against the flow. We are moving in opposite directions. And I am like a salmon swimming perilously upstream, looking for home. Which is, of course, what Gwen was doing: risking everything to find somewhere she could anchor herself. From this walk on, she was discreetly rebellious all her life, determinedly pursuing her own path, pushing against the grain, always swimming against the current.

Everything about this ambitious, reckless walk went against the grain. Because walking through foreign countryside—penniless, weighed down with easels and paintboxes, singing for centimes, sketching male portraits in exchange for bread and beer, sleeping beneath haystacks, all of it without a chaperone—was disreputable and dangerous. It was not what the daughters of well-heeled, aspirational solicitors did. In 1903, middle-class women were expected to sit inside their airless houses, strapped into the latest hip pads and S-bend corsets—contraptions designed to thrust forward the bosom while shunting back the bottom, simultaneously skewing the lower back, pushing on the hip and knee joints, crushing the kidneys, chafing the hip bones, and blistering the soft flesh beneath the breasts.

And here's another thing: women were expected to truss up like chickens not only to protect their own reputations but to protect the reputations of their entire extended family. A wild-walking woman besmirched all within her bloodline, adding another insidious obstacle to any ambition she might have. Lizzie Le Blond, an avid Alpine hiker and climber, expressed this with panache in her memoir, writing of the "frantic" telegrams from her great-aunt to her mother: "Stop her [Lizzie] climbing mountains! She is scandalising all London...."[4]

Hardly surprising that, for most women, a walk meant little more than a tottering stroll in all their finery.

So what was it that made Gwen do something so brazenly transgressive?

⌒

The Johns were an isolated family, unable to integrate with the upper reaches of Haverfordwest society and unwilling to integrate with the lower reaches. In his meticulously researched biography of Augustus, Michael Holroyd explains that "the children were at ease only in the sea or roaming the wilds." The family's position became still more entrenched after the death of Augusta John, an amateur artist and mother to Thornton, Gwen, Augustus, and Winifred. Augusta had been withdrawing from family life ever since the birth of Winifred, frequently absent, searching for a cure for her poor health. Eventually she died, aged thirty-five, among strangers and hundreds of miles away in Derbyshire. Her death certificate cited rheumatic gout and exhaustion. She left behind some of her own artworks—pastoral scenes and seascapes, a muralled nursery—and a talent for painting, inherited by both Gwen and Augustus.

After Augusta's death, Gwen's father, Edwin John, withdrew still further, becoming increasingly distant and leaving the children to run wild. Augustus's memoir, and Gwen's rare references to Edwin, paint a vivid picture of him as rigidly Victorian, a man whose "cult of the clothes-brush" meant that appearances were more important than anything else. His stiff upper lip, exaggerated by bereavement, resulted in all four children being denied parental love and affection, compounding any sense of abandonment from the abrupt death of their mama. Edwin installed his two pious and pathologically cruel sisters, who fired the children's nanny, breathed fire and brimstone into Gwen and her siblings, then disappeared.

Sharpening the sense of loss and dislocation, Edwin then moved the family from their home "with all its old associations, its family traditions" to a new house in a new town. The house was "dark and cube-like, with a peeling façade . . . in a dreary little street." Although Gwen rarely spoke of her childhood—and never with any happiness—Augustus described their new home as "a kind of mortuary where everything was dead, like the stuffed doves in their glass dome in the drawing room and fleshless as the abominable skeleton clock on the mantel piece: this museum of rubbish, changing only in the imperceptible process of its decay, reflected the frozen immobility of its curator's mind." The children's bedroom was so cold they piled furniture onto their beds to keep warm on chilly nights. Meanwhile Edwin, a stickler for rules as well as for appearances, insisted that Gwen swallow every mouthful of the rice pudding she so loathed, down to the very last scraping.

Marooned in his own grief and anxiety, Edwin was unable to show love, affection, or emotion. In their cold, gloomy, and silent home, Gwen and her sister invented a language based on touch and facial expressions, but this too was forbidden by Edwin.

Unsurprisingly, the children made an alternative home in the cliffs, woods, and wet shingle beaches where Augustus and Gwen would fling off their clothes and throw themselves in and out of the waves.

All of this Gwen carried inside her. The early and sudden loss of her mother, the chill neglect of her father, a new house that was more mausoleum than home, the stark juxtaposition of indoor authority with outdoor liberty.

What does that do to a child of eight? Or a woman of twenty-seven?

~

As Gwen walked, brashly sketching men in bars along the way, Sigmund Freud sat in his study a thousand miles away, making the first connections between the experience of loss in childhood and later manifestations of melancholy (depression). Since then new branches of science, from neuroscience to developmental psychopathology, have led to an explosion of knowledge on the effects of trauma. And hundreds of studies have linked the premature loss of a parent with depression, anxiety, or other psychiatric disorder, as well as physical illness. We now know that trauma produces actual physiological change, including, according to leading trauma researcher Bessel van der Kolk, "a recalibration of the brain's alarm system, an increase in stress hormone activity, and alterations in the system that filters relevant information from irrelevant."[5]

The early death of a parent is repeatedly cited as a particularly profound form of adversity, one that becomes dramatically exaggerated if the surviving parent or caregiver simultaneously withdraws any love or affection. A 1980s study conducted by Karlen Lyons-Ruth found that emotional withdrawal had a disturbing and long-lasting impact on children. It wasn't the finding she expected: she had assumed hostile and aggressive parenting would be more damaging. Instead she identified a "striking and unexpected link" between a parent's emotional withdrawal and later feelings of disconnection and depression.[6]

In his book *The Body Keeps the Score*, Van der Kolk describes how our brains are fundamentally rewired by early exposure to trauma: "Trauma is not just an event that took place sometime in the past; it is also the imprint left by that experience on mind, brain, and body. . . . It changes not only how we think and what we think about, but also our very capacity to think." Of particular interest is Van der Kolk's identification of a consistent profile among children suffering from trauma—a profile that seems to reflect many of Gwen's later traits while seeping into her art in unexpected ways.

According to Van der Kolk, traumatised children often grow up to show a pervasive pattern of emotional dysregulation, problems with concentration and attention, and difficulties getting along with themselves and other people. The physical alteration of their brain forces many to "try to shut themselves down and develop tunnel vision and hyperfocus." They often repeat the same behaviours, he adds, finding it hard to learn from their experience. To boot, the endless pumping-out of stress hormones makes them prone to numerous physical problems, from poor immunity to headaches, sleep disturbances, and premature death.

All at once, much of Gwen's idiosyncratic behaviour begins to make sense: her omnipresent battle for concentration; her disordered eating; her dislike of social situations; her enduring and often inexplicable poor health; her obsessional love—first of Rodin and, later, of a woman called Vera Oumancoff, both of whom she frequently stalked and cringingly abased herself before.

More striking still is the way in which Gwen found ways and means to master the stubbornly disruptive feelings that threatened to overwhelm her. Van der Kolk identifies three strategies for countering trauma: talking therapies that can help process difficult memories; medication that closes down certain pathways; and experiences that effectively "contradict the helplessness, rage, or collapse that result from trauma." One such experience, he explains, is physical movement. Another is art. Gwen had no access to medication or to a skilled psychotherapist. Instead she used her art, her love of rural walking, her deep connection with the sea, her letter writing and extensive journaling, to explore who she was, to imaginatively unconfine herself, to symbolically reorder herself, to provide a much-needed sense of calm and control. Her journals and letters make it abundantly clear how difficult this was, the struggle and dedication it required, the toll it took on her health. For Gwen was frequently unwell, lamenting how "much time is lost by ill health." She littered her letters with references to being ill (headaches, colds, lassitude, fevers) and complaints of her "great great depression," noting that "the terrible depression has passed" or "the cloud of depression" was descending.

And yet her creation of such monumentally beautiful paintings was—paradoxically—the result of her psychological disequilibrium. Her overriding need was not to make friends or cultivate family but to make sense and order of her life, to repair, recreate, and *free* herself. For this she needed solitude. And in that solitude she threw off her past, forgot the future, and existed only in the moment—immersed, engrossed, and mistress of herself.

⌒

Gwen's need for solitude tolls through her letters and her journals: "I must stay in solitude to do my work"; "Every moment alone makes me what I am"; "I am better alone"; "I should like to go and live somewhere where I meet nobody I know"; "Be alone."

And then, her best-known words: "I may never have anything to express except this desire for a more interior life." No wonder her introspection became the focus of her painting. No wonder the solitude that became so central to her life was so central to her art.

By the time she left the Slade School of Art in 1898, Gwen was already showing the first signs of her fascination with pictorial space and with depicting the interior lives of her sitters. She left London for Paris, studying with the American painter James McNeill Whistler and consolidating her understanding of paint. Here she began making self-portraits, perhaps tasting for the first time the power of the portraitist to recreate herself through the medium of paint. "Gwen John is sitting before a mirror carefully posing herself," wrote Ida, who was studying alongside Gwen in Paris. "She has been at it for half an hour."[7]

Gwen loved Paris—its sense of freedom, its artistic possibility. She wanted to stay, but when her father visited to discuss a prospective allowance, she responded with fury to his greeting: "You look like a prostitute." Showing the sense of autonomy that was to mark her life, she retorted that she could never take money from someone who thought like that. Her pride and stubborn independence meant the end of Paris.

She returned to London, to a bleakly miserable time that she called her "subterranean period," and that Susan Chitty, her first biographer, termed her "disturbed years." Later Gwen recalled, "I saw nobody." She needed other people, but she also recognised in herself a growing compulsion to be alone: "People are like shadows to me and I am like a shadow," she wrote to a friend. She was becoming aware of the circumstances necessary for her to make art: "It requires a quiet mind for me to paint," she wrote a few years later.[8]

Despite being frequently homeless or confined to basement flats where, according to her brother, "no ray of light ever entered,"[9] Gwen produced two of her best-known portraits—and it's here that we find her reinventing herself, beginning to turn inwards. Her *Self-Portrait*—now hanging in the National Portrait Gallery—shows Gwen as the woman she wanted to be: modern, assertive, affirming and flaunting her identity as an artist. She famously described herself as a waif, but there is nothing waiflike in this portrait. Gwen dazzles with her modish dress, her bravura, her technical abilities, her knowledge of the conventions of portraiture.

Within a year, Gwen had painted another highly accomplished self-portrait. Now hanging in Tate Britain, *Self-Portrait in a Red Blouse* startlingly and dramatically reveals a new version of Gwen John: more introspective, less sure of herself. Her clothes—flamboyant and fashionable in her first self-portrait—have become neat and demure, less distracting. She no longer looks the viewer in the eye. Instead she asks us to look not *at* her, but *into* her.

Gwen's professor at the Slade was so impressed by this painting that he bought it, hung it in his studio, and then painted himself in front of it. But despite the painting's technical brilliance, Gwen felt no satisfaction, no pride. She might as well not have done it, she told a friend, for in all the time it had taken her, she hadn't derived more than a few seconds of pleasure.

When my children learnt to walk, I sometimes took them to Tate Britain to look at animal paintings. I'd stopped scrutinising Gwen's painting of Dorelia by then, but we always left the gallery via Gwen's *Self-Portrait in a Red Blouse*. There were days when I found it deeply unsettling, when I could barely look at her and we would hurry past. But on the days when I stopped and gazed, I tried to fathom what it was that disconcerted me. Was it the black velvet ribbon that gripped her throat like a noose? Was it the blood red of the blouse? Was it the tartan on her blouse that looked more like the struts and bars of a cage than the markings of a pattern? Was it the arms pressed so tightly to her body? Or the hair flattened so neatly against her scalp? Or the smallness of the canvas? Or was it the paintwork, at once so iridescent and so scratched out?

Beneath the splendid surface shimmer of *Self-Portrait in a Red Blouse* lurked something uncomfortable. Gwen was painting herself in confinement.

One hundred and twenty years ago Gwen's decision to seek out solitude—to make solitude the bedrock of her life—was dangerously radical. It continues to be radical. But it seems to me that, especially in our hyperconnected age, solitude is also essential. In the last few years I'd watched my teenage daughters accrue huge webs of online "friends." I'd felt their pressure to "like" and "share" on social media. I'd started to feel it myself, vaguely resentful of the time appropriated by all this digital socialising, of the unspoken expectation to foster online communities, to *join in*. Studies confirm that the pressure on women is particularly acute. Already constrained by the additional burdens of caring for others,[10] we also feel more duty to engage online, to reply (promptly) to the never-ending scroll of images and comments from our swelling panoply of "friends." It reminded me of my earlier working life—the unceasing injunctions to network, to behave like a team player.

Living in London, cheek by jowl with millions of others, compounded my sense of never being alone. As did having an iPhone, which, despite being immensely useful, seemed to have thrown me into the digital arms of thousands more. My feelings were ambivalent—social media and the internet have introduced me to many wonderful people—but I couldn't help thinking that all this obsessive togetherness made solitude both more intimidating *and* more necessary. Meanwhile, the media ran repeated stories on the damage (invariably dementia) wreaked by being alone, by social isolation. It seemed to me that admitting to a desire to be alone was both contrary and freighted with implication.

Reading through Gwen's letters, I'm reminded that society has never trusted a woman alone. A woman who enjoys solitude, who needs time apart from others, is viewed with deep suspicion. Either she's alone because she can't find a companion, in which case there's something wrong with her—is she weird? a narcissist? or just sad and lonely? Or else she's alone *because* she's actively hunting for a mate. A clandestine prostitute perhaps. Or—worse still—she's shirking her responsibilities. Women are expected to care for their offspring, their elderly parents, their partners. They're expected to sustain the fabric of communities. So it stands to reason that a woman demanding time alone is not only potentially deranged, shamefully lusty, or tragically lonely and abandoned but utterly selfish to boot. In her letters, Gwen repeatedly records the public response to her walking alone: men followed her in the street, they frightened her in forests, they accosted her, wanting to know why she was on her own.

Things have improved, but as I was about to find out, many people were still baffled by my solitary walking. Even in an age and culture that values the individual and her autonomy and liberty beyond (almost) all else, women are not allowed to admit a love of solitude. Ironic, really.

It was to be another seventy years before a woman could publicly champion her need for solitude. The writer May Sarton wrote that "loneliness is the poverty of self; solitude is richness of self." In her groundbreaking memoir *Journal of a Solitude* (1973), Sarton explained that without time alone, she lost her centre: "I feel dispersed, scattered, in pieces." Even the smallest interruption threatened her periods of "happy and fruitful isolation."

The psychiatrist Anthony Storr in his seminal book *Solitude* described a creative person's "most significant moments" as those in which "she attains some new insight, or makes some new discovery; and these moments are chiefly, if not invariably, those in which she is alone."* But time spent alone does more than enhance our creativity. It gives us a greater sense of freedom. It deepens our relationship with the spiritual and the natural. It helps us understand who we are. According to Storr, the capacity to be alone is "an aspect of emotional maturity." As she walked along the banks of the River Garonne, Gwen was moving closer and closer to that emotional maturity.

---

*Storr used "he." For obvious reasons I have changed it to "she."

I like thinking of my old crisis of confinement as the onset of "emotional maturity." I roll the words round in my mouth, taste them, savour them. "Emotional maturity" feels so much better than the churlish, shameful guilt and the raging claustrophobia that struck on short, wintry days when the rain wouldn't stop and the babies wailed and the washing machine spewed dirty water over the kitchen floor and rats scuttled out from under the fridge.

Gwen had a similar experience, crystallising her desire for exile, for art over domesticity, for open space and solitude. Ida gave birth to her first son (Gwen's first nephew) in Liverpool, and Gwen hurried to help. Ida was struggling. "[He] howls," she wrote to a friend. "He is howling now. I have done all I can for him. . . . I think he would very much rather not have been created." In another letter, she wrote, "Baby takes so much time—and the rooms we are in are not kept very clean, so I am always dusting and brushing." Gwen escaped the domestic chaos and Ida's incoherence by pushing her new nephew round Liverpool, writing snappishly to a friend, "I have been very busy with the baby."

There's a photograph taken at this time that I return to again and again. It shows a profoundly awkward Gwen, at the very edge of a picture that includes Augustus, Ida, and their new baby. The picture is dominated by Ida's and Augustus's hats—voluminous and carefully centred within the frame. Gwen, who loved hats, is bareheaded, her hair drawn tightly back. As a result her head appears tiny, like the baby's. She stands slightly apart from the family trio, her neck and arms rigid, her shoulders braced. Everyone looks into the camera, except Gwen, who looks stubbornly into the distance. Refusing to meet our eye. Refusing to be a part of this Happy Family. Refusing to play along, even for the camera. Already she was exiling herself.

⌒

As I walk through the valley of the Garonne, the messy daily urgencies of life evaporate. The twitchiness of the city fades and a sense of calm settles deep inside me, as if I'm moving not outwards but inwards.

The countryside is empty, abandoned. Occasionally I see a man on a machine—a digger or a tractor. This is not the countryside Gwen and Dorelia walked through. There are no hedgers, ditchers, fruit pickers, tramps, tinkers, drovers, or shepherds. The river is deserted, the old ports little more than bleached posts and slimed bricks. No pleasure boats, fishing tugs, gravel dredgers, or reed pickers. The canal is quiet. No barges, tub boats, mules, gypsies, or labourers. There are just enough cyclists on the towpath to make me feel that I haven't entirely disconnected myself, that I'm quite safe. And in this eerie emptiness, I realise that I'm not alone. Beside me the river runs, my guide, my steadfast accomplice, whispering sweet nothings in my ear, throwing needle-brilliant shafts of light my way. And in this muted bubbling companionship I'm reminded of my children, their chitter-chatter, the way they toss me sweets and chocolates as we walk together. How can I be alone when I have a river beside me?

Only when I arrive at my room for the night do I feel peculiar for being by myself. The vulnerability that plagues the solo female walker, that makes our experience infinitely more complicated, springs to life.

"You are all alone?" My host's gaze sweeps over my shoulder and I find myself involuntarily turning my head, as if I've somehow misplaced my walking companion.

"*Je suis toute seule*," I say. "*Moi et mon sac à dos!*" I laugh nervously. Already he has made me feel slightly ashamed of being without a companion. Ashamed enough to convert my rucksack into a sort of friend-substitute.

François tells me that he usually cooks for his guests. For twenty euros he'll cook three courses and provide two glasses of wine. I've not eaten since a lunch of wild figs, a stolen apple, and a handful of blackberries, so I agree and head off for a shower.

In my room is a visitors' book, full of enthusiastic comments from couples with names like Eric and Monique, Pierre and Patricia. "Wonderful food from François and marvellous hospitality from Violette," I read, with a jolt of relief. I feel better knowing there's a woman floating around, although I'm not sure why. Perhaps it's the peculiar artwork on the walls—charcoal sketches of naked females with amputated breasts and dismembered feet. Or perhaps it's the penholder—a moulded pair of buttocks between which a pen has been decisively wedged.

I go down at the appointed hour of 7:30 PM, keen to meet Violette, keen to explore the sensibilities of a wife who has images of mutilated women up and down her stairs. Gwen swims back into my mind as I recall Rodin's cast, for which she modelled. It was left incomplete, both arms amputated above the elbow.

But there's only François in the kitchen, a glass of wine in one hand and a half-emptied wine bottle in the other. I scan the room, looking for my table.

"We shall eat overlooking the Garonne." He gestures outside to a large table on a balcony.

I wonder if he's drunk and wish Violette would turn up. There are more mutilated women hanging on the kitchen wall, their limbs chopped up and rearranged in a disturbing collage of body parts. François sees me eyeing them.

"Voodoo art," he says, and then adds, "We will eat together."

I peer through the gloom to the balcony, expecting the table to be laid for three. It isn't. It's laid for two.

"Normally I serve my guests," he continues. "If you were two, I would serve. I would not join. But you are all alone . . ."

I want to tell him that I'm rather enjoying being *all alone*, but it's dawning on me that there is no Violette, that perhaps Violette has been dismembered and disposed of. Perhaps it's the remains of Violette staring down at me from every wall.

"I have four children," I blurt, as if this will protect me.

"By four men?"

I'm so startled by his question—which I have never been asked before—that words flee me. François fills the sudden silence with another of his unnerving questions. "And now you are divorced?"

"No!"

"No? So what are you doing here on your own?"

François looks utterly bewildered until I tell him I'm researching a book. Then he gives a loud exhalation, smacking of comprehension—and relief. "You are a writer doing research! You are on a pilgrimage!"

I nod vigorously. That's right, I think. I'm not a woman roaming around for the sheer pleasure of her own solitude. I have valid *reasons.*

He points his finger at me, waggles it, and says, "You are a terrible mother."

⌒

One hundred and sixteen years earlier, Gwen and Dorelia arrived in the same town late in the evening, tired, hungry, and in search of a room. In a letter to her friend Ursula Tyrwhitt, Gwen explained that they rarely took rooms, being unable to afford them, except when they arrived after dark because then "it is rather dangerous." The men, she continued, "want to know where we are going to sleep and follow us."

At the first inn, the landlady refused to give them a room, saying "she had not got one, which was a lie." The two girls tried every inn the town possessed but were consistently turned away: "They did not like us in that village, they thought us *mauvaises sujets.*"

Gwen and Dorelia sang and drew portraits in return for a few coins with which they paid for meals. But still they were treated with either hostile suspicion or lewd curiosity. "And what do you think the woman charged: two francs for our dinner and we had hardly anything—I called her a thief," wrote Gwen. After this spartan supper, the inevitable happened: "We left in haste and fear," and "we were followed by two men" who left Gwen and Dorelia alone only when Gwen "spoke like an angel" and promised to meet them later. That night they slept "under some haystacks," until Gwen was "woken by Dorelia saying there was a man looking at us.... We had a little congregation."

Their journey, during which they were "frightfully hungry and tired," continued in much the same vein: "Things turned out badly again for us because they [the local people] could not make us out ... the people were very inhospitable ... they would not sell us bread.... When we were sleeping some people from the town came and saw us.... I cannot write any more now as two *mauvais sujets* are sitting by us and will not go away."[11]

Young women didn't walk—unchaperoned, unescorted— through the countryside beneath "half a hundred weight" of easels and painting equipment. They didn't visit inns and try to eat alongside the male clientele. These were men's spaces unaccustomed to the presence of bold young women whose bodies weren't for sale. Gwen and Dorelia were inexplicably different, brazen outsiders that aroused fear as much as they did bafflement or licentious curiosity.

⁓

Progress has—thankfully—intervened. Although a woman backpacking alone is still subversive, still a little challenging, I inspire no suspicion or hostility. But plenty of bemused curiosity: "Why are you on your own?" "Aren't you bored of your own company? Lonely?" "Don't you have any friends that like to walk?"

One day, as I'm crossing a narrow humpbacked bridge, a white car slams to a halt beside me amidst an impressive squealing of brakes. "Where are you walking?" demands the driver, in French, from beneath her helmet of white hair.

"Toulouse," I reply.

She thumps her palm against the steering wheel and roars with laughter. "*Bravo! Bravo! Toute seule?*"

"*Oui.*"

"*Vous avez du courage! Beaucoup de courage!*" She leans over to the passenger seat and shouts to the elderly man beside her, "*Elle va à Toulouse! À Toulouse! Toute seule!*"

"*Bravo!*" shouts the man. "*Vous avez de la bravoure!*"

"*Bonne chance,*" they screech in unison, the car jolting forward and disappearing into the distance.

"Did you hear that?" I look over my shoulder at my *sac à dos.* "We have courage and valour."

Later, a bicycle stops beside me and a man in a flat cap asks the same question. I give him the same answer.

"*Vraiment? Toute seule?*"

I nod and he punches the air with excitement. "*Vous avez du courage! Vous êtes une aventurière, madame! Anglaise?*"

"*Oui.*" I nod. He waves and wobbles off, shouting, "I lived once in England . . . terrible bread . . . terrible weather . . . only apples to eat!"

⌒

I'm sitting on an isolated stretch of untrodden path a short way from the canal, and studying my map, when a man in a red T-shirt cycles past. I blink, startled. The cycle path is on the other side of the canal, and my path—which is more of an

overgrown track that I've beaten aside with my walking pole—
is rutted and fringed with tangled briars and knotted willows.
I've not passed another person for three hours, so I'm already
thinking of this as *my secret route*. Besides, how can he possibly
ride a bicycle without being whipped and torn to shreds?

For a second I wonder if he's been stalking me, following
me quietly while I thrashed about in a skirmish of thorns and
thistles. But he cycles on, so I breathe a sigh of relief and return
to studying my map.

But then I hear a rustling, a bumping . . . the jolting of wheels
and the brushing of willow boughs. I look up. The man is lurching
towards me, his red T-shirt flashing like the eye of a police siren.
Why is he coming back? My body stiffens. Even before I've asked
myself the question (why *is* he coming back?), images are swirling
round my head. My mind races through the contents of my rucksack. Dirty clothes. Books. What else? What else? No time—it's
too securely fastened. And then with relief I remember the whistle attached to the strap of my pack. Which strap? Underneath or
on top? But there's no one to hear my whistle, I think, panicked,
groping around for the miniature plastic whistle that had seemed
such a clever device when I bought the rucksack. I reach for my
walking pole, everything inside me fizzing with inarticulate dread.

Calm down, I say to myself, trying to muster some rational thought process from all this bodily shaking and rattling.
He's probably lost. He's probably cycling back to find the track.
If I helpfully point him back the way he came—"*Le route de
vélo, c'est là-bas*"—he'll be gone. I can hear his wheels juddering
through the runnels, his angry curses as he pushes aside brambles and saplings.

But then I look up and my hands freeze. My breath stops, forming a sort of gag of terror in my throat. The man has dismounted from his bike. Just ten feet from me. Why would he do that? Why would he stop here?

I wait for him to walk towards me, guessing that he'll either want directions (says my rational, optimistic brain) or attack me (shrieks some other part of me that is also urging me to run, now!).

Instead he sits down. Just ten feet from me. In the sudden silence my breath begins to return to normal and I wonder why he's taking so long to attack. Still shaking, I pack away my map and stand up. My plan involves walking away, very fast. If I head through the undergrowth and towards the canal, I can throw off my backpack and jump in—perhaps a boat will save me. In these strange, uncertain moments of planning my escape, time seems to elongate, the seconds passing with hideous sluggishness.

I come out of this odd, fearful torpor when I notice he's talking to me. He's apologising. In French he's apologising for having frightened me, disturbed me. And I notice why he's chosen to pause beside me—he's sitting on a sawn-off tree trunk. And swigging at a water bottle. He must have cycled past, then turned back thinking it might be the only place to sit along this prickly, overgrown path.

I'm so relieved, I smile and tell him I'm going to Toulouse.

"Are you a pilgrim?" he asks. "Are you doing the Compostela?" He gestures into the distance and tells me I have strayed considerably from the ancient Catholic pilgrimage route to Santiago.

I explain that I'm a sort of pilgrim, an answer I've learnt people like to hear. It means I'm neither weird nor deranged nor friendless.

We chat, we compare routes, we look at my ragged map. Eventually we walk on, together. I beat back the overgrowth with a stick, he threads his bike through my beaten path. By the time we reach the bridge, we're almost friends. He points to the left and turns his bike to the right. "*Au revoir et bonne chance,*" he says, offering me his hand, which is flushed pink with sunburn.

I head off through the slanting September light, a new buoyancy in my step. I feel . . . invincible. As if I have mastered some obtuse fear, proven it irrational and unworthy.

Being alone in remote places makes us feel vulnerable. It's one more anxiety we juggle as we walk, another emotion in a complicated series of emotions peculiar to women. Will I be harassed or assaulted? Will I arrive before dark? Is this area safe? Can I stop here or should I keep marching? Where can I go to the toilet?

Women of the past walked with amplified fears for their personal safety, compounded by worries of how they would be perceived and whether their reputations could survive intact. Long skirts, petticoats, and notions of "femininity" and "decency" made disappearing behind brambles for a wee more complex than it is for me. I've never forgotten Frieda Lawrence explaining how, in her first marriage, she wasn't supposed to be seen *opening the door* to the WC, something echoed by the English writer Flora Thompson, who wrote in her memoir that every "Victorian child . . . had been taught that no one must even see her approach the door" of the privy.[12]

In spite of progress, I have expended far too much mental effort on finding suitably discreet locations. On one treeless day, when Lycra-clad cyclists were shooting past me every few minutes, I took a thirty-minute detour simply to find somewhere to pee.

As I mull over this, a boat swings past me. At the wheel is an elegantly headscarfed woman. I raise my hand in a salute of post-survival vigour and optimism, sister to sister. As the boat passes, I notice a man standing on deck. From the back of the boat, he is peeing into the canal, making careless arcs of urine in the air. And grinning at me.

⌒

What is it about being a religious pilgrim that makes a walking woman suddenly acceptable? Is it because there already exists a tradition of women going on pilgrimages as companions and bearers, making the idea less alien? Or is it because the very word *pilgrim*—in its religious context—denotes qualities of surrender, submission, and deference, making a walking pilgrim woman so much less threatening? After all, if she's on a religious pilgrimage, she must be pure and dutiful, not a runaway abandoning her female obligations, threatening the social order. It's surely no coincidence that wealthy Japanese women of the past were totally housebound except for the rare occasions when they were permitted to go on a pilgrimage. For countless women throughout history, a pilgrimage was the only time they left their homes.

To walk in the spirit of freedom, independence, adventure, to walk for oneself, is as transgressive today as it was for our mothers and grandmothers. This is changing, slowly, steadily. But too slowly for my puzzled and perplexed hosts.

On the next night, when I'm asked why I'm walking to Toulouse, I sigh and say, "I'm a pilgrim." I don't want to have to explain—in broken French—that my sort of pilgrimage is infinitely more complex, more unpredictable, more nuanced than the faith pilgrimage they have in mind.

Pilgrimages are a splendid reason to walk long distances, be they secular or religious. But why can't we simply walk?

⌒

In 1985, when I was twenty, I vented in my diary about being unable to walk alone in the country. I had come through a period of profound disequilibrium and I wanted—more than anything—to hike in solitude. I found my diary recently—this is what I had written in my embittered rancour:

> Why can't I walk on my own? How come I can vote, get married, have children, get a job, go to prison—but not go for a simple walk? It pisses me off. I could go, I suppose. But I would be terrified. So what's the point of that? Why must I always be terrified?

My teenage years unfolded against the backdrop of the serial rapist and murderer Peter Sutcliffe, or the Yorkshire Ripper. Young women were disappearing, their bodies turning up horrifically mutilated. We grew up fearing nightfall, darkness. We came to believe that, come twilight, we needed to be inside, behind closed doors. We came to believe that we could not walk alone. Although Yorkshire was his territory of choice, we were warned that nowhere was safe. For five years he was hunted by police. How could one man outwit hundreds of detectives? The question compounded our dread.

Meanwhile, I experienced the usual unwanted male attention—the whistling, the catcalling, the endless following. As soon as I began going out without my parents (around the age of thirteen), I discovered what it was to be propositioned. It seemed that any man could approach me, regardless of my circumstances or age. I was accosted as I returned from the shops, on escalators in the London Tube, in the cafe where I waitressed after school, while pedalling on my bike. On my first trip to the hairdresser the (middle-aged, balding) stylist rubbed himself hard against me for the entire duration of my haircut. I was flashed at, leered at, groped at. On and on it went.

Several years later, in a tent on the southern coast of Turkey, I woke to the sharp press of an unfamiliar body. Muzzy-eyed, I wondered where my boyfriend was, what was happening. Hands were inside my clothes, but I knew they weren't his hands. Besides, he was on my right, asleep. To my left a man was burrowing into my sleeping bag and pushing his hands under my T-shirt. I recognised him—he was one of the Turkish students who had befriended us over supper.

Even then, something prevented me from shouting out. As if I was frightened of hurting his feelings, or of aggravating him. Instead I shook The Boyfriend, who shoved the man out in a spew of curses, dirty clothes, reeking trainers. It was the middle of the night, but we packed up the tent and walked away, trudging through the darkness until a saffron sun rose out of the sea.

⁓

It took another two decades before I felt able to walk alone. I was helped by a large black dog, acquired expressly for the purpose of feeling safe while I ran along a London towpath or walked over the Sussex Downs at dawn. I credit my dog for the slow return of my ability to feel safe on my own.

Another fifteen years and here I am, exquisitely and powerfully free, walking in my own time, at my own speed, with my own thoughts. And utterly alone. And yet terror—which is profoundly constraining—lies skin-deep.

The unwanted harassment that has historically accompanied a woman walking in remote landscapes—described by Lillias Campbell Davidson in her 1889 *Hints to Lady Travellers* as "the danger . . . of annoyance from impertinent or obtrusive attentions from travellers of the other sex"—raised its ugly head throughout the years I spent researching this book.

In letters written in her early twenties, Frieda Weekley (as she was then) wrote of "strange men" following her and her children when she took them to the beach. "On the day your last letter came," she wrote to a friend, "I was in a cove alone with the children when a huge blond country lad began hanging around us, followed us, where the path became dark and narrow he propositioned me, I walked straight past but then I hear him making a strangled sound like the bellowing of a bull, he's about to attack me, I turn round and, happening to have the children's spades in my hand, wave them in the air and shout out, go away, you are mad. . . . Afterwards I was completely exhausted by the moral effort."[13]

Gwen John complained, throughout her time in France, of unwanted male attention. In Paris, when she sat in cafes to draw or write letters, she was invariably approached. Her love of wild and solitary walking was dampened by the need to think of her safety: "I did not go far from the path for the sake of security. . . . (This is because there are many men who always go around, but if you are in the open they don't dare come near you.)" On one particular country walk, she was pursued by a man with his penis on display. No wonder she wrote, "I am not myself except in my room" (which was blatantly untrue), and sought refuge for a while in the repeated painting of her room.

For the Anglo-German writer and poet Mathilde Blind, an "evil-looking French man" destroyed her solitary Alpine walk, following her repeatedly and pulling at her skirts so that she had to swing "such a blow right in the face that he fell back, the blood streaming from somewhere, probably his nose—but I did not stop. I simply raced along as if I had wings to my heels."[14]

For the writer Mary Eyre, in 1863, it was Spanish men: "A respectable, quietly-dressed woman, walking quietly alone, is subject to insult and outrage in the streets. . . . Even accompanied by a guide, I was yet subjected to hooting and insult," she wrote of her long-distance walks in the Pyrenees. This constant unwanted male attention obstructed her chosen pursuit, making it "absolutely impossible to gather the rare and beautiful plants that adorn [the] mountains."[15]

But harassment wasn't solely the prerogative of French or Spanish men, of course. In 1934, the Dutch journalist and author Odette Keun wrote, "Again and again I have been amazed at what happens to me in the parks, when I am sitting quietly in a chair with a book. An Englishman arrives, bows and squats down on the grass by my side. . . . He talks to me about the weather—so politely that it is impossible to reply only by a grunt. After two minutes: 'Won't you come for a drive in my car?' he asks. . . . Or: 'Won't you come and have tea in my flat, it's just round the corner.'" Keun was surprised that nothing, not even her age, deterred men from accosting her, saying emphatically, "I am *not* a young woman."[16]

In parks and on urban streets, women were able to find (some) safety by staying near other people, as Gwen did. In the wilds there were fewer people, so walking alone required another layer of audacity and courage. In 1938, the Finnish author and artist Tove Jansson took an early morning walk to the Italian seaside, a mile and a half from where she was holidaying. Despite the early hour, she was waylaid almost immediately by a bearded farmer riding a horse with its ears sheathed in red knitted ear warmers, and a pink silk bow tied round its neck. The usual questions began: Signora or signorina? All alone? Why alone? Jansson answered honestly—she was unmarried, she was alone. The hairy farmer whipped out a wallet stuffed with grubby notes and invited her to become his wife. Jansson was subjected to repeated harassment in Italy, and finally invented a fictitious husband for herself. But it wasn't only men who harassed her for being alone and different. A few months before in Brittany, she'd made the mistake of swimming after 4:00 PM, when the local school disgorged its pupils. Spotting a woman in a bathing costume (something they'd never seen before), the children chased her, pelting her with stones.[17]

The truth is that there are many more assaults on women in urban areas than in rural areas. We are safer—from dangerous men at any rate—in the wilds than in the city.[18] Most attacks are committed by people we know, indoors. We are safer outside than inside. We read about horrific rapes and random murders of strangers in wild places, but in reality these are few and far between. We know about them because they garner a disproportionate number of lurid headlines—headlines that inflame our nascent feelings of fear and vulnerability.

The graphic images these violent crimes provoke are exceptionally hard—if not impossible—to shift. For years I wouldn't take my children to a nearby park because a mother and her child had been brutally attacked there. Others felt the same way, none of us able to shake off the disturbing images lodged in our brains. The park was abandoned, making it more dangerous than ever and denying us the opportunity for exercise, fresh air, trees, sky.

Instead of letting fear restrain us, we must remind ourselves of the facts and press on, reclaiming the countryside and the wilderness for ourselves, for our daughters, granddaughters, and great-granddaughters. We must also press our governments for change. In 2018, France introduced a law to curb the harassment of women in public places. The first of its kind, this legislation means men can now be fined for wolf-whistling, shouting insults, making sexual noises and gestures, following women, and other forms of pestering. Twelve months after the law was passed, 731 fines had been handed out, ranging from €90 to €1,500. While many French women believe this is merely the tip of the iceberg and that most women still won't report this type of chronic everyday harassment, it is a move in the right direction.

Liberation comes in many guises. It's a constantly shifting goal requiring dogged and sustained effort and work. So now, when I'm walking alone and I feel that familiar prickle of fear, I think of Simone de Beauvoir's memoir, her words of bravura: "I had no intention of making my life a bore with precautions . . ."[19]

Or I remind myself of the American writer Mary Lee Settle, who one day walked alone up a deserted Turkish hillside. The path was so overgrown she had to push aside weeds, brambles, tangled vines. All of a sudden she saw a man, looming out of the overgrowth. "He stood there in front of me, smiling, quite silent, a large strong Turkish man," she wrote. But instead of attacking her or insulting her, he offered her a "small bunch of sweet wild thyme." The man—who was deaf—then led her to some hidden ruins, where he gave her a guided tour, miming the purpose of each stone, of each ruined room. At the end of the tour, he put his arms around her and kissed her on both cheeks. Settle was so deeply moved, she took the bunch of thyme home, pressed it, and kept it for the rest of her life.[20]

In the village of Meilhan, I stay in a house where everything is so *loved*, so *attended* to, that I feel myself at risk of being dusted, polished, and arranged on a shelf. The house feels almost oppressive beneath its weight of ordered choreography. An antique spoon with a corkscrew handle has been fastidiously placed so that the light from my bedroom window catches on the well-polished silver, projecting a stippled flurry of brightness onto the ceiling. A sherbet-yellow ribbon has been tied round a rolled bath towel with satin edging. The bed, which is of old mahogany in the French Empire style, is layered with cushions in coordinating sizes and scrupulously ordered throws. Every picture, every book, every *objet* has been located for effect. I tiptoe through the room, reluctant to touch or move a single item, and wondering how I am to lie—let alone sleep—in such an immaculately dressed bed.

Over breakfast—a crystal glass of orange juice, a cut-glass butter dish the weight of a brick, croissants on antique linen and gold-painted bone china that must be washed by hand—I talk to the owner, Pierre. He likes my interest in his paintings, in his thin Wedgwood porcelain, in the composition and curation of his dining room.

After half an hour of talk, Pierre asks me—in a hushed voice suffused with mystery—if I would like to see his studio. "When you have finished your *petit déjeuner*, knock here," he says, pointing at a door hidden behind a potted palm.

His voice—its lowered tone so rich with promise—piques me. I feel utterly safe with Pierre, so I finish my croissant, meticulously collecting every flake and crumb on a dampened fingertip, and knock on the secret door.

Surprisingly, it opens into a dark, dishevelled den—maroon walls, heavy drapes—stacked with canvases. Pictures cant from every wall, giddily, with none of the precision of the public rooms. I feel as if I've stepped backstage—from a brilliantly lit theatre set to the disordered hubbub of a dressing room.

Pierre appears, soundlessly, from a connecting room. "My collection," he announces. I glance round the room at pictures that seem oddly familiar. I peer through the gloom at a small pencil drawing. Is it a . . . ? No, it can't be. I peer again, seeking out a signature. It is! It's a Chagall. My gaze moves to the next, a small painting on an easel. A seascape in shades of turquoise, signed by—I peer more closely—Gustave Courbet! Above the Courbet is a drawing by Jean Cocteau.

He goes to a corner and pulls out a square canvas, the size of a small window. "My current restoration project," he says. The signature on this frayed and peeling canvas is in red paint and as clear as anything: "A. Lhote."

"Gwen John went to André Lhote's classes in the 1930s," I say breathlessly. It occurs to me that somewhere in these stacks of unrestored art there could be a Gwen John drawing, one of the many she did on her walk in exchange for beer or bread.

"Gwen John," he repeats, frowning and rubbing at his nose. "A woman? Not many women painting then." This, of course, is nonsense. Hundreds of women were painting then: when Gwen John started at the Slade School of Art in 1895, the women "outnumbered and outshone" the men.[21] The Paris art schools overflowed with talented female pupils from as far afield as Australia and America, a few of whom are finally beginning to be recognised, but most of whom have slipped silently through the cracks of the artistic canon.

"No," he continues, "I do not know your Gwen John." His collection, he explains, has been amassed from *les brocantes* and *les marchés aux puces* (junk shops and flea markets) and consists of his speciality, French masters between 1870 and 1930. He prefers *les marines* (paintings of the sea and the seaside), he adds, sweeping his arm round the wine-dark walls of his studio.

This was a period when the painting of water and sea was much favoured as a subject. Rivers and seascapes appear frequently in the works of Pissarro, Sisley, Whistler, Monet, Bonnard, Courbet, Sickert, and many others. Boats, canals, oceans, streams, lakes, bridges, ports, beach scenes—a proliferation of (male) artists experimented with the technical complexities of painting water flow, reflections, dappled half-light falling on churning waves, the gleam of seawater on skin, the swelling of tides, the motion of ripples, the cascading of waterfalls. The sea and water were male spaces, the preserve of male painters. Portraits and interiors were suitable subject matters for women. Not for them the vast and liberating infinity of the ocean.

Gwen painted her only known beach scene in Tenby when she was twenty. And yet her painterly eye wasn't focussed on the sea but, predictably, on a mother and child dressed in mournful black. In spite of—or perhaps because of—her deep and enduring love of the sea and rivers, she made no further attempt to capture it on canvas. This wasn't because she feared painting outside—we know she drew *en plein air*. Nor was it because she didn't visit the popular seaside haunts of her fellow painters: indeed, she often went to the coast and did many of her most arresting drawings at Pléneuf in Brittany. Perhaps she was loath to convert something of such emotional significance into a "technical challenge." Perhaps she had no wish to risk denuding water of its powers by rendering it on canvas, weakening, if not destroying, one of the greatest and most visceral loves of her life.

Perhaps she had more important things to conquer in paint. Like herself. For in painting herself, over and over, she confirmed the perpetual rebirth of her identity.

One of the most pernicious effects of trauma is the way it disrupts our ability to *read* other people, making social interaction acutely difficult. Gwen's social anxiety made it impossible for her to find peace or pleasure among groups of people. But as much as she needed solitude, she also—like all of us—needed human contact.

Portraiture was a way of engaging not only with herself but with others. With a model in her studio she had an opportunity for human connection, in an environment where she held control—a far less risky proposition than having to navigate a social occasion. In the safety of her own space, with a paid model, she could avoid the conflict and loss of control that Van der Kolk identifies as a primary fear of traumatised people. Gwen never completed a commissioned portrait. She was often asked, and although she occasionally began one, the struggle was too great and each attempt was eventually abandoned. She could work satisfactorily only when she had full mastery of her subject.

No wonder so many of her paintings invoke a curious sense of unease, of tension. Her models—flattened against the wall, tightly framed within the boundaries of the canvas—are rarely named, exude no character, are "like shadows." On closer inspection, her models resemble her. They wear the clothes she wore. They have the same hairstyle. They hold the items she valued and that belonged to her (books, flowers, cats). They sit in her chair. Their hands are clasped—just as her hands are clasped in her childhood photographs. Like her, they were single women, without husbands and without children.

Jeanne Foster, who sat for a commissioned (and uncom-
pleted) portrait in 1921, wrote of Gwen: "She cannot endure
having the pose changed by a hair's breadth after she has arranged it. She takes my hair down and does it like her own. . . .
She has me sit as she does and I feel the absorption of her
personality as I sit. . . . She is more myself than I am."²² As
Mary Taubman says in her book *Gwen John*, "Self-portrayal . . .
pervades her work, no matter what the style or the medium."

The sea is a lonely place. Painting is a solitary profession.
And the line between solitude and loneliness is wisp-thin. In
portraiture, Gwen evaded loneliness. In her preference for paid
models and children (whom she paid too), she found a sense of
mastery, of control. Not of them, but of herself.

There's a current line of thought that portraiture represents,
in the words of the sculptor Antony Gormley, "the conquest of
the hunted by the hunter."²³ When I think of history's endless
portraits of naked, supine women, this seems breathtakingly clear.

But Gwen's case was infinitely more complex: she was both
hunter and hunted.

⁓

Gwen treated her models well. She knew what it was to stand,
naked, hour after hour in a chilled studio. As I make my way back
to the river, I look for the stable where her modelling career began.

On September 2, 1903, Gwen and Dorelia reached Meilhan,
perched high above the Garonne. They had walked for miles
that day, arriving after dark, hungry and thirsty. They began
marching the main street, singing loudly. Singing sometimes

brought them a few swift centimes, and they needed money for an inn. On this particular evening they were turned away from every door, eventually finding a stable where they slept on a layer of hay, their portfolios spread over them like a stiffened blanket. A young artist heard that two beautiful English girls were sleeping rough, and came to look at them. They woke. He introduced himself. They talked art, poverty, hunger, painters, Paris. He handed over his card, inviting them to look him up if they came to the city. He told them, breezily, they could be artists' models . . . in the City of Light.

Models were usually poor, uneducated women of a certain age. But Gwen wrote down his address and slipped it into her belongings.

A single, fleeting moment—but one that was to change the trajectory of her life forever.

⁓

What is it about water? Why do so many feel the urgency of its tug? Over and over I come across the same sentiment: people who *must* live beside the sea, artists *impelled* to paint or photograph water, musicians *inspired* by the sounds of oceans, families who will holiday *only* beside the beach or among lakes or on a canal boat, retirees who have saved *all* their lives for a sea view.

My father is no different. "I have to be near the sea," he says. "I'm not myself when I'm not within walking distance of an ocean." Even Rousseau, whose preference was for mountains, recognised the need for water in his perfect landscape: "I need torrents, rocks, firs, dark woods, mountains," he declared.[24]

I had always considered myself immune to watery obsessions. Not for me the pull of the river, or the call of the sea. I saw myself as more of a mountain girl. But on my self-allocated rest day, halfway between Bordeaux and Toulouse, something startling and slightly odd happens. Something that makes me reconsider the significance of water in my life.

It's day five, and my blistered feet have tramped sixty-two miles, treading between river and canal. But instead of waking up buoyant and bubbling at the prospect of a day off, a day in which my poor, sore muscles can lounge around and recover, I wake up bereft.

For a reason I can't explain, I feel a deep and visceral longing for *my* river, *my* canal. It feels like homesickness, a gut desire to be beside my watery companion. The ancient charms of the little French town I'm staying in—golden-stoned chateau, churches, cafes, croissants—pall.

In the porous light of early morning I peer at my map. I fold away my day-off clothes and put on my walking trousers, my walking boots, my backpack. I feel elated. And—in spite of my pack—peculiarly light. Like a dandelion seed released from its clock. I'm going back to my river. Back to the reflections that pull the whole world into a single shimmer. Back to a day of nothing more onerous than putting heel to ground, over and over and over.

I slip out of my B&B, smiling, my heart dancing in its cage. I have this perverse feeling of rebellion, of having broken my own rules, of being complicit with a tract of water. I like it—it feels curiously right. As if I'm returning home. How else to describe it?

Writing from Toulouse, Gwen lamented, "We shall never get to Rome, I'm afraid—it seems further away than it did in England." Toulouse, with its bedroom where they slept "like any bourgeoisie," had none of the thrills of being on the open road. And yet they decided to spend the winter there, working and painting from a rented room. Gwen wrote about the compelling beauty of the surrounding countryside, of the Pyrenees in the distance, of the "wonderful" sunsets and the "sublime" scenery: "a red sun—livid."

And yet only her masterful portraits of Dorelia have survived, portraits suffused with a tenderness and intimacy that rarely appear in her later work. Her Toulouse paintings pulsate with mystery and novelty reflecting Gwen's new sense of liberation. Released from her past life, Gwen began discreetly challenging the traditional practice of portraiture: in one portrait Dorelia is not standing but moving, as if passing through the painting. When her paintings of Dorelia were finally made public, they were applauded by critics and compared to Whistler, Degas, and Vuillard. The casting off of her old, frail life, the strange serenity of her novel environment, the sweet promise of something new gave Gwen a sense of urgency and vigour. She wrote to Ida saying she was working manically, doing five portraits an hour. To her painter friend Ursula Tyrwhitt she wrote, "I do nothing but paint. . . . I have discovered a few little things about painting."[25]

The long, arduous walk from Bordeaux to Toulouse unleashed something within Gwen. The wild, open space, the continuous presence of flowing water, the wide skies left her with a love of sleeping beneath the stars, of walking among trees and beside rivers. Like her letter writing and her painting, her love of wild walking and her recognition of its capacity to heal never left her, becoming a defining theme of her life and a vital prop in her identity.

Her Paris letters are littered with references to walking in the countryside and its ability to make her feel better. In 1904 she wrote to Ursula, saying, "I should like to be in the country, if only for a short time. I feel more at home in the country than in the town always."

One of her favourite excursions involved taking a boat down the Seine to Suresnes in the countryside (it's now a suburb of Paris), where she would walk, read, and draw. "I feel better since I have been out for a long walk in the country. It is strange how walking . . . relieves my heart," she wrote, after one such outing. On these trips—and in spite of the inherent dangers—she frequently walked alone in forests and slept out beneath trees. "I often don't come home for three or four days," she wrote in a letter. Elsewhere she described how she "walked in the forest in the dark and rain, it was lovely walking through the fallen leaves."

She fearlessly walked alone at night, saying, "I am happier when I walk in dark," and that in the darkness she could "think in tranquillity, looking at the sky, where there is no noise and not much light." She regularly slept in the Luxembourg Gardens, "in a little copse of trees." Here, among the plants, she was able to think more freely, more fluidly, than she could in her room or in the tumult of the city. Because the gardens were locked at night she felt safe here, among the shrubbery, away from prying eyes and roving hands.

⌐

Within months of leaving Toulouse, Gwen was in Paris, living alone and modelling for Rodin. He was sixty-three—dazzling, powerful, a celebrated genius. She was twenty-seven—floundering, shy, socially ill at ease. In spite of this, they became lovers.

She began calling herself Mary, rearranging her name from Gwen Mary John to Mary Gwendolen John. Confusingly, and a little bizarrely, Rodin often called her "*ma petite soeur.*" She called him "*mon maître,*" and told him he was "all that is beautiful and romantic in my life." Her love for him was wild, irrepressible.

For Gwen the affair was epiphanic, painfully all-consuming. For Rodin, who lived with another woman, it meant nothing. Reading accounts of their relationship, it's easy to feel sorry for Gwen. It's easier still to wince at the way she belittled herself before her "*maître*": pleading with him to see her, freezing in order to save the coal for his promised visits, lurking outside his house simply to catch a glimpse of him. But to do this would be misguided. Her choice in Rodin meant she was never burdened with the domestic drudgery she so disliked and that destroyed swathes of her fellow female painters. She had seen the demise of other Slade students. The hugely talented Edna Waugh had married a man who denigrated her art, and all but forbade her to paint. Ida, once a rising star at the Slade, had become Mrs. Augustus John, drowning in domesticity, writing, "I am miserable," and "I am quite foolish nowadays," and, "How I wish I were with you. . . . You have Rodin and work and streets and museums."[26] Ida died shortly afterwards, days after giving birth to her fifth child.

By contrast, Rodin recognised Gwen's talent, encouraging her to draw, paint, and write. He recognised her inability to organise herself and taught her how to timetable her days. He paid the rent so that she could have a room of her own. He encouraged her to eat properly, to walk every day. He lent her books. He introduced her to the Catholicism that was to become such a pivotal part of her later life. He may even have read the two thousand letters she sent him, sometimes two or three in a single day. But most importantly, he had no desire for another wife or child. Did Gwen somehow sense this? Was it the reason she emotionally yoked herself to him for the best part of her childbearing years?

In choosing Rodin, Gwen was able to live freely in the convention-defying manner that suited her. There was no one to stop her sleeping in parks, drawing and reading alone in cafes, walking at night, modelling nude, collecting cats. Which is not to excuse the fact that Rodin was often callous and cruel, of course. Only to say that theirs was a complicated relationship—for Gwen at any rate. In a curious way, her submission to Rodin gave her a childlike permission to do as she pleased.

She hadn't forgotten her dream of walking to Rome. The notion was resurrected, but with Rodin in place of Dorelia. She tried persuading him to join her, promising to keep him warm with her body, to organise the entire trip, to make it as comfortable as possible. But Rodin didn't take the bait. And Gwen never walked to Rome.

Every morning, wherever I am, an immense heron clatters out of the rushes, all spikes and bones and yellow beak. Its wings unfold, a vast shuddering pair of curtains, and it disappears into the distance, leaving its reflection trembling and fading.

From this point on, my mind drifts and flows, always travelling, never quite arriving. Much like water. The more I look at the canal, at the quavering reflections of sky, trees, birds, at the eel weed shimmying beneath its surface, the less cryptic Gwen and her paintings become. Walking between the untamed, rebellious river and the calm, trammelled canal, I feel as though I'm straddling the two versions of her. And finding a new version of myself at the same time.

After five days of river walking, my Water Thoughts flow thick and fast. I carry with me copies of Gwen's portraits, sensing that—with their drubbing refrain of Who am I? Why am I?—they contain the key to Gwen. Every night I spread them out, alongside my notes. I start to feel as if I'm walking not only in her footsteps, nor merely along a river and canal, but through her life in all its glory and tragedy.

Little facts are starting to join up in ways that are both illuminating and disquieting. Gwen painted her last self-portrait when she was thirty-five. She never painted herself again. Thirty-five. The age her mother died. Was it coincidence that she bid farewell to the self at the very age her mother bid farewell to life? Or have I missed something in all that introspective intensity?

Rodin's name—Auguste. Her brother's name—Augustus. Her mother's name—Augusta. Rodin called Gwen "*ma petite soeur*" and "Marie," so like the name of his adored dead sister,

Maria. Marie. Mary. Coincidence, no doubt. The human brain seeks out patterns, after all.

The most curious coincidence occurs on the last day of my walk. As I head towards Toulouse, I realise that I have no idea where Gwen lived in the city. We know she and Dorelia spent the winter there, falling out of love with each other and becoming bored and restless. We know they rented a room from a woman who would appear at night, having somehow passed through their locked door. We know Gwen often walked to a local hill and sat there, drawing the city and looking out to the Pyrenees. But the street they lived on, where was it? I pull my phone from my rucksack and type "Gwen John" and "Toulouse" into Google. Up she pops with some rudimentary biographical information: her date and place of birth, her date of death, her more famous lover. Her date of death looks oddly familiar: September 18, 1939. I've lost track of time, but I know it's September. It was September when she walked to Toulouse, and it's September now. I look at my phone and see today's date: September 18, 2019. The hairs rise on my arms.

In an eerie act of synchronicity I am completing my pilgrimage eighty years to the day that Gwen died her solitary death in the seaside town of Dieppe. I have a sudden sense of the past collapsing into the present, of my river and her sea converging outside of time and space.

"Coincidence," says Matthew when I call him.

"But I'm not supposed to finish the walk today," I protest. I don't tell him about the call of the river, how the water enticed me back. I don't tell him the water has become *a friend*. How can I explain something so inexplicable, so peculiar, to someone as rational and empirical as Matthew?

⌒

That night I dream of my river, its milky depths, its puckering pearly surface, the luminous beckoning blue of beyond. All night long the river is with me, curling in and out of every dream, of every waking moment. As if water had seeped into my brain.

Gwen often dreamt of water, of the sea. In one of her watery dreams, she and Rodin stepped out of an ocean-submerged Eiffel Tower and swam naked, blissful and ecstatic. Until a man appeared and forced them to leave the water and put their clothes on. Freud might have had something to say about a dream so obviously priapic. But who needs Freud when a dream is as wrenchingly clear as this?

⌒

When I reach Toulouse I feel, for the first time, a sharp loneliness. Toulouse is a city of youth, its hundreds of cafes and bars thronged with beautiful people. Such a vibrant city and yet I feel devastatingly alone here. I was happy to eat by myself in the country (my book propped up against the breadbasket, my phone flashing from behind my wine glass), but here I disappear to my room and nibble on nuts and bananas. The urban loneliness is so paralysing that I'm unable to settle, unable to work at the little desk in my dark, dingy room.

The countryside is a far better place to be alone, providing—perversely—a sense of intimacy lacking in the confinement of a city. I think wistfully of all the people I met beside the river and the canal, of those fleeting moments of connection: the cyclists I shouted "*bonjour*" to, the fishermen I chatted with, the boat owners I waved to. Each day my solitude was punctuated with these tiny currents of connection, reminding me that I was part of the immense wash of humanity. But here, in France's fourth-largest city, I feel isolated and disconnected.

My flight home is in forty-eight hours, but I begin yearning for my river, poring over my map. Do I have time to return there, to my heron, to the fig trees with their bounty of purple splitting fruit? I think of the reeds and bulrushes, the pink clover and creeping Jenny, the honeysuckle and wild peppermint, the jade-green water of the canal, the silver sweep of the Garonne. I remember the turquoise flash of the kingfisher, the wheeling buzzards, the fat blackberries, the yellow mirabelle plums. And all at once I no longer want to be in Toulouse.

Virginia Woolf believed women needed a room of their own. May Sarton believed they needed time of their own. Me? I think women need a route of their own. Outdoors. Away from the concrete circumscriptions of the city. Between earth and sky. Close to water.

⌒

August 1918. The war had been dragging on for over three years and Rodin had recently died, plunging Gwen into sickness and misery. Her notebooks from around this time show relentless self-injunctions ("rules") to better "control her mind," and her rigorous self-timetabling as she struggled to feel "normal" again.

6–7.30 breakfast and housework
7.30–8.30 prayer

Ursula wrote urging her to go to the sea, and Gwen replied saying she had come to the same conclusion. The sea was calling to her, and—conveniently—she had friends staying in Pléneuf, a tiny village on the wild coast of Brittany where she had spent the four previous summers. Here, she felt "very happy" and "immensely liberated, organic and free . . . peaceful, untroubled and focussed," according to her biographer, Sue Roe. The empty Breton coast, with its rugged rocky paths and its clear light, "inspired and calmed" her. The day before leaving Pléneuf to return to Paris, she took a different direction on her morning walk to the sea. In a stroke of serendipity, she stumbled across a crumbling manor house, hidden away in the green shade of horse chestnut trees amid a tangled, overgrown garden and a meadow through which flowed a small stream. She knew instantly that if she lived here, she could draw as she wanted to, rendering perfectly the moods and feelings she wanted to express.

She returned in the new year, taking rooms in the isolated, crumbling Chateau Vauclair and writing to her patron, John Quinn, "It is such a wonderful place. . . . There is a wild lonely bay . . . and beautiful places to walk . . ." The war had ended and the chateau was to be her "*chez-d'oeuvre*," her work home, her place of spiritual solitude. She was enthralled by the silence and by its humble, sad beauty. Her time here was to be a remarkably creative and productive period where she could work, undisturbed, to the sounds and scents of a coastline that bore a great resemblance to her childhood coastline of Pembrokeshire.

She began each wintry morning by walking to an isolated beach. Here she stripped off her black dress and her dark woollen coat and threw herself into the surf, just as she'd done as a child in Tenby. She became utterly absorbed by the endless breaking of waves, counting them and discovering they came in groups of ten: nine smaller waves followed by a single crashing breaker. She applied this pattern to herself, declaring her heart also an ocean with numerous waves of sadness and pain, but inevitably followed by a breaker of great joy.[27]

Two months later, the owners of the chateau decided to sell it, giving Gwen only a few more months in this house and landscape which had assumed such significance for her. She wrote to the new owners' solicitor asking if they would sell it (despite them having just bought it); she begged Augustus to find the necessary 50,000 F. She wrote to her father about it. She wrote to John Quinn suggesting he might want to buy it. She made plans to visit a moneylender. She refused to leave, in spite of its new owners.

Her year of living alone, walking daily on the remote Brittany coast, changed how she painted. As her biographer, Sue Roe, explains, Gwen's portraits from this point on put even greater emphasis on inwardness and reflection, using technically and psychologically complex techniques. Her more meditative style was to take the depiction of spiritual serenity (she often used the French word *recueillie*) to dizzying heights.

What strikes me about Gwen's Chateau Vauclair period is how the landscape released her, enabling her to continue excavating herself, to continue the process of stitching herself back together. She drew and painted prolifically during this time, working mainly in pencil and watercolour, and frequently using children as her models. Usually using girls (around the age she was when her mother died), Gwen posed them in the sartorial style of her own childhood—ribboned hats and best dresses—and with their hands neatly clasped, as hers were in every one of her childhood photographs. Almost as if she was recasting her own early childhood, willing it back into life. Her drawings of this period are among some of her finest work, with their mood of innocence, tenderness, and vulnerability.

But without her sea walks, without the wind-scrubbed peace and solitude of Chateau Vauclair, how was she to continue? When she returned to Paris, she was so homesick for the Brittany coast that she would go out at night and pick leaves and grasses from the hedgerows "all dark and misty and when I took them home I sometimes found my hands were full of flowers." By November, her state of mind—that had been so creatively productive, so calm and composed at Pléneuf— was once again spiralling out of control. "All the other things I knew before have gone away, now, from my memory," she wrote, as her health deteriorated into fever and fatigue. She resumed her journaling, urging herself to greater piety, to greater self-discipline even as she grew increasingly unsettled and fragile, with repeated bouts of delirium and chronic exhaustion. She couldn't shake Pléneuf and its briny, brackish wilderness from her thoughts. She consoled herself by walking in the forest near

Meudon, always taking a tiny notebook in which she sketched wild flowers, ferns, and grasses. Walking, in spite of her weakened health, was a means of thinking clearly. As she walked between the trees, she noted down possible motifs and ideas for forming pictures alongside her miniature sketches. She jotted down colours and thoughts.

But her heart was still beside the sea. She kept herself abreast of developments at the chateau, noting that "new windows had been put in and a wall built between house and farm." A year after leaving she was still convinced that this was her natural home, and she was still trying to persuade John Quinn to buy it, writing to him, "It is very wonderful. You can walk miles . . . when the tide is low." He didn't reply to her letter, leaving her in a state of "profound disappointment" contributing "to the stress and nervous tension that made her ill."[28] "I think I shall live there again some day," she wrote in a letter, bravely bolstering any last vestiges of hope.

It was to be a year before she began to recover, finally reconciling herself to the loss of Chateau Vauclair and writing to Ursula, "I'm like a plant that was dying and nearly dead and begins to grow again."

But she never returned to Brittany. Indeed, there's no evidence that Gwen returned to the sea until 1927, when she crossed the English Channel to see Gus and Dorelia in England, and where she insisted on taking a bus each day to Bournemouth so she could look at the waves. And then in September 1939, beset by illness, she began to dream of "fresh air and the sea."[29] On September 10, she summoned a local solicitor and asked him to draw up her will. The following day, despite her stomach pain, she took the train to Dieppe, "and freedom."[30] She had no luggage but had made provision for her beloved cats, as if she knew that she was dying and would never return. She stepped off the train, collapsed in the street, and was taken to the Hospice de Dieppe. Again, she summoned a lawyer to draw up her last will and testament, leaving everything she owned to a nephew.

At 8:30 on the morning of September 19, she was pronounced dead, causes unknown. She was sixty-three. Like her mother, she died far from home, and alone.

Her grave lay undiscovered for seventy-five years, until it was found in a cemetery outside Dieppe. It had eluded biographers for decades because the name carved into the small, simple headstone was not Gwen John but Mary John.

It's possible she was returning to England. But it's far more likely that she dragged her dying body to Dieppe to feel the sea air one last time. To bask in that carousel of light that only the ocean offers. To end her life beside the waves in the sort of spiritual convergence that had always been so important to her.

As her life began, so would it end.

⌣

What if Gwen's father (who was discovered, on his death, to be hugely wealthy) had lent her the money she needed to buy Chateau Vauclair? Could years of clifftop walks and ice-cold plunges have saved her flagging health? Might she have continued painting?

On these tiny twists of circumstance our lives are shaped, altered irrevocably.

The evidence for living beside the sea or close to water is unequivocal. Numerous studies now suggest that those living near water are healthier and happier.[31] We don't know why—the omega-3 fatty acids in oily fish? the bacteria and minerals in seawater? the inevitable presence of food? the abundance of light? We know only that in the presence of water and oceans we relax, we let ourselves be taken out of ourselves. Water sluices clean our overwrought minds, explains marine biologist Wallace J. Nichols. It offers "regularity without monotony . . . the inverse of our current condition of monotonous suffocation."[32]

Willa Cather, walking on the coast of southern France, put it perfectly: "It is good for one's soul . . . to do nothing for hours together but stare at this great water that seems to trail its delft-blue mantle across the world."[33]

⁓

In a letter to Gwen sent a few months after her river walk ended, Ida asked, "Are you much altered?"

She was.

And so am I.

In escaping the prison of the city, of the daily surge and fester of everyday life, I have also escaped the prison of myself. I have shaken off long-held fears of being alone in unpeopled places. I have unpeeled and discarded a sense of vulnerability that has constrained me for decades. I have learnt that solitude is not only for other people, that wild, rural spaces are not only for men, that water has the capacity to profoundly affect me— as it did Gwen—if only I let it.

When I return home, I feel enriched but also emboldened. It's not only myself that's altered. My future looks different: it's acquired a tantalising rosy glow, the glow of promise and possibility and hope.

I've taken down all the copies of Gwen John paintings from my walls now. All but one: *Girl by a Window*. One of her last paintings in oil. Like all her paintings, it's tiny. Seven by six inches. In it, a woman stares out of a small window. She's wearing an oversized hat and a voluminous skirt. Her hands are held loosely together in a book that's open on her lap. Here are all the trademarks of a Gwen John painting: the plain, humble background; the window; the swaddled, anonymous sitter butting up against the rim; the open book; the sense of stillness.

But the element of deflected suffering, of anguished oppression, is absent. Gone. As if Gwen had finally made a fragile truce with the world. As if she knew that one day the window would open, and like herons, we would unfold our heavy wings and fly away. No wonder the gallerist Cecily Langdale observed that Gwen's painting "has been more greatly admired by women than by men."[34] Because although Gwen painted for herself, she also painted for anyone who has felt the press and grip of constraint and confinement.

And right at the end, she shows us a way out. *Girl by a Window* is a painting of self-reliance, of independence, but—above all—of solitude.

4

The Weight of Complexity

Clara Vyvyan and Daphne du Maurier

Not Walking. Walking as Catharsis. Journeys of the Imagination. Gynaecology. The Older Walker. Walking Companions. Sketching and Photographing. Obscurity.

A feeling persisted that I never should discover what I sought for unless I could travel in the wild, unpeopled parts of the world.

—CLARA VYVYAN, *Roots and Stars*, 1962

When I return from my Gwen John Walk (as I call it), several girlfriends quiz me on what it was like to be all by myself for ten days: Wasn't I bored? Wasn't I lonely? Did I miss my family? Did I have to fend off any men?

My replies are scanty. I'm ashamed to admit that I didn't miss my family, that I was never bored, that any male attackers existed only in my lopsided imagination. But most of all I'm ashamed to admit how much I enjoyed my own company.

Eventually I confess to Matthew that I rather liked walking with myself, more than I had expected to. He looks at me, horrified, then tells me I'd better keep that quiet: it makes me sound . . . His voice peters out, but I can smell the words on the tip of his tongue: *self-satisfied, narcissistic, smug.*

OK, perhaps I wasn't entirely alone, I add quickly. I had Gwen with me. And a grey heron. Matthew rolls his eyes.

It takes courage to enjoy one's own company for an extended length of time. But perhaps it takes even more courage to admit to it.

The truth is, being on one's own is not the same as being alone, or being lonely. Being on one's own is a confronting of oneself. And if we don't confront ourselves, how do we stop clinging to the habits of our past? How do we change, progress, develop? How do we *become*?

⌒

Three weeks later, I trip in a rabbit hole and break a bone in my foot. A small bone, but the break is serious enough to necessitate a gargantuan, square-toed plastic boot. After five days I'm promoted to a strange open-toed sandal with a back-to-front heel. I call it my geisha girl shoe because it looks—very slightly—like the platform-soled clogs traditionally worn by Japanese women. I hop around with a pair of crutches that leave red welts across the palms of my hands. Within days I feel hemmed in, stifled by the walls of my house and the unbearable uselessness of my foot. I cancel everything in my calendar, then sit with my leg raised—as instructed—and stare out of the window like a Gwen John woman. I try to think about Gwen, about her journey into solitude and her unfolding realisation of the essential place of aloneness in her life and her art. But being unable to walk is affecting how I think. I feel ragingly imprisoned in my alien footwear, unable to think beyond my own plight.

I start taking small, hobbling walks, during which I feel at once extravagantly visible and quietly impotent. Knowing I can't escape means I think for far too long about when and where to hobble. Dusk and dark are out of the question. As are uneven surfaces and routes where roads must be crossed. It's not only the sense of restriction that's affecting me—it's that I'm not sure who I am. How we move is part of our identity, part of who we are. This tottering, toppling person I've become feels all wrong. As if I've woken up and found myself—bafflingly—in someone else's ill-fitting clothes.

⌒

My friend Alice emails me with the name of a tireless female walker and writer I've never heard of. "It's criminal, but hardly anyone knows about her," Alice writes. "She's called Clara Vyvyan and she walked with Daphne du Maurier."

I scour second-hand shops from my laptop, ordering battered books with dented spines, and maps that smell of dust and damp. It's my new non-walking project: to imaginatively follow in the footsteps of an unknown walker using only maps, books, and a laptop. A journey of the mind. No movement required.

For days I run the tip of my finger down rivers and up contoured mountains, tracing roads, canals, railway lines, rivers. I prod at villages and churches and ponder thin dotted lines, fat red lines, meandering green lines. There's something about the mystery and promise of maps, the way open roads unfurl, connecting hamlets with cities, farms with towns, the coast with the hinterland, the mountains with the metropolis. In maps we find what Rebecca Solnit calls "the language of the earth." Even though I cannot walk, I feel connected to the world again.

And yet something nags at me: the unblinking ease with which I tripped and broke a bone, the feeling of being trapped in my body, the sense that I cannot get away. As if old feelings of vulnerability are resurfacing all over again.

⁓

A successful journey on foot requires an acceptance of, and a refusal to be bound by, the complexities and vulnerabilities we live with. Our fear of rape, assault, and twisted ankles hinders us from being alone, just as it hinders us from venturing into unpeopled places or dark spaces. As we grow older, our fear of physical risk balloons, making us even more frightened of being by ourselves or of taking the sort of bodily risks we ignored in our youth. Older women, according to clinical psychologist Dr. Karin Arndt, are particularly frightened of being alone, often to the extent that it dictates the life choices they make, or fail to make.[1]

Evolutionary psychologists speculate that our fear of being alone lurks deep in our DNA. For millennia we lived, foraged, and walked in groups, helping each other with menstruation, pregnancy, childbirth, and the communal feeding and raising of children, while protecting each other from wild beasts and oversexed males. To be cast from our Stone Age group meant certain death. Fast-forward to the twentieth century, and being a lone woman continued to be a frightening experience. A lone woman invited male attention, indicating that she was unprotected, available. Hardly surprising then that women have typically travelled in groups, and that the prospect of time alone can provoke overwhelming fear and anxiety.

It doesn't need to be like this.

When the Australian-born writer and market gardener Clara Vyvyan followed the River Rhône from source to mouth, she was sixty-seven. In 1952, the year of her three-month river hike, sixty-seven was the average age of death. Today's equivalent would be an eighty-two-year-old woman walking 562 miles with a backpack. For me, Clara is a thrilling beacon of hope and possibility. A reminder that age cannot extinguish our thirst or capacity for adventures on foot.

I make a promise to myself: when I'm sixty-seven, I too will walk the length of the Rhône. For now, I walk her route on a map, sliding a fingertip down the winding line of the river, and looking at Rhône landmarks on my laptop—glaciers, lakes, vineyards, flamingos. Although Clara's Rhône riverscape is held before my inner eye rather than felt beneath the soles of my boots, it's a walk of sorts, and I take to hobbling up and down my garden in a paltry simulacrum of her wild riverside hike.

Clara's river walk, like Gwen's, demarcated the end of one chapter of her life and the beginning of another. But Clara's walk was also a means of symbolic purification, quite literally an attempt to flush out elements of herself she had come to dislike.

⌒

"I am going forth on a pilgrimage to lose myself in a river," Clara wrote in her travel memoir, *Down the Rhône on Foot*. Europe was reeling in the aftermath of World War II, but Clara had other concerns. She called them her "personal pygmy troubles," anxieties that needed scrubbing away, discarding. The truth was more complicated: Clara was weighted with grief. During the war she had lost her mother and her adored husband, watched the wanton destruction of her garden with its ancient trees and rare shrubs, and handed over the keys of her beloved home to a distant heir who had carelessly and greedily consigned her to a few cold rooms at the top of an impossibly steep staircase.[2] But to mourn a husband and home so keenly felt churlish and self-indulgent when others had lost so much more. Her grief became tainted with feelings of guilt, shame, and self-loathing.

Clara hoped that following a river from source to delta would "purify" her, wash away and drown her "old self" that was buckling beneath "bitterness" and "self-pity." She longed to escape, not only from the "wretched, frustrated, disillusioned person" she had become but from the circumstances of her life which seemed to be closing in on her, trapping and diminishing her. And she longed for solitude, writing, "I wanted more than ever to be alone.... I wanted to stride away ... to go where there would be no intimates, only valleys and mountains and strangers."

This was not to be a mere riverside stroll. To lose herself, Clara knew she needed "one of the mighty cosmopolitan rivers of Europe," a river she could follow from its initial "drop of flowing water to its apotheosis in the sea." In 1952 the Volga and the Danube were behind the iron curtain, making them largely inaccessible. She ruled out the Rhine—a mere six and a half years had lapsed since the cessation of war with Germany, and she didn't feel comfortable with the notion of walking in recent enemy territory. That left the Rhône, a river with its source in the Swiss Alps and its mouth in the South of France. To follow the full course of the Rhône meant walking 460 miles, not as a conqueror, exploiter, or explorer, she stressed, but as a pilgrim, surrendering body, soul, and spirit to the great river, its moods and meanderings. She allowed herself only minimal possessions, deciding to wear the same clothes every day, with a single nightgown and a single change of underclothes which she planned to wash in the river. And there would be no cheating, no taking lifts. When a friend suggested she do so at the "dull parts," Clara was outraged: "I shall walk every mile from beginning to end," she declared.

I type out Clara's packing list and pin it to my wall beneath a picture of her route, which is now an asphalt cycle lane. Although born and raised in the Australian outback, Clara had married into the British aristocracy. She was now the widowed *Lady* Clara, freighted not only with her own cares and suffering but with *stuff.* Dilapidated and derelict stuff at that. She referred to it as "the bondage of familiar things," and her intention to walk for three months with a single set of clothes was an eloquent plea to be purged of it all. Not only had their "wanton destruction" brought her suffering and guilt, but she was preparing for a life in which she was no longer mistress of the house, lands, and "familiar things" she had once shared with her husband, Sir Courtenay Vyvyan.

Isn't this half the joy of backpacking? To realise how little we need? To know that we can exist in body and soul with little more than a packet of Band-Aids, a bar of soap, and a single change of clothes? Of course, it's more freeing when we have a home to return to, and a little money in our pocket (Raynor Winn's *The Salt Path* is antidote reading for any overly romantic interpretations of being entirely footloose).

Even so, backpacking reminds us of the modesty of our needs. Raising the question: If we need so little, why do we spend so long accumulating so much?

⌒

I can see Clara now ... squeezing her book of poetry (Matthew Arnold's *Selected Poems*, if you're interested), her felt rain hat, and her wind-resistant beret into her knapsack. As she does so, she finds the bits of herself she likes, folds them, tucks them into the side pockets. Such a neat way to discard the bits she dislikes. Simply leave them behind, along with the *stuff*. And if they persist in following, in clinging on, she can outwalk them. Discard them along the way. Let the river take them.

⌒

For weeks Clara had fretted at the prospect of knocking on strange doors each night in search of a bed. For weeks she had pacified her incredulous friends. "You're really going to walk ten miles a day or even more? At your age too?" demanded a horrified neighbour.

In truth, Clara was dreading going alone. "Stepping out from that glacier hotel to face many weeks of hopelessness ... a nomad life wherein each evening I would have to summon all my weak reserves of resolution and judgement in order to find a pillow and a crust," she wrote. It would be far less daunting to have someone with her, if only to commiserate with when doors were slammed in her face. She began searching for a companion, and eventually her friend and neighbour, the author Daphne du Maurier, agreed to join her for the first thirteen days of hiking. Daphne was a lifelong walker who left her study every afternoon to amble through the Cornish countryside, accompanied until recently by her three children.

Like Clara, Daphne was emerging from a period of tumultuous emotion. Having resigned herself to a platonic relationship with Ellen Doubleday, her American publisher's wife and someone she'd allegedly been in love with for years, she was now (according to her biographer, Margaret Forster) in the midst of a relationship with the actress Gertrude Lawrence. But Gertie was unwell and Daphne was worried about her (Gertie would die from liver cancer a few weeks after Daphne returned from the Rhône, prompting profound grief and "suicidal thoughts"). All this had to be kept under wraps, for Daphne's husband and children had no inkling of the true nature of her love for Gertie. Meanwhile Daphne felt restless, writing to her publisher, Victor Gollancz, "I wonder if it is the change of life? But isn't forty-five a bit young?" She was dismayed by the lines lengthening and deepening in her face and the sudden thickening of her waist. Moreover, her children had recently left home and she was feeling the sharp disorientation that accompanies a newly emptied nest. Could two weeks tracking the course of a river restore some of her serenity?

She packed a belted Norwegian rucksack with a vast assortment of clothing, a hot-water bottle, and multiple bottles of cosmetics—vanishing creams, sunburn lotions, wind-protection creams, mosquito-bite lotion, and tiny glass bottles of perfume. They set off, Clara in her green corduroy skirt, woollen jersey, and beret, and Daphne in her white jockey cap, mountaineering boots with yellow laces, and a linen skirt, only to be told by the hotel receptionist that they couldn't follow the river because "men are working there." This was to be the start of multiple detours which added over one hundred miles to Clara's journey.

As soon as the pair were entirely alone, Daphne whipped up her skirt to reveal bare knees protruding from white cotton shorts. The skirt was hastily rolled down when a rooftop appeared on the horizon. Together they made instant coffee in a billycan, which they boiled over a fire of twigs and drank from a shaving mug. They washed their clothes in the Rhône, drying them on sun-warmed rocks. Both frequently wandered off on their own (Daphne had a saying that one should always see dawn and sunset alone). Night after night they were turned away from door after door. And yet Daphne was exultant, writing to a friend that it was "one of the best holidays ever . . . we lived like two tramps." She added that she had never—in all her life—felt so free.

But bound up with Daphne's feeling of freedom was an awareness of the additional complexities women carry when they backpack. Unlike Clara, Daphne couldn't countenance sleeping "in a haystack." She wrote to a friend explaining how desperately she needed her "awful ritual of creaming my face, and my hair in pins." Later, she flew into a panic when her period arrived: How was she to "walk up a mountain" while bleeding into a sanitary pad? "What shall I do ...? I see myself furtively changing behind a glacier," she wrote in a letter.[3]

⌒

So what *do* we do? It's not merely the inconvenience of having to find discreet places to change and having to carry both new and used sanitary wear: it's also the cramps, headaches, back pain, diarrhoea, and sickness that can accompany menstruation. Rather than walk through blood and pain, Daphne chose to go by car on these occasions, leaving Clara to walk alone. But earlier walkers didn't have this luxury. Their writings rarely refer to such things, but inevitably they would have had to grapple with changing rags behind trees, grinding abdominal pain, and lower backache to complement the shoulder ache that came from carrying a wooden-framed canvas rucksack with iron buckles.

The arrival of one's period meant not only extra laundry but potential social humiliation. In *The Second Sex*, Simone de Beauvoir describes the mortification felt by women picking up their used sanitary towels that had loosened and escaped as they walked. On long hikes, menstrual rags had to be discreetly washed and dried, while pads had to be surreptitiously disposed of. And if one's period arrived unexpectedly, one had to rustle up a pad from whatever materials one could find. In the Cairngorms women often used sphagnum moss, a hugely absorbent plant capable of holding many times its own weight in liquid. Discarded sheep's wool was another option: Roman women used wool not only to make pads but to compress into primitive tampons. Before this, Egyptian women used material from the papyrus plant. Meanwhile grass and other plant fibres were fashioned into rudimentary sanitary wear, although bulky rag pads (often attached to belts, from where they frequently slipped out of place) were more commonly used. As recently as 2010, according to an article in the *New York Times*, girls in Kenya whose families couldn't afford sanitary pads were still using rags and even mud in their knickers, and inevitably missing four or five days of school each month. "How can I come to a place when I am bleeding?" they asked.[4]

Nowadays, most of us have access to period-tracking apps, the pill, menstrual cups, tampons, ever-thinner sanitary pads, and powerful painkillers. Our ancestors had no such luxuries. In spite of this, they walked, climbed, and travelled, often strenuously, and frequently in the face of social opposition. Bleeding women were, after all, supposed to bleed in the clandestine confines of home. Pregnant women were also deterred from robust walking, which was thought to trigger miscarriage. In 1922 when the American poet Edna St. Vincent Millay wanted to lose an unwanted pregnancy, her mother made her take long hilltop walks to urge the foetus out.

Our gynaecology continues to hinder us: several friends told me they couldn't possibly countenance a long-distance hike because of post-childbirth incontinence or conditions like fibroids, endometriosis, menorrhagia, and polycystic ovarian syndrome, which meant grievously long, heavy, and painful periods. Biology, like fear of assault, is yet another factor in the complexity of female walking.

Shortly before Daphne arrived to meet Clara in Switzerland, her most enigmatic, spellbinding story was published. Bizarrely, and presciently, *Monte Verità* (*Mountain of Truth*) is a tale of "mountain fever," of "that urge to spill all energy, all thought, to be as nothing, blotted against the sky." In Daphne's eerie, haunting novella, a young woman called Anna makes the dramatic decision to leave her husband and the life she knows in order to live high up in a secluded mountain sect alleged to have a nirvana-ish immortality. It's a powerfully unsettling story, resistant to easy explanations.

Before she loses herself to the mountains, Anna marries and—to the male narrator's surprise and confusion—clears out her new husband's ancestral home, "the multiple odds and ends, and the collection of furniture handed down from [his] forebears," the *stuff*. This stripping back of possessions is the first sign that Anna is embarking on a journey of spiritual independence and truth, turning her back on men to become *herself*.

Monte Verità is a story about women rejecting domestic married life. It's a story of what happens when we betray the things we love "for baser things, for comfort, ease, security." It's a story about ageing and betrayal. But most of all it's a story about the male punishment meted out to women who dare to climb their own path. Female freedom, suggests Daphne, comes at a cripplingly high price.

When Daphne returned home from her Rhône walk with Clara, she wrote to a friend, "I had a *heavenly* time. I wasn't sure how I would get on, you know, with a rucksack on my back, and tramping the road, and sleeping at different places each night, but I adored every moment. . . . The strange thing is I found a village up a side valley so much like the valley village in the story, and a great rocky mountain that could have been Monte Verità. I tried to get up it but it defeated me."[5]

There's no right or wrong way to read *Monte Verità*, but I read it, in part, as a reflection of Daphne's struggles in her own search for truth. And, of course, as her affirmation of the way walking in empty landscapes propels us towards a sort of inner truth. Even if, on occasion, the landscape defeats us.

⁓

After Daphne left, Clara continued down the Rhône alone. A savage bite from a dog left her hospitalised for seventeen days, with a leg that she had to dress and bandage for weeks after. As she recovered, a letter from Daphne arrived that Clara read over and over. Their walk had unleashed a restlessness in Daphne who wrote, impassioned, "I can't get the itch of the road out of my system. What have you done to me? I walk and walk. . . . I haven't lived hard enough. I yearn to pull up beans from the earth and sleep in dung."

I love this image of Daphne: sitting among the polished silver and buffed crystal of her well-swept home, lusting after a life of dung. Because here's the thing about *comfort, ease, security*—it can topple into insipid inertia in a nanosecond. And when that happens, we are trapped. Enslaved by our own sweet-smelling laziness. Our inherent courage morphed into a soft and easy cowardice. I know: I've been there.

And so, I suspect, had Daphne.

When two friends arrived to join Clara on a later stretch, they were so short of money they resorted to stealing tomatoes and apricots from French orchards and scrabbling potatoes from the earth with their bare hands. "My shoulders ache . . . and my feet are blistering and sweat trickles down my back," wrote Clara's friend in her diary, "but it's a wonderful life of freedom."

Like Gwen and Dorelia fifty years earlier, the three women had to contend with constant rejections in their search for accommodation each evening, even when hotels obviously had rooms available. The landladies "did not see us as we saw ourselves" wrote Clara, noting that they were "the only rucksack people on those roads . . . the only lunatics who walked in the heat, sane men moved about . . . on wheels."

They slept on hard, dirty floors. Often, they washed from a cold-water tap in a courtyard or a shared single drip tap beside an outside toilet. They were rarely offered pillows. Dogs rushed at them. Swamps and broken bridges forced them to locate new routes, involving hours of extra walking. Hurricanes nearly cast them into the frothing torrents of the Rhône, while "French [men] . . . full of 'amour'" continually propositioned them. After her friends left, Clara tramped alone, her boots in pieces, their soles peeling away. This caused her acute anxiety because she had badly fallen arches requiring specially built insoles: her boots had been handmade and weren't easily replaceable in the remote valleys of the Rhône. Without her boots, how could she walk?

But Clara pressed on, "clopping along in my flattened shoes." She was, she realised, in the imaginative grip of the river: "To

follow the river, mile by mile, day by day, that was now my life. . . .
The Rhône had become . . . an incarnation of the great give-and-
take rhythm of the world." She was determined to follow the
Rhône to its final destiny in the Mediterranean. When she could
follow it no farther, she persuaded a fisherman to row her through
the vast briny lagoons of the Camargue delta and out to sea. Only
then, with her journey complete, did she feel able to return home,
writing, "I knew suddenly that my quest was ended. . . . I was ready
for return with a quiet mind to those fine things of everyday life."

⁓

There's something about this journey of Clara's, about the way
she follows the river so methodically, so determinedly. Not
back to front, like Gwen John. But from the glacial gush of
first life to its final satisfying splutter, far out to sea.

Rereading her account, I can't help feeling she was doing
more than purging herself of difficult, disliked emotions. On
this stunningly courageous walk, she was ordering her life,
making peace with her own mortality.

When we choose a river journey, we choose a landscape
that reflects back to us. I'd noticed this as I wandered along the
Garonne. It wasn't merely the sky and trees that were reflected
but myself, my journey. For ten days my world, my life, existed
in duplicate. When we follow a river from source to mouth, our
life is reflected in its circuitous passage. The tentative beginning. The twisting, turning middle. The immutable end.

Confronting one's mortality is more difficult than it's ever
been. We live in a society desperate to sweep death into the

cobwebby corners of care homes. And yet when we confront our demise, when we look it in the eye, accept it, don't we live fuller and more meaningful lives? The Dutch writer Etty Hillesum certainly thought so, writing in her diary shortly before she was killed in the Auschwitz concentration camp that "by excluding death from our life we cannot live a full life, and by admitting death into our life we enlarge and enrich it." Frieda Lawrence made the same point, a decade earlier, writing, "Life is life only when death is part of it."[6]

As I sit with my leg propped up, indignant, grumpy, and sorry for myself, I think of Clara, her leg gouged by a potentially rabid dog, lying alone in a mountain hospital thousands of miles from home, "faint with terror . . . thinking in despair: 'This is the end.'" If she hadn't confronted her own mortality before, it surely happened then. Death, she wrote later with considerable bravura, is "the last adventure . . . perhaps the greatest one of all."

Clara's river journey burned brightly as she grew older, a memory of absolute liberty, of chequered, dappled light dancing on water day after endless day. She couldn't shake it from her thoughts, and, eleven years later at the age of seventy-eight, she returned to the source of the Rhône to pay a "tribute of remembrance." Walking through snow, scrambling over glaciers, and tramping up and down mountains, she fell upon her beloved river with affection and relief. She followed the river partway, noticing with mingled sadness and fury how changed it was: "It had been drained, diverted and dammed for human purposes." The villages had changed too, "each having now its own tourist hotel."[7]

Never go back. Never go back.

And yet, Clara finished her trip with "a feeling of veneration and deep peace." She felt surrendered, lost for a second time "entirely in the river." This was her last mighty hike, her swan song to the river that had "purified" her a decade earlier, her "old self carried away and drowned by that swift current."

But she didn't retire to her couch with her favourite Egyptian cigarettes. Instead she tramped the Cornish lanes in her black oilskins, her frayed black beret, and a pair of unravelling black mittens, almost until her death, half-blind, at ninety.

⌒

Clara's love of wild, solitary walks had begun, quite by chance, in 1907: she was twenty-one and staying with a friend in Ireland. One day, she left the house merely to take a few breaths of air. Black clouds skulked overhead and the foliage gleamed in the green half-light. It began to drizzle and the birds fell silent. The drizzle thickened into rain. The rain grew heavier and a mist blew in. Instead of turning back, Clara trudged on, as if pulled by some invisible thread. The rain dripped from the ends of her hair and splashed from the hem of her coat. The mist grew denser until she was pushing through wet whiteness, breathing in the smell of damp birch trees and crushed sodden bracken. On and on she went, not knowing where she was or how long she'd been walking, but feeling oddly elated and without any desire to find shelter or company. This walk, alone in the rain, was her epiphany. She had a sudden feeling of freedom combined with a Zen-like sense of being absorbed by the landscape. "I felt as if I possessed the whole country or as if it possessed me. . . . On and on I went, ecstatically alone in my one-dimensional world of mist," she wrote in her memoir. She returned home changed, having experienced a completely new sense of autonomy. "I was an atom, lost, not in empty space but in a new and rich universe," she wrote. "I was an atom that could feel a wild exhilaration in its newly won freedom."[8]

Ten years after her Irish epiphany, Clara began her restless hunt for "the wild and sublime," a search that was to characterise the rest of her life. The interim years had been devastating: she had seen extreme poverty first-hand as a social worker in the slums of East London; as a nurse she had witnessed the horrors of World War I; finally—in the space of four years— she had lost a brother, a sister, and her father.

She escaped her inner desolation by embarking on the bravest of all her treks, utterly unfazed either by her age (she was in her forties) or by warnings that the journey would be "neither pleasant nor easy." She and a girlfriend took a steamer bound for Canada, where they planned a river route, from Aklavik inside the Arctic Circle to Fort Yukon in Alaska. Some of the journey was done by canoe but much was on foot. For nine days they pushed their way through towering grasses and tangled willows, often walking over swamps that undulated terrifyingly beneath their feet. They scrambled along riverbanks that fell sheer to the water, hanging on to roots and branches as black swarms of mosquitoes massed round their netted faces and chomped at their flesh. In spite of this they "felt a great longing to . . . spend the rest of our days wandering about the unknown, cruel, magnificent land."

The two women arrived in Fort Yukon to find themselves a tourist attraction. No lone women, it seemed, had previously walked the snarled treacherous banks of the "rough, cold, swift, mosquito-haunted" Rat River.[9]

After World War II, and several years before her Rhône walk, Clara changed tack. She decided her struggle for inner composure would be best served by walking routeless and planless. This time the sea beckoned. Her mind in disarray, her heart broken and bruised from a surfeit of loss, she packed a rucksack and a walking stick, took a train, and then simply began walking along the coast of Dorset. She craved open space and felt a compulsion to walk alone, "day after day to an unknown destination . . . with only a rucksack and a walking stick for company." Outside, between heaven and earth, she felt the enlarging of herself, as if she were "keeping time with the beating pulse of the country." This was her favourite way to travel, "without obligations, restraints, set plans or time limits . . . alone . . . and on foot."

There's something about wandering off, with neither expectation nor intention. Without responsibility of any sort. As my foot healed, I began taking walks—slow and short—along the

River Thames, which lies at the bottom of my road. My Garonne River walk had opened my eyes to the possibilities of water. I was shocked at how I had taken the Thames for granted: its proximity, its bird life, its preposterous beauty. For two decades I had walked beside it without *seeing* it. The story I told myself—that I was a mountain girl—had blinded me to the startling and wondrous complexity of something that lay virtually on my doorstep. I blamed *Heidi*, the formative book of my childhood, a book steeped in the miracle of peaks and pine trees. But I also wondered if it was the *how* of my previous river walks.

For years, I had struggled to find any sense of inner stillness. Surrounded by young children, then teenagers, I rarely had my eye on the present (and certainly not in a still way). I was perpetually pulled towards an indistinct future—usually one in which I had damaged them deeply by not making them wear a bike helmet, or have braces, or do eye exercises, or floss nightly, or practice the piano more, or study for an exam, etc., etc. I hadn't been raised with a mother who did this. I had no role model for operating in our age of maternal anxiety.

Because the river was so close, when I walked beside it I often had children or a dog lurching towards the low-level wall that ran between the path and the water, filling me with fear. And the sheer proximity to home meant my brain was still blundering with *the bondage of familiar things*, what Clara recognised as the mind's "wavering disquiet and pettiness." No milk in the fridge, paperwork undone, dog food not ordered, dentist appointments missed. For decades, every walk was a rush, an attempt to squeeze too much activity and responsibility into too little time, to hurry home for this or that.

For Clara, water—particularly rivers—was the supreme symbol of freedom, offering both physical and cognitive liberation. Which is exactly what women need. Frequently burdened and busy with parents, children, partners, work, and homes, women rarely have the chance to feel both bodily and cognitively *free*. But on my Garonne walk I'd achieved this, and when I returned to the Thames, I saw it through a new lens. A single long-distance river journey had snapped me from my stuck-in-the-mud way of being and thinking. Of course, my children were older. I no longer fretted about them drowning. But as I swung along on my crutches—I was as deft as Long John Silver by this point—I noticed the black-headed gulls crying, wheeling, diving. I noticed the cormorants and herons, the white poplars, the light mantling on the water.

In these swinging, hobbling forays I started to appreciate walking without expectation, intention, or responsibility. I had no need to write about the Thames. I took no phone or camera, removing any self-expectation to frame a shot or post on social media, or count my steps, or know what time it was. I walked merely to be with the river.

⌒

Clara never travelled with a camera. Her companion on the Rat River trip sketched throughout, but not Clara. And yet her memories of walking were so deeply etched she was able to write this trip into a book thirty-five years after the event, claiming that the "rivers, mountains, forests, glaciers, birds and rapids, remain as vivid as if I had seen them this morning."

The memories of her Irish travels were even more impressive, written after a lapse of forty years.

In our Instagram epoch, hiking without taking endless pictures feels almost maverick. Walking the Garonne, I had sometimes sketched rather than taking a snapshot. Not because I am any good at drawing (I'm not) but because I wanted to understand Gwen John. Much later I discovered that the landscapes or scenes I'd drawn were welded in my mind, high-definition memories that superseded all others.

Behind a camera we're outside of the moment and the landscape, separated by the obstacle of lens or screen. But sketching or painting pulls us into the moment, into the spirit of the place. When I looked at my little drawings in the months that followed, I remembered the weight of sunlight on the nape of my neck, the taste of wild fig on my tongue, the cool moss beneath my legs, that inner stillness—sensations that didn't return when I looked at images on my iPhone. My rag-and-bone sketches weren't pictures or mementoes—they were portals to my imagination.

Our profligate use of cameras—too easy, too fast, too careless—means that instead of capturing the moment, we lose it. When we draw or paint, we expand the moment, creating space for all our senses, and fixing the memory with blade-sharp clarity.

Incidentally, neuroscientists think our sharpest, deepest memories are those we make when alone. These are the memories that stay with us in glorious Technicolor rather than sepia. Fewer distractions, apparently.

In the same year that Clara walked the length of the Rhône, the American writer and critic Lionel Trilling wrote of "the modern fear of being cut off from the social group even for a moment."[10] For years I too was constrained by the fear of being alone and *cut off.* Because I was so determined to avoid time on my own, I had lost all capacity for solitude. Moreover my fear caused me, insidiously, to make choices I might not otherwise have made. It weighed on me, pressed at me, much like wearing a straitjacket. I often used my fear of assault and my gynaecology to justify my fear of being alone—a strong cocktail of restraint and evasion.

I think about this when I dip into the carefree walking adventures recounted admirably and eloquently by so many men: Laurie Lee, Werner Herzog, Bruce Chatwin, Patrick Leigh Fermor, Edward Thomas, Henry David Thoreau, etc. I once lived (and walked) vicariously through their books, but their easy, uncomplicated swagger—encapsulated in lines like Werner Herzog's "Where I'm going to sleep doesn't worry me"[11]— made it plain these were not men or adventures I could emulate. It is women like Clara Vyvyan—casting off untold fears, dealing with additional complexity and danger—who encourage us to live not *vicariously* but fully and in the flesh. She reminds us that the courage of others is contagious, that valiant women can breathe hope and fortitude into other women.

Thanks to the lost writings of innumerable women like Clara, I've discovered that walking alone, day after day, can be euphoric. It's quite possibly the most poignant and liberating discovery of my life.

And yet walking with others can be deeply rewarding. Clara recognised this and walked in company as frequently as she walked alone. A couple of years after her Rhône trip, she walked the Pindus Mountains of Greece, again with Daphne du Maurier. "The wilds had never ceased calling us," wrote Clara. Daphne was the perfect walking companion: adventurous, enthusiastic, fit, drawn to wild, remote places, but perhaps most importantly of all, "calm and silent." While walking, Daphne would often wander off and "settle herself into some stony hollow" where she could meditate silently, sometimes for hours, which suited Clara perfectly.

The subject of walking companions weighed heavily on women, most of whom felt compelled to travel with somebody else. Clara wrote at length about the "friend" dilemma. Her preference was to walk alone during the day and have company during the evening. She wanted to share the punishing humiliation of being turned away from door after door, but she also wanted to discuss her day over supper. Nan Shepherd thought the conundrum was solved by walking with "the right sort of hill companion." Indeed, Shepherd thought the silence of the mountains was "enhanced" by the "perfect" companion. For her, this was someone able to merge his or her identity with the mountains. In other words, someone able to respond to the landscape exactly as she did, someone who let "the hill . . . speak."[12] Clara and Shepherd agreed that the worst companions were "chatterers."

New studies have found that walking in silence with another person can be a deeply rewarding experience, in which our bodies communicate without any need for talk. When we walk in rhythm with another person, we subtly communicate by falling in step. Researchers call it "step synchronisation as a form of non-verbal social communication."[13]

Clara realised that her long-distance, sometimes silent treks with Daphne had developed an unbreakable bond between them. "Together we had forged a link of shared experience, a link which can ... withstand all the tests of friendship, time and change and separation," she wrote, after returning from the Rhône. Her book on hunting for wild flowers in the remote Greek hinterland was dedicated to "My good companion, Daphne."[14]

The funny thing is, distance walking ameliorates distance. Walking day after day—with the right companion—brings us closer to those we're walking with than anything else I can think of. If we hadn't hiked for all those years as a family, I suspect we might be a different sort of family, less close perhaps. And when I think back through the many boyfriends of my youth, the only one embossed on my memory is the one I trekked with.

Not all Clara's walking companions were as like-minded as Daphne. In her books she derided unnamed friends for being either too bossy or too passive. Both types wrecked her hikes. For Daphne, what made Clara the perfect walking companion was Clara's easy-going nature, and it strikes me that easy-going (which is not the same as *passive*) is the most important quality in a walking mate.

In many ways, the necessity of finding and having a companion merely added to the complexity with which women of the past walked. Few could declare, as William Hazlitt did, "I like to go by myself." Or as Robert Louis Stevenson did, "A walking tour should be gone upon alone." Few had the luxury of rejecting *all* their friends for not having the "right combination of personal tastes and characteristics," as Petrarch did when considering a companion for his ascent of Mount Ventoux.

⌣

By the time I finish my Walk of the Mind with Clara, my foot has mended and I am ready to embark on a real walk. While I prepare and pack, I wonder what I should do with Clara, whether I should edit her out of this book. Whenever I mention her name, the response is always the same: Who on earth is Clara Vyvyan? In spite of her books and her walks, she is missing from every single book on walking—including tomes like *The Illustrated Encyclopaedia of Walking and Backpacking*, which referenced every man who had ever converted his "walking tour" into a book. Moreover, Clara has no biography, no archive, and no Wikipedia page.

But isn't this the point?

5

In Search of Being and Meaning

Nan Shepherd

India. Scotland. Mountains. Vertigo. Disappointment.
Navigation. Self-Belief. Silence. Roots. Hope.

For an hour I am beyond desire. It is not ecstasy, that leap out of the self that makes man like a god. I am not out of myself, but in myself. I am. To know Being, this is the final grace accorded from the mountain.

—NAN SHEPHERD, *The Living Mountain, 1977*

It's always the same. I'm moving through a space. Not a place, but a space. Blank, indistinguishable, apocalyptically empty. Time is indistinct, blurred. Sometimes spires of morning light mark my way, but at other times the light is grainy, charcoaled—a sort of twilight. Always I'm alone, often running, occasionally saunter-ing. The only certainty is that my journey will end as it always does: on an edge, ahead a plunging pool of nothing. As if I've reached the earth's end. Sometimes I stop walking before I reach that precipitous, vertiginous void, turning back effortlessly into another dream. Frequently I wake up, perched upon the thin blade of land, heart hammering. At other times I walk right off the edge and feel myself falling, my legs cycling, my arms wind-milling. As if I'm trying to catch at the air with my fingers and toes. I wake tangled in the sheet, sodden with perspiration, the breath scratching in my throat.

Not a nightmare, says my psychologist friend. A night *terror*. "How long has this been going on?"

I tell her it's been twenty years now. She purses her lips, nods. I don't tell her I can trace my night terror back to a very particular point. A point that has wedged itself deep in my mind. Unyielding. Unshiftable. Trapped.

⌢

When I was twenty I dropped out of university and fled to the mountains. I had an urgent need for height, open vistas, space. I wanted to be far, far away: from people, civilisation, myself. In an odd, inarticulate way I needed a landscape that could mirror the wild, messy emptiness I felt inside. And after months in dark, smoky, and very small rooms, I craved air, light, and height. Above all, I longed for height.

What is it about height that promises some form of salvation? I thought that with altitude I could look out at life, at the tumbling bits of me, with a generous sense of perspective. Somehow I felt that only the remote heights of the Himalayas could provide the clear lines of sight I needed, while simultaneously offering distance and wilderness.

So I and my boyfriend—a mountaineer whose life had conveniently unravelled at exactly the same time—set off for the remote foothills of the Pir Panjal, far away from the usual traveller trails and treks. We camped below the snow line, where the night temperature plunged below zero. Every morning we watched the sun rise beyond the ridge, flinging its buttery rays over peak after peak, until every snow-tipped mountain for miles and miles glistened rose gold. We'd pack up the tent, throw on our backpacks, and set off, mapless, routeless, always heading north.

We skidded down ice-bound ridges and scrambled up ramshackle tracks of scree. We stumbled through unclaimed valleys of pine, spruce, juniper, and wild apricot, and, when the track disappeared, we navigated through thickets of bamboo, or along abandoned riverbeds, our huge, unwieldy rucksacks swinging from our backs.

In the evening we ate with the Gaddi shepherds, sharing their dahl and chapatis. The light fell swiftly in the Himalayas, dropping into darkness without any lingering dusk or twilight. As we unrolled sleeping bags and mats, the Gaddis roamed through the thick blackness with torches made from the long roots of pine trees. We lay in our sleeping bags and watched them leaping around in their plastic sandals, collecting up stray goats, the orange tips of their beedi cigarettes fading and flaring, and their broken teeth gleaming, white and jagged.

For three months we lived like this, our days stripped bare. The knotted mess of my past life receded, but in its place came something I'd never encountered before: fear. I discovered a quaking, paralysing horror of heights; an ungovernable fear of falling, of dying. I was convinced I'd tumble into a crevasse and die. On narrow tracks, little more than shelves hacked into the rock face, I became so overwhelmed my muscles went into spasm. With my entire body shaking I crawled on hands and knees, inch by excruciating inch, never looking down at the ravine that lay thousands of feet below.

Often we crossed dizzyingly steep canyons on swaying, fraying rope ladders with missing treads and crude knots where the rope had worn through and been casually repaired. Merely looking at these bridges paralysed me with terror. But there was no alternative route, so I developed a habit of looking fixedly ahead and moving painfully slowly—a technique that was bearable until I reached the middle of a rope bridge. Here, the swaying became rocking. The cliff edge I'd left was miles behind me. The cliff edge I wanted was miles ahead of me. A rung was inevitably missing, leaving a yawning aperture over acres of empty air. Below, water dashed violently over sharpened rocks. Panic gripped me. Every limb, every muscle seized up. Sweat dripped into my eyes. The fierce, uncontrollable shaking began again. My long-suffering boyfriend—who always went ahead—would shout his now-familiar mantra: "You have nothing to fear but fear itself." Eventually I'd find myself on the other side of the canyon. A jellied, quivering blub of terror.

I never felt the pride of conquest. I never thumped the air or whooped with victory, like reality TV contestants. The emotional effort, the physical strain, left me depleted, exhausted. Besides, I hadn't conquered anything. I knew full well the next time I crossed a skimpy, broken rope ladder or crawled along a greasy ledge the width of my hips, terror would rise up, just as it had before. And next time I really might slip and die.

The disappointment was devastating. I realised then that I'd never be the daring mountaineer I'd dreamt of becoming, that I was possessed of a debilitating frailty over which I had very little control, and that my body couldn't be trusted or relied upon. At the same time, I became aware of something pressing inside me: a feeling of fragile optimism. In finding myself so acutely frightened of dying, I came to realise how desperately I wanted to live.

The Scottish writer Nan Shepherd scrambled up mountains with impunity. But she also had her own version of vertiginous terror, a sort of after-the-event paralysis which struck from the comfort and safety of her single bed. Tucked up under her bedspread, she'd think over the day's daredevil antics and go cold with horror. As soon as she was back in the mountains, she became, once again, oblivious to her fear: "When I go back, the same leap of the spirit carries me up."[1]

I envied Shepherd's fearless *leap of the spirit*, and longed to understand how she transcended her horror at exactly the moment I succumbed to it. But I shared her passion for the "tang of height." Although I had confronted my puniness there, the Himalayas had given me an enduring taste for altitude, for vast panoramic vistas, for the unfolding drama of mountains, for their thin, scoured air with its sharp, mineral taste. And—perhaps less predictably—for walking uphill.

The Himalayas had also given me a new sense of my future. From their peaks, the world had looked different: clearer, more certain. And my place in the world had looked simpler, less anguished. I worked for a few weeks with Mother Teresa, hung around some Buddhist monasteries, then returned home, paper-thin and with a chronic autoimmune disease. I finished my degree and found a job in the fledgling technology industry, working with computers the size of houses and mobile phones the size of *War and Peace* (the hardback version). But in my London flat and my matt-black office, I yearned for space and height. Over the next decade I explored hills and mountains at every opportunity: Snowdonia, the Peak District, the Lake District, the Black Mountains, the Alps, the Dolomites, Kilimanjaro, the peaks and plateaus of the Spanish Sierra Nevada. But never the famous Scottish Munros.

I'd been to the Scottish countryside only once—to a tiny island off the west coast where Matthew was banished to work, uninterrupted, on a strategy document. I was allowed to go too, on condition I didn't speak to him. For five days I stalked stags through wet heather, watched the rolling grey ocean from slippery rocks, and read. That was it. A reputation for biting midges and endless rain meant that Scotland disappeared from my radar.

Until I discovered Nan Shepherd. And her living mountain.

⌒

What makes a woman stare so fixedly, so curiously, that she sees the leanest of veins in a leaf or the lightest of flecks on a petal? What makes her sniff, taste, touch the crinkled leaf, the fading petal, the crizzled crust of ice—the earth, moss, lichen, sand—that the rest of us pass by? What makes her listen so closely, so attentively, she hears "the movement of the midnight owl" and the "low far-off murmur" of water?

Shepherd has been described as a woman deeply and passionately in love with the physical world, enthralled to the physical reality of life, to the "sticky and rich" ripeness of it.[2] But I think her story is also the story of a woman's hunger. The story of what happens when hunger swells to the point of semi-starvation.

During my years of susceptibility, I once put myself on a ridiculous fast. Throughout my four days of so-called cleansing, I thought of little but food. When I finally came to eat, something peculiar happened. My meal—a vegetable stew I often made—acquired colours, smells, subtle flavours that I'd never noticed before. It was the same old recipe, but this time it burbled and crooned in the pan. On the plate, its hues of scarlet, violet, pale green seemed brighter, more vivid. The herbs smelled richer, more earthily pungent. The slick of oil shone green gold. My inflamed appetite had subtly altered both me and the dish itself. For all its crude and homely qualities, that vegetable stew remains one of the best meals I've ever eaten.

So here's the question: What made Shepherd so hungry?

At the end of World War I, Marie Stopes's book *Married Love* (essentially about sex and birth control) was a bestseller, and in its fifth edition. But Stopes's postbag contained more and more letters asking for advice not on contraception but on sexual frustration.[3]

The war had wiped out almost an entire generation of young, single men, leaving millions of women without the future they'd expected and been raised for. Those born between 1885 and 1905 were the most affected.[4] Shepherd was born bang in the middle, in 1893. As far as marital prospects went, she couldn't have been born at a worse time.

Two million such women existed in the UK alone, and millions more across Europe. Cruelly labelled in the British press as "surplus," these women faced a future deprived of husbands, children, intimacy, or romance. The burden fell disproportionately on middle-class women like Shepherd. Not only because a higher proportion of the officer class had been killed but because middle-class women had been raised to marry someone of an equal or superior social class. Marrying down was unthinkable.

In daily newspapers Britain's young women were also described as "a problem" and "a disaster for the human race." Other words used to describe this generation of unmarried females included "thwarted," "jealous," "bitter," "deficient," "wretched," "on the shelf," "old maid," "sex-starved spinster." And so on.

As Virginia Nicholson points out in her seminal book *Singled Out*, this epidemic of surplus women had a seismic effect on marital behaviour. Suddenly, the arena of courtship became a competitive battleground. Good looks and femininity were at a premium. Failure to scoop a husband meant a future in which one was irrelevant, isolated, and a figure of fun.[5] Worse still, it threatened a life of servitude: as late as 1949, Simone de Beauvoir was writing about single women remaining a servant in the father's, brother's or sister's household, a source of free housekeeping or childcare.[6]

Being unmarried also meant a life without intimacy, a life of "withering into virginity," as the writer Winifred Hodgkiss so bitterly put it.[7] No wonder Marie Stopes's postbag was full of letters from women troubled by intensely strong sexual feelings. Letter writers wanted advice on masturbation, and tips for satisfying sexual urges. Many were overcome with shame and guilt, unable to stop masturbating and begging for permission to continue. Stopes suggested a "really hot bath" to dissipate "the electric energy which accumulates."

Electric energy. Appetite. Hunger. Where does it go?

Shepherd was no stranger to explosive feelings of desire, to *electric energy*. She wrote about it in *The Quarry Wood*, her autobiographical novel: "Through [Martha's] body there ran a tantalising irritation. She thought: 'It isn't pain—but what is it? It's in me. It hurts my body.' And she writhed, twisting herself upon the bed. . . . Her wants felt inordinate and she too small and weak." Martha realises what she wants: "Just to touch his hand: that would allay the agony that tore her, the pain that gnawed and could not be located, that was in all her body and yet nowhere. She knew now. She wanted Luke. . . . She wanted Luke with an animal . . . ardour."

At last the female capacity for *animal ardour* was being acknowledged, compounding the anguish of *surplus women*. Frieda Lawrence played her part: thanks to her, D. H. Lawrence had discovered the profound pleasures of a robust sex life. More importantly, he now had an inkling of female desire, combined with the encouragement of a woman equally keen to impart her secrets of sensuality to the world. He made it his life's work to change the prissy English attitude to sex, writing stories of women who found their true ecstatic selves through physical union with a man. The time of women living in sexual ignorance until their wedding night was over. Between them, he and Frieda had opened a Pandora's box. Sex was no longer something to be fearful or ignorant of. Nor was it merely for procreation. Instead it was a means of liberation, ecstasy, and quasi-spiritual transcendence.

Shepherd, like all well-read women of her generation, read Lawrence.[8] I too read Lawrence as a teenager, thumbing through *Lady Chatterley's Lover* for the rude bits (which now seem excruciatingly tame), imagining myself frisking naked among the violets in a transformative glut of passion. It never occurred to me that I wouldn't have a taste of Lawrentian bliss at some point in my life. But many women of Shepherd's generation recognised that the allegedly earth-shattering experience of sex (or even kissing in Kirk-constrained Scotland) was to be nothing more than a fantasy. There simply weren't enough men to go round.

Shepherd took her *animal ardour* into the mountain, transmuting her disappointment, despair, and desire into the landscape and, later, into her writing. No wonder *The Living Mountain* has been described as having "a shudder of eroticism."[9]

For many "surplus women," the incessant, aching longing for children was infinitely more painful than the need for sex. The maternal urge, the biological clock—call it what you will—is an appetite of its own, often acutely painful and frighteningly ungovernable. Whether it's hormonal or existential is largely irrelevant: for both men and women procreation lies at the very heart of who we are. None more so than for this generation of women, bred to breed, and given no time to adjust, to plan, to imagine a different future for themselves. It mattered little that Shepherd had excelled at school—middle-class women were educated for wifedom and motherhood, not for illustrious careers.

Shepherd's unpublished notebook reveals the weight of her maternal expectations. At around the age of sixteen she copied out, in her scrupulously neat handwriting, pages and pages of poetry, hymns, and proverbs on the rapturous state of motherhood and the devastating loneliness of being "barren." It's difficult for those of us who grew up in the bright light of feminism to understand quite how deeply this sort of literature affected women, how it set hard inside them, shaping their expectations, their self-esteem and sense of purpose. Shepherd's notebook contains poems with titles like "Motherhood, the Blessed Barren" (about a woman unable to have children who "will go her silver lonely way / Towards heaven . . . There God shall bring her little ones"); "Old Mothers" (a poem about "sweet, old mothers" with "white hair and kindly eyes" who murmur "blessings over sleeping babes"); "Madonnas" (from a volume called *Songs of Motherhood* and including the memorable lines "Mothers' hearts do always hear / Divinest music ringing clear / And peace and love, good will on earth / are born with every baby's birth"); and "The Cradle" (featuring a mother "lovingly" and "steadfastly" making a cradle "with all her would-be mother's wit").

A rabbinic quote ("The Lord could not be everywhere so he made mothers"), and several carols featuring the Virgin Mother, Mary, compound the raison d'être of women-as-mothers.[10] Meanwhile a much later copying of a poem about a childless woman who dreams of becoming a mother only to wake and find herself cruelly deceived ("unloved, alone," and "the dream of happiness destroyed . . . / What tongue can speak the dreary void?") hints at Shepherd's own feelings of unspeakable sadness.[11]

So where does all that longing go? All that aching, unfulfilled love? Many women had nieces or nephews, but Shepherd's only sibling, Frank, died in 1917 on the other side of the world—a "senseless" death from tuberculosis that had devastated the Shepherd family.[12] He left a wife and daughter, but six years later the daughter also died.

Shepherd had already witnessed the disappointment wrought by infertility—and its consequences. Her mother loved babies and, according to Shepherd's biographer, Charlotte Peacock, had wanted more than the two she had. Unable to become pregnant again, she'd taken to her bed—and there she stayed until her death at eighty-five, rarely leaving her room. Neighbours suspected her of being a malingerer.

When World War I ended, Shepherd was only twenty-five, and the opportunity for adventure, romance, and love should have stretched glimmeringly before her. But this was post-war Aberdeen, a city riddled with unemployment, inflation, strikes, and flu epidemics, and spitting with ex-servicemen unable to find work and inevitably carrying the physical and psychological baggage of war (a subject Shepherd later explored in one of her finest pieces of fiction, "Descent from the Cross").

Any gleam of escape was extinguished when Shepherd's father died in 1925. With him went his pension, leaving Shepherd as the sole carer and provider for her bed-bound mother. At the age of thirty-two Shepherd was shackled to her mother and her childhood home, to a future gapingly empty of intimacy, love, adventure. Where does all that emotion go? All that loss, longing, disappointment, regret?

Suppressed and crushed into a hard, festering tumour of pain? Onto paper? Or into the mountain?

～

April. My first trip to the Cairngorms mountain range, Britain's largest tract of untamed country. No roads or railways pass through it. No pylons or telegraph wires traverse it. No other part of Britain is so vast at such height. With five of Britain's six highest peaks within its boundaries, the Cairngorms National Park in the Scottish Highlands is the size of Luxembourg, but barely inhabited. Perhaps this isn't surprising given winds on the plateau can reach speeds of more than 170 miles an hour, snow falls every month of the year, and people have been swept away by rivers, blown off their feet, frozen to death.

Hugo and I step off the train at Aviemore after a seven-and-a-half-hour train journey. The light has drained from the sky, and as we walk from the station to our guest house, it starts to rain. Within seconds the rain turns to barbed sleet, stinging our cheeks, clinging to our clothes.

"It always rains ice in Scotland," Hugo mutters. "Everyone knows that, Mum."

The following morning a blizzard is blowing, snow swirling thickly in every direction. The sidewalk is a thick, white crust, the roofs of Aviemore are draped white. Dense white cloud obscures the mountains. The silence is heavy, muffled: snow-silence. "There'll be no buses or trains today," declares the guest-house owner.

We decide to walk, regardless. By the time we set out, the snow has turned to rain and the ground is a swimming tide of melting brown slush. Trucks send arcs of filthy meltwater that drips down our trousers and into our walking boots. Hugo forgets to put his hood up but by the time he realises this, his hood is a pond and his hair lies wet against his head, sleek and seal-like. Our feet grow damper and damper. Water seeps behind my backpack, through my coat, right through to my shoulder blades.

We walk to the ancient pine forests of Rothiemurchus, rain-sodden, dripping from every brim, every hem, every eyelash, our feet slurping in our boots. On the edge of Loch an Eilein we find Shepherd's "enormous venerable Scots firs," and giant pine trees with runkles of bark a "foot and a half in length and thick as books." We crouch down beneath one and breathe in the smell of pine needles, damp earth, wet moss. Hugo pokes around in the tree's twisted roots, and I think about *how* Shepherd walked: like Clara Vyvyan, she liked to absorb the feel of a place, to let its sights, scents, and sounds soak into her. It's a way of walking—of being—I'm learning to love, but not one that lends itself to relentless rainfall.

We splash back to our guest house in shared silence: we are nothing but two wet bodies, barely human, shivering with cold. In our room we tip the water from our boots and peel off our clothes, every single layer streaked and puddled with wet, with Shepherd's "black pitiless unceasing rain."

We drape our sodden clothes over the radiator and our tiny room fills with steam and the smell of black peat, making the space feel tight and oppressive. Quite suddenly I think of Shepherd's bedroom—the room she slept in all her life. A tiny, cramped room beneath the eaves—too small for a wardrobe, desk, or chair—with a narrow single bed pushed against the wall and a window looking out to the Deeside valley. The room was so small Shepherd had to keep most of her clothes in the maid's bedroom.

The house had at least four other bedrooms. Her mother's room—which became available when Shepherd was in her fifties—was spacious, turreted, and in possession of sweeping views. Her brother's room was empty. Her father's room was empty. Even the maid had a bigger room than Shepherd. But she chose to stay in her own room. For eighty-seven years she slept in the same choked space, in the same narrow bed, overlooking the same view.

⌒

I often imagine Shepherd in her little room. She liked to read until the early hours, sitting on a cushion on the floor. The smallness of her room (her biographer described it to me as a cell)—and the idea of sleeping in one's childhood bedroom all one's life—induces a mild sense of panic in me. As if I can't breathe properly. But Shepherd refused to be constrained by it. Like Ellen Falconer, a Shepherd-like character in her novel *The Weatherhouse*, she "shut herself in as to a tower and was safe; or rather, she felt, shut herself out from the rest of the house. The room seemed not to end with itself, but through its protruding windows became part of the infinite world. There she lay and watched the stars; saw dawn touch the mountain; and fortified her soul."

Shepherd's novels, like Gwen John's paintings, brim with doors and windows, forever opening and closing on a succession of women. Gwen's painted women sit inside looking out, but Shepherd's fictional women move restlessly, ambivalently, and often confusedly between the two. Uncertain of where their place is. Unclear about how to break free. Unsure of how to escape or how to belong.

There's a photograph of Shepherd as a toddler that crystallises this straining for freedom, this sense of being caught between two worlds. It's a conventional family picture where she looks as if she's about to slide from her mother's lap and run away. "As though I were demanding to get at life," wrote Shepherd later. "I swear those limbs move as you look at them."

But there's something about her mother's grip, the way she's pinioning Shepherd's arms with her own, fixing her with a steely gaze. Isn't this the story? Not Shepherd's toddlerish squirming—what toddler wants to pose for a photograph?— but those maternal fingers digging into her chubby arms.

In a later family photograph, a grinning Shepherd stands in front of her unsmiling mother. Shepherd looks away from the lens, out of the picture. Again, the maternal hands grip at Shepherd, like claws on her shoulders. Although Gwen John evaded the obligation of an unmarried daughter to care for a single elderly parent, Shepherd's sense of propriety was deeply ingrained, shaped by the prevailing Calvinism of twentieth-century Aberdeen and compounded by her strong sense of duty and compassion. In an age when unmarried women were passed around as a source of free domestic labour, marriage was the only way to escape family ties.

Many years later, one of Shepherd's students asked her advice on caring for mothers. Shepherd's reply was unequivocal: never do it.[13]

⌐

"Every book is, in one way or another, an appeal for help," wrote Simone de Beauvoir, reflecting Lawrence's famous line that "one sheds one's sicknesses in books." They're suggesting that we can exorcise ourselves through the therapeutic process of writing, but they're also suggesting that we can *transcend* our sickness, freeing ourselves from pain, trauma, confusion. Both of them used fiction to examine, unpick, and order the thoughts and emotions that floored them.

Shepherd was no different: between the ages of thirty-five and forty-one, in a frenzied rush of creativity and catharsis, she published three acclaimed novels and a poetry collection. Here everything spilled out, despite her attempts at concealment. She used the writing process to interrogate herself, to hold elaborate dialogues with herself, to untangle how she felt and thought. Hardly surprising that her subjects range from desire, education, sickness, shame, and humiliation, to female identity, old age, home, and self-determination. Hardly surprising that her novels are characterised by ambiguity, conflict, and discord.

At the same time, she taught at Aberdeen's Teacher Training Centre. She also lectured to local societies in the evenings, worked on a study of Rupert Brooke's poetry, cared for her bedridden mother, and dealt with the aftermath of her father's death. Small wonder that she wrote in rabid snatches, fragments that she later stitched into beguiling prose.

The need to *shed her sickness*, to *appeal for help*, must have been overwhelmingly strong. How else does one work with such undiluted frenzy?

Shepherd suffered, throughout this period, from a "revulsion against"[14] herself, and from thoughts and emotions that "tormented" her, leaving her "miserable." She never disclosed the source of her torment, but it appears that Shepherd had a secret she harboured all her life. A secret that, for fourteen years, brought anguish and bewilderment. A secret that made her tremble with fear, because she knew if word slipped out, her world would "blaze up and perish."[15] This was not bohemian Paris. This was Scotland, with its Calvinist distrust of emotion and its tightly laced culture of duty, piety, conformity. Shepherd knew exactly what happened to sinners.

⌒

We take a bus ten miles south, to see Shepherd's first view of the Cairngorms, the view that "thirled" her to the mountain, that she later described as "that great gashed cleft above Glen Feshie, which I watched, year after year, filled with depths of a blue that made my heart turn over."[16]

When we find the house where her family spent their summer holidays, a woman in a denim dress answers the door and says she's never heard of Nan Shepherd. I whip out a Scottish five-pound note and point at Shepherd's face, which gazes wistfully from beneath a jewelled headband. The woman beams at me and says we can go anywhere we like. Hugo goes in search of ptarmigan and I find a damp tussock, perch on it, and gaze across to the mountains, which are drowned in mist and rain.

Shepherd didn't walk in the mountains until the tail end of those pivotal years of frenzied, purging writing. In the spring of 1930, she took a month-long walking break, writing that her "whole nature" had "suddenly leaped into life" and she was "making poems at about the rate of one a day." From these poems pour the silent anguish that Shepherd had been living with.

Meticulous detective work from Shepherd's biographer suggests she endured fourteen years of desperate, unrequited love for a married man: John Macmurray. Once an Aberdeen student and later an eminent philosopher with radical ideas about freedom, Macmurray was enormously attractive to women, highly intelligent and deeply thoughtful. He shared many of Shepherd's shattering experiences, including the fracturing of his Presbyterian faith. Unfortunately he was married to one of Shepherd's closest and oldest friends, Betty.

But theirs was a complicated marriage. Betty had a lover who provided a physical passion she'd never felt with her husband. Her carnal awakening encouraged her to press Macmurray for an open marriage, persuading him that this was simply another stage in his evolving philosophy of freedom. And so Macmurray and Betty permitted each other to stray sexually from their marriage vows.

In theory this offered Shepherd an opportunity for intimacy with the man she adored. We know that Macmurray had a few dalliances, and judging from Shepherd's "raw, vexed, and yawning" sonnets,[17] she was one such (unsatisfactory) dalliance. Charlotte Peacock speculates that they made love during a holiday Shepherd spent with the Macmurrays in South Africa. And yet it seems he couldn't reciprocate her ardour. He later confessed to feeling "a trifle Victorian in my habits. I can't get my instincts to change to keep company with my ideas." Much as he wanted to emulate his wife's sexual freedom, he couldn't. "I don't trust myself in sex very much," he wrote. "I was too deeply damaged there when I was young."[18]

Or perhaps Shepherd simply wasn't his type. Macmurray's biographer describes a Scottish camping trip where the Macmurrays, Shepherd, and a friend called May spent an evening discussing sex. May plucked up the courage to ask Betty if she could sleep with Macmurray: "She wanted to be able to say, even to herself, that she had been in bed with a man at least once in her life." While she spent the night with Macmurray, Shepherd shared Betty's tent.[19]

Either way, Shepherd's broken-hearted sonnets are testament to a storm of emotions: shame, humiliation, pain, desire, anger, and, finally, a quivering acceptance.

Her autobiographical novel, *The Quarry Wood*, suggests Shepherd sabotaged herself, becoming a victim of her own feelings of fear and restraint. The Shepherd character, Martha, is set alight by a "secret and impossible love." She ricochets from feeling "splendidly alive" to being gripped by "cyclones of desire," until—utterly overwrought—she has to pass "the time in restless walking," eventually sleeping in a field, then walking into a wood where she finds Luke (the character based on Macmurray). "An intoxication seized her. Her blood raced; her heart thumped." She walks towards Luke, determined to take him, to have him, but, at the last minute, "her habit of self-control and silence was too strong to be broken."

No one knows what happened between Shepherd and Macmurray. She carefully cut away half the pages from her notebook of this period. The Macmurrays burnt all their letters when they left Britain for South Africa. The notes and early drafts of Betty Macmurray's unpublished memoir have disappeared. The memoir itself was "edited" after her death.[20] All that remains are Shepherd's works of fiction, her sonnets (she dedicated her volume of poems to the Macmurrays), and a series of enigmatic comments alluding to her "greatest friend," or "a man" for whom the sonnets were written.

But here's the point: Shepherd walked into the mountain fuelled by anger, pain, and frustration. She had witnessed the devastation of the Great War, grieved over the deaths of her only sibling, niece, and father, taken full responsibility for her bedridden mother, partially purged herself through the frantic writing of three novels, and suffered fourteen tortured years of unrequited love and thwarted desire. A heavy burden of heartache, disappointment, and physical turmoil for someone who claimed to be "not physically very strong."[21]

She was ready for the curative powers of the Scottish landscape: "It was a country that liberated. More than half the world was sky. The coastline vanished at one of the four corners of the earth, [she] lost herself in its immensity. It wiled her from thought."[22]

⌒

For the last few years we've delegated the art of navigation to our phones, to Google Maps. But even I know that a mobile phone won't cut it in the Cairngorms. Our Ordnance Survey map is laminated so it can double as an emergency ground sheet (at least that's what the online reviews claim). Just looking at it provokes a brief stab of nostalgia: for the days when I travelled with an A–Z, when a set of dog-eared Ordnance Survey maps accompanied us on every walk. We engage with the landscape quite differently when forced to use a map. We see our journey in its entirety. We exercise the place, direction, and grid cells in our brains as we calculate distances and timings. And when we run our fingertips over intriguing routes, rivers, bridle paths, contours, and cul-de-sacs, we sense the narrative arc of our expedition, recognising the joy of the journey rather than the destination. Pinching in and out of an on-screen map can never compete. Nor can blindly following a moving red dot that so cleverly orienteers, navigates, *thinks* on our behalf.

Hugo and I spend our next day in the Cairngorms learning navigation. Our instructor, Fred from Kent, takes us on a ten-mile hike through knee-high snow. Armed with maps and a compass, we are charged with locating the route and identifying the places and symbols on the map. The snow lies on top of springy, waterlogged moss, creating the wavering sensation of walking across a waterbed. As we go, each foot plunges through twelve inches of sifted-sugar snow, then sinks another four inches into invisible sodden moss. With great effort we retrieve our ice-laden boots and repeat the full manoeuvre, step after exhausting step. My boots begin to leak, and soon my feet are freezing and soggy. Above us, buzzards circle in lazy loops. Below us, white mountain hares sprint and bound, disappearing into the horizon.

Snow begins to fall again and I'm struck by how very white it is, by the kaleidoscopic shades of white. The gashes made by our feet leave a greenish-white hue where the snow has broken through to the moss below. The hills in shadow have a bluish tinge, while the flank of the hill glitters, silver white, in a sudden shaft of light. The sky above us ripples through soft shades of grey white to a pearly white and finally to a bright, gilded white where the sun lurks. And now we are white too, the shades of our jackets—orange, red, black—disappearing beneath falling snow.

There's something intently tranquil about a landscape denuded of colour. I feel my mind becoming slowly unmoored, its usual fizz and buzz melting away.

I reach over and take Hugo's hand. He gives me a snowy grin. And in that moment I love him with a breathtaking ferocity. It's as if this stark, frozen landscape, drained of colour and form, sharpens the edge of my feelings, giving them an additional intensity. The moment is swiftly followed by a pang of sadness, a suspicion we'll never walk like this again, hand in hand. He's almost as tall as me, already beginning to assert his independence. Which is as it should be. Having him beside me—both of us lost in this Narnia whiteness—makes me feel braver, less alone. Would these hills have the same exalting emptiness if I couldn't reach over and take his hand?

We seem to have been walking round the same white hill for some time, and when I catch the instructor's eye, he admits that we're lost. We crouch over our maps, poking and exclaiming. Our mortified instructor coughs awkwardly, then pulls out his phone to check the GPS—which is exactly what we're not supposed to do. We're supposed to be navigating without technology, which—as our instructor has warned—is fallible, prone to losing power when we most need it.

And here's the other thing about mapping technology: researchers think that by outsourcing navigation, we destroy the parts of our brain responsible for spatially locating us. Several parts of the brain are thought to be crucial for directing us through space. Together they form a sort of navigational hub, receiving and processing a string of information from our place, grid, and direction cells. It's an intricate and fantastical piece of engineering, linking our joints and muscles with our senses, our memories, and the land around us. Crucially, this navigational hub is the first part of the brain to fray and fade in those with Alzheimer's disease.

A few years ago I lost all spatial cognition. It was a bewildering and terrifying experience, which began on a bus when—for reasons no neurologist ever uncovered—the view from the window became oddly and vividly pixelated. Although I was within minutes of my home, suddenly I didn't know where I was. I couldn't recognise any landmarks. Despite the blurred miasma all around me, I got off the bus and found the sign for my street. I'd lived there for twenty years, but nothing looked familiar. My terror turned to panic when I couldn't recognise my house. Lost on my own street and unable to recognise my own front door, I stumbled in and out of the wrong front gardens, my heart rattling with fear. I felt as if I was helplessly witnessing my own descent into amnesiac madness. Eventually my brain shut down completely and I fell into a short coma, cracking my head on the sidewalk as I collapsed. But the point is this: not being able to spatially locate yourself is frightening; not being able to remember familiar places is terrifying.

Navigation is particularly important for women. Not because we are any less navigationally capable but because, as girls, we weren't always encouraged to roam freely or to explore alone.[23]

Our unexercised, discouraged navigational brain muscles led many of us to misguidedly believe males had superior skills. By delegating map reading to men, we further weakened our navigational abilities in a cruel self-fulfilling prophesy. Could this be why almost two-thirds of Alzheimer's sufferers are female? We don't know, but it's a compelling reason for learning to navigate before it's too late.

Fred explains that a white-out is almost impossible to navigate. With no path or landmark of any sort, our brains struggle, our place cells flounder. This, he reminds us, is how people die. We feel duly grateful for his iPhone which has—perversely—oriented us in a way no map or compass could.

Just as Shepherd had begun to navigate herself into the mountains and out of her emotional heartache, she experienced another hammer blow, one that hit at the very core of her fragile self-esteem.

In 1933, her third novel was published. The *New York Times* wrote glowingly of her as one of the few writers to attain "a complete and individual" art, a writer who excelled at "bringing vividly to life rugged and remote and ingrown corners of the earth." By this point she had been acclaimed on both sides of the Atlantic, compared to Virginia Woolf, and lauded as a leader of the burgeoning Scottish literary revival. This was her springboard to literary fame and fortune. She put the finishing touches to her book of poems and disappeared to the Cairngorms to hike with friends.

She returned home to a savage review in a literary magazine, written by Lewis Grassic Gibbon, a feted Scottish writer who moved in the same literary circles:

"Miss Nan Shepherd writes about farm life in Kincardineshire, a farmer's pretty granddaughter, a prima donna who disturbs the peace, and God alone knows who. I extend my sympathy to the Almighty. This is a Scots religion and Scots people at three removes—gutted, castrated, and genteelly vulgarised."[24]

After years toiling at her novels, to be dismissed so thoughtlessly, so vindictively, must have devastated Shepherd. Despite the praise heaped upon her, she had always suffered from self-doubt, feeling a "profound dissatisfaction" with everything she'd written and believing her talent to be mediocre.[25]

A month after the review appeared, Shepherd was interviewed for the *Scotsman* at her house in the suburbs of Aberdeen. She laid a table in her garden with a tablecloth, a home-made cake, and a large pot of tea. Her mother was invited to join them, and the afternoon passed in a vigorous discussion of modern Scottish literature, the use of dialect, the place of Scottish humour, and other subjects that fascinated Shepherd. When the interviewer got up to leave, Shepherd walked him to the garden gate, where she said something startlingly unexpected: "I don't like writing really. In fact I very rarely write. No . . . I only write when I feel that there's something that simply must be written."

She rarely spoke of her novels after this. A few months later her only volume of poetry was published and then it was another decade before she published anything, disappearing into long years of silence. She didn't publish another book for forty-three years. And that was it. The end of her literary output.

"I've gone dumb," she'd written to a friend earlier, expressing her dissatisfaction not only with all that she'd written but with her very grip on life. "I think I'm afraid. . . . I suppose there's nothing for it but to go on living."

There's an illuminating line in *The Second Sex*, in which Simone de Beauvoir says, "Artists care about what people think more than anyone else; women narrowly depend on it: it is easy to imagine how much strength it takes for a woman artist simply to dare to carry on regardless; she often succumbs in the fight."

Beauvoir knew all about the obligatory fight for self-belief, for success. But she's wrong when she suggests this is *easy to imagine*. Quite wrong.

Succumbing in the fight for self-esteem, or writer's block? Nothing else to say, or frightened that she lacked talent? We can only guess at the reasons behind Shepherd's decision to put down her pen. Likewise we can only guess at why, a decade later, she picked up her pen once more, wrote her masterpiece, *The Living Mountain*, but submitted it just once. After a single rejection she consigned it to a drawer, where it gathered dust for thirty years.

Friends urged her to find another publisher. A neighbour who managed a local publishing house nagged her to hand over the manuscript. She refused. An odd decision perhaps, because *The Living Mountain* is—above all—a book that lives and breathes. Mountain air blows from its pages. High winds gust from its jacket. The very smells of the Cairngorms—honeyed heather, spiced juniper, cool, clean bog myrtle—burst from its spine. It is not a book for a dark drawer.

Writer Kathryn Aalto believes Shepherd feared the misogynistic scrutiny of the walking and climbing community: she "worried her sensual book about being and feeling in the mountains would be dismissed and shut down by the dominant culture of male climbers, data-driven scientists, and quest-obsessed mountaineers." Shepherd's fears would be borne out.[26] As late as 2016, a well-known scientist, climber, and writer derided *The Living Mountain* as "fanciful, contrived, and fundamentally anthropocentric," mocking her as an example of someone seeking salvation in the hills.[27] "Snide mansplaining," retorted Aalto in her book *Writing Wild*.

I can't stop mulling over Shepherd's words: *I think I'm afraid.*

⌒

Shepherd was both insider and outsider in her Aberdeen suburb of Cults—a rigid, insular community, tightly bound by church, convention, tradition. A community where dancing with your hair unplaited caused scandal and malicious gossip.[28] Although Shepherd grew up breathing in its values, she was a closet outlier in many ways. An impassioned teacher, she described her job as an attempt "to prevent a few of the students . . . from conforming altogether to the approved pattern."[29]

But to be both insider and outsider is to walk a very tight rope—precariously balanced, never revealing enough to be cast out, yet living always with a sense of oneself as other, as different. A straddled, anxious life. Like Martha in her auto-biographical novel, Shepherd did "not wholly belong to the world in which she sat." She was "a wild thing trapped."

⌣

In my early forties I came across a poem—"The Girl Who Goes Alone"—by the American poet Elizabeth Austen. Reading it for the first time, I felt the hairs on my arms rise, and for a few frozen seconds I seemed to stop breathing. In those compressed, com-pacted lines everything I felt about walking, about being in the wilds, about being female, coalesced into a sharp shaft of hope.

The girl who goes alone says with her body
the world is worth the risk.

In that catalysing moment I realised that I didn't have to be trapped by fear. Nor did I have to overcome it (in that heroic way of reality TV). I just needed to befriend it, accommodate it, apprehend it. The problem was, I'd become more fearful than ever. Fear lived inside me like a cyst, corrosive and enfeebling.

⌣

Having children had magnified all my fears. When I first hiked with them, my dread of heights bloomed. I had vertiginous terror not only for me but for them. Being in the grip of over-whelming panic was humiliating and demeaning, so I tried to hide it. Besides, I didn't want them to absorb it, to become unnecessarily fearful, as I was.

They found me out. On a skinny, crumbling ledge in the Dolomites I had a sudden vision of all four children tipping to their deaths. Dealing with fear of my own imminent demise was bad enough. Having it compounded with fear of their deaths was crushing. I knew I shouldn't watch them. But to look away—to fix my gaze into empty space—was impossible. I had a vague and irrational idea that if I could just keep them in my line of sight, I could keep them safe. As I shook and sweated, they pranced around, peering over the edge, stopping to inspect fungus or ants. In my mind's eye, I saw them slip, slide, topple. How easy it would be. Just one misjudged step. A single wet stone. And dead!

I called croakingly to Matthew, "Tell them to stay away from the edge . . . to hurry up and get to the end."

He couldn't hear me over their cries and shrieks of delight. Pulsing with fear, my heart leaping in and out of my mouth, I got down on all fours and began crawling, groping the path with my hands and knees, keeping my eyes on the children ahead of me.

And then Matthew pointed at the sky, shouting, "Look! A buzzard!" All four children leant back, their bodies arched perilously, precipitously, over the cliff edge.

"No!" I yelled, with a sudden surge of panic. "Don't look up! Just look ahead and walk. Just fucking walk!"

For a minute there was silence. And then Hugo, who was eight at the time, said, "Why is Mummy crawling? And why is her face all wet and white?"

My daughters, who were older, knew instantly. "She's scared! She's scared!" They started to skip and skitter, darting across the path, pretending to lurch to their deaths, pushing and shoving each other, and shouting, "I'm falling! I'm falling!"

Inside my rib cage my heart thumped. My vision was dissolving, like a pointillist painting, so that I could no longer see clearly. I gripped at little prickly shrubs with my shaking hands and shuffled my knees along, inch by inch. "Please get them off this path," I whimpered.

"Your mother is not good with heights," said Matthew calmly.

Later that night the children climbed into bed with me. They stroked my hair and snuggled into my neck, whispering, "Don't worry, we'll look after you, we're not scared."

Fear doesn't always propel one into courage. But if it propels others into kindness, or bravery, isn't that enough?

It wasn't just plunging mountain paths. At the beach I was convinced my children would be swept away by a tidal wave. On London sidewalks I felt sure they would fall beneath the wheels of a thundering truck. In forests my anxious eye hovered over them, lest they disappear into the undergrowth forever. This was nothing to do with my own vertigo, and I often wondered where this fear had come from. Studies show that pregnancy and lactation can have powerful and long-term effects on our brains and hormones—effects that aren't yet fully understood. Researchers think the anxiety felt by many new mothers peaks in the first few weeks and then fades, very slowly. They also think that the newly awoken maternal brain circuit with its instinct for preservation could linger until menopause or beyond. Fear, it seems, is hardwired into the maternal brain.

⌒

A few years later, I thought back to our stomach-turning walk in the Dolomites and realised that all my terror-inducing vertiginous experiences were seared so brightly into my mind that they'd acquired a dramatic life of their own. It struck me that during these petrified pauses I was utterly present in my body, electrifyingly alive in a way that never happened in my day-to-day life. Sometimes these moments became the sharpest memory of an entire walk: high-resolution images that led me back to more blurred recollections, a sort of memory key. And in an oblique way these long, merciless moments of fear—in which my world shrank to a single square foot of rock or shale—widened my emotional range. Afterwards, I comprehended things differently: a growling dog, episodes on the news, incidents from the past. And I stopped perceiving my fear of heights (sometimes known as height intolerance or, at its most extreme, acrophobia) as shameful or inhibitory. It was simply part of who I was.

Up to 5 percent of the population suffer from a fear of heights, and twice as many women as men. Some scientists believe fear of heights is genetic, perhaps accounting for a third of cases. But research also suggests that people with a fear of heights are more likely to have physiological conditions affecting their balance—abnormalities in balance control or an underlying balance dysfunction (such as an inner-ear issue).

According to a neurologist friend, my history of childhood earache suggests I could fall into this category. Being on a mountain ridge generates a different set of sensory and physiological responses in me than it does in others. For evolutionary psychologists, a fear of heights is little more than a protective mechanism bestowed on us by distant ancestors. As our forebears walked out of Africa bearing precious babies, food, and water, a fear of high and narrow ledges encouraged them to find a safer route or to take extreme care when crossing. I exist only because they exercised supreme caution in high and perilous places.

Research suggests we can overcome our irrational fears by repeatedly exposing ourselves to them.[30] Which is exactly what I intend to do.

⁓

It's August when I return to the Cairngorms alone to walk Shepherd's favourite routes and to wild camp. I've not slept on a mountain since a disastrous hike up Mount Kilimanjaro, when severe altitude sickness forced Matthew to turn back and I dutifully followed him.

I want to trial Shepherd's theory that "no one knows the mountain completely who has not slept on it."[31] She dedicated a full chapter to mountain sleeping, a state in which "one neither thinks, nor desires, nor remembers, but dwells in pure intimacy with the tangible world." Still, the prospect unnerves me. She also wrote unflinchingly of the dangers of this vast wilderness, of schoolchildren freezing to death, of boys beaten dead by howling winds, of skiers disappearing forever, of a student of hers found lifeless "on abraded hands and knees as she clawed her way through drift."

Shepherd first climbed the highest Cairngorm peak, Ben Macdui, with a mountain guide who used a whistle when thick white mist rolled in. I'm also with a guide, Sam, and a fellow walker, Claire, who has multiple sclerosis and whose brother died of the same disease in his forties. Like me, she doesn't want to be afraid any more. Like me, she knows how autoimmune disease alters the relationship we have with our bodies. Already Sam has made us vault a fast-flowing river. Much to our surprise, our inelegant leaps on shaking legs landed us firmly on the opposite bank.

We pitch our tents high on the plateau, four thousand feet above sea level and beneath a ridge of scummy snow. From either side, two sources of the River Avon rush down immense slabs of stone, plunging over vast boulders, pouring through gullies and chasms. My ears thunder with its roar. Already the wind is rising, snatching at our tents and whipping at our hair. Sam has warned us that torrential rain—possibly a storm—is forecast. He has double-checked our tent pegs, tightened the ropes, instructed us to sleep in everything we have, including our waterproofs.

We're just crawling into our tents when we hear an avalanche of tumbling stones. I peer nervously from beneath the tarp. Above, on a wide ledge, ten reindeer are browsing at the moss. They see us and turn away, cantering across the boulders.

I lie in my sleeping bag, rigid with all the layers I'm wearing. It's after ten o'clock but the sky is yellow with light. Rain begins to fall, softly, then thumping against the tent roof, as if hundreds of small feet are running over it. The tent feels minuscule and flimsy. Cold seeps up through the mattress, through my arctic sleeping bag, through my thermals, fleeces, waterproofs, into my spine. I push in my earphones and listen to Tilda Swinton reading *The Living Mountain.* "Mankind is sated with noise; but up here, this naked, this elemental savagery, this infinitesimal cross-section of sound from the energies that have been at work for aeons in the universe, exhilarates rather than destroys." Swinton's voice stops abruptly. My phone has died, which happens with continuous exposure to freezing temperatures.

Am I exhilarated? No, I'm uncomfortable. And cold in obscure parts of me. And yet, this is not like my London sleeplessness. I feel . . . for a second the word eludes me. And then it finds its way, slowly, to the tip of my tongue. Here, in this bare and lonely place, deafened by driving water and yowling winds, the iced earth pressing into my limbs, I feel . . . altered. As if I am metamorphosing in some strange way.

⁓

We expect to live cocooned in comfort and convenience now. We complain when deprived of the *comfort, ease, security* that we've become accustomed to, Daphne du Maurier's *baser things.* But what if the austerity of our ancestors' lives helped give them shape and meaning? What if the progress that eliminated the silence, hunger, cold, heat, and darkness of the past has also eliminated an essential part of us? Electricity, central heating, twenty-four-hour supermarkets, freezers, microwaves, cars, computers, air conditioning . . . haven't they made our lives a little flatter and blander?

Some of my most vivid memories are of swimming in floe-cold sea, my bones blue with chill, of gnawing, panic-inducing hunger, of thickly smothering darkness, of silence broken by a single thread of birdsong. In the Cairngorms I experience these sensations again, dimly reconnecting to a past that has come untethered, that is slipping from me and from so many of us.

Our bodies benefit from a little hardship. Recent studies suggest that when we're under certain amounts of physiological stress—hot, cold, hungry, physically tired—new pathways open, improving our health, honing our brains. According to the biologist David Sinclair, our bodies respond positively to tiny bursts of adversity, switching on genes that defend us from disease and illness: a little bit of heat, a little bit of cold, a little bit of hunger, some exercise, some hypoxia [lack of oxygen] are all ways of activating defence pathways that turn on our body's repair systems.[32]

It's strange, but all the women in this book seemed to know instinctively that their bodies and brains had nothing to fear from short bouts of physical hardship. As if they knew that sometimes we have to say yes not to what we want, but to what we need.

⁓

No one knows what prompted Shepherd, at the age of eighty-three, to have *The Living Mountain* published. After all, her previous novels and poems had been out of print for decades. But shortly before sending off her manuscript, she'd been interviewed by the *Aberdeen Evening Express*, subsequently becoming the subject of a newspaper headline that surely rankled, that surely turned her thoughts to her impending mortality, her legacy, her mountain.

Under the inflammatory headline "Writer of Genius Gave Up," the article began: "Over forty years ago Nan Shepherd was acclaimed as a writer of genius. . . . Such accolades and yet since the '30s, Miss Shepherd has published no major works."[33]

This wasn't the first time Shepherd had been quizzed on her aborted literary career. But it was the first time she'd been accused of *giving up*, with its implications of indolence, apathy, and defeat. Besides, Shepherd hadn't entirely given up. She'd written occasional articles for journals and newspapers, a handful of new (unpublished) poems, and a short story. Most importantly, she'd written *The Living Mountain*, a breathtakingly radical paean to a mountain range.

"I confess it was with some considerable delight that I reread the manuscript," she wrote to a friend. In the months after the "Writer of Genius Gave Up" article, Shepherd wrote a new introduction and found a new publisher. Ten months later, on October 27, 1977, Aberdeen University Press published three thousand copies of *The Living Mountain*. A local newspaper described it as "exquisite prose . . . a little masterpiece."

And that was it. No further reviews. Meanwhile, boxes of the book lay around Shepherd's house. Tens of copies were given away to friends and neighbours. By the time it was reviewed in a national newspaper ("a stunning and loving analysis of the lure of high and lonely places," according to the *Guardian*), Shepherd had been dead for two years.

It was another quarter of a century before *The Living Mountain* was reprinted as a single volume.[34] But by 2008 it was almost out of print and on the brink of disappearing yet again.

Since then Shepherd has achieved the recognition she deserves, becoming the first female, excluding the Queen, to appear on a Scottish banknote. She—and *The Living Mountain*—has inspired numerous performances, artworks, retreats, treks, even health initiatives. *The Living Mountain* has been lauded as a masterpiece ("the finest book ever written on nature and landscape in Britain"[35]), translated into tens of languages, and published across the world. Her novels have been read on national radio, her poems reprinted. Indeed, Shepherd has acquired a global cult following that grows and grows.

But why did it have to take so long?

⌐

Women have, of course, been walking all over Scotland for centuries. Sarah Hazlitt—wife of the acclaimed essayist, painter, and walker William Hazlitt—walked in the Highlands for several weeks in 1822, covering between twenty and thirty-two miles each day, and recording her experiences in a journal. Like Shepherd's, her account languished, unpublished for over seventy years. Finally, it was attached as an appendage to her ex-husband's book. Even there it was obscured, belittled, seen as nothing more than an extra window into her husband's "great" mind.

Sent to Scotland by her husband to organise a divorce she didn't want (William had become besotted with the nineteen-year-old daughter of his London landlady), Sarah used the time to redefine herself as an autonomous, courageous woman. In her journals she described walking over "a narrow alpine bridge without either a ledge or handrail," then across "a profound ravine, through which, at a great depth below, a foaming torrent dashes over disjointed masses of rock." Later she crossed "a rustic footbridge, of about three feet in breadth and without ledges, which is scarcely to be crossed by a stranger without awe or apprehension." She was frequently terrified, writing of her "violent perspiration." She scrambled up slippery crags, crossed swampy and pathless mountains, waded through dreary moors full of bogs, and walked "lonely places" while storms raged.[36]

Women of Sarah's class typically toured towns and cities by carriage. But walking in the Scottish Highlands provided anonymity and distance, both geographical and emotional, from her husband and from her past. More importantly, it allowed Sarah to test her own resilience as she prepared for a new life as a (scandalous) divorcee. Among the crags and bogs of Scotland, Sarah found and became an empowered version of herself, in a liberation which found voice in her only known writings: *Journal of My Trip to Scotland 1822.*

From then on she lived independently with her son, never remarrying.

~

As I near the summit of Ben Macdui, Scotland's second-highest Munro, I feel a wind at my back. Nudging, pushing me upwards. I feel it most firmly in the small of my back. As if strong flat palms are urging me on. I'm about to call out to Sam, to ask him why the wind is most insistent at the base of my spine, when I realise these are no ordinary winds. These—I decide—are the spirits of Nan Shepherd and Sarah Hazlitt; of the farmers' wives who regularly walked twenty-five miles through these very mountains with baskets of eggs balanced on their heads; of all the other valiant, forgotten women in whose footsteps I walk.

When we reach the bouldered plateau of Ben Macdui—a bare, fleshless place—mist drops from above and wraps itself around us, rolling over the rocks, smothering the views. I'm just wondering if the mist might also hold the spirits of these women who have taken such grip of my imagination, when I look down and see, almost beneath my foot, a small, fat bird, black and white and dancing over the huge boulders on tiny, skinny claws. That something so exquisite has flown to these barren heights and is dancing with such grace and elegance makes me laugh aloud. The bird—a ball of puffed-up fluff—opens its beak and sings, its trill rising above the wind. All at once the mountain seems friendlier, gentler. The bird is a snow bunting. Shepherd spent long periods of time in some of "the loneliest and most desolate crannies of the mountain" watching and listening to snow buntings, reflecting on their "delicate perfection that is enhanced by the savagery of their home." She likened the experience to "[tasting] a pleasure of the epicure." The snow bunting is now a protected bird, and this is one of a mere sixty pairs breeding in Britain, all of which can be found only in Scotland.

"The mountain has given you that privilege," says Sam, who likes to remind us of the many gifts of the mountain: air for our blow-up mattresses, water to drink, blaeberries to eat, wildlife to watch.

The mountain gives us something else, too. Descending from Ben Macdui, I listen for a snow bunting. This time I hear nothing. Not the trickle of water nor the lash of rain or wind. Not the rattle of falling rock nor the crunch of footfall on scree. Sam and Claire have gone ahead, leaving me with the most profound silence I have ever heard. It shocks me, and I strain to hear . . . something, anything. In the emptiness, Shepherd's words sidle into my head: "To bend the ear to silence is to discover how seldom it is there. . . . Listening to it one slips out of time. . . . It is like a new element."

I *bend my ear*, let the silence slip through it, feel it spread through my head, my brain, and down into my body. I seem to empty myself into it so that for a few seconds I am no one, and nowhere.

Sam calls my name. As if snapped from a trance, I see the rocky path descending steeply beneath me, hear my walking poles as they clatter against stone, my boots slipping and slapping on loose pebbles. When did I last hear silence? For years, the relentless assault of city noise has lodged inside my skull, a part of me I can neither shed nor escape.

⌒

Modern-day noise affects more than just our mood. According to experts, it's killing us. On an average London day, I'll hear: a pneumatic drill, aircraft, sirens, car alarms, the thrum of streaming traffic from a nearby road. Inside, the washing machine bleeps, bathroom fans drone, and the fridge door whines if it hasn't been properly closed.

We take noise for granted, optimistically believing we've adapted to it. But a growing body of evidence suggests that the perpetual cacophony of modern life is threatening our physical and mental health. Constant exposure has been linked to hearing loss, sleep disturbance, stress, learning impairments, heart disease, obesity, tinnitus, and diabetes.

Even the noises we've adjusted to—and no longer hear—continue to affect us. According to one expert, they still have an effect on our pulse, our heart rate, our blood pressure. At night, noise slips into our ears, even as we sleep, and passes to our brain. It may not wake us, but our bodies are alerted, our circadian rhythms disturbed, our sleep fragmented.[37]

For the next few days among the mountains I bend my ear into the silence at every opportunity. As I become more used to it, I discover that the greater the apparent silence, the more I can hear. Minuscule sounds unfold from within the silence, sounds I'd never normally hear, sounds that remind me I am never alone.

I hear the thinnest trickle of water from somewhere deep within the earth. I hear the snap of a twig, the crackle of dry leaves, the slightest of breezes, the lightest of rain, the muted whinge of a single midge. In silence, with one's ear bent to it, every sound is amplified so that even the quietest of spots suddenly seethes with the hubbub of life—insect life, tree life, the goings-on of weather and birds and underground brooks.

Only high on the plateaus when the weather stills is there absolute silence, dense and lonely. After a few moments, the silence—its echoing emptiness—begins to unnerve me. As it did Shepherd, who wrote of how "that awful loneliness / Received our souls as air receives the smoke."[38]

Even her love of altitude couldn't always compensate for the loneliness of the high plateau.

⌣

It seems to me that nothing is as freeing as prolonged walking. To step out, with one's possessions on one's back, unburdened by car or bicycle or horse . . . But walking also takes us *beyond* freedom. In the "long rhythm" of walking, we move through successive self-revelations into a meditative state where we are someone else entirely. For Shepherd it was "hours of steady walking . . . hour after hour" that helped her discover "what it is to be."

What is it about walking *hour after hour?* Again, science suggests that Shepherd had an instinctive understanding of what our bodies need. We were made for endurance. Our bodies, with their springy tendons and shock-absorbing joints, were built to walk for hour upon hour, day after day. The human heart, say experts, "evolved to facilitate extended endurance activity."[39] Sedentary people have smaller hearts with thicker walls, less able to pump quantities of blood for long periods. But we can rebuild and reshape our hearts merely by adopting an endurance activity, like hiking.

This is, after all, how our ancestors lived. Paleontologists believe we left the great plains of Africa around ninety thousand years ago, walking along the Great Rift Valley until we reached the Levant. Many of us walked on, into Asia, Australasia, Europe, the Americas. On and on we went, always on foot, always laden with babies, cooking pots, animal skins, the few belongings we needed to set up camp, to survive. As persistence hunters we may not have been able to outsprint a deer, but we could pursue it for days and days until it dropped dead from exhaustion. This ability to *endure* was a hallmark of our long-distant relatives. It's also the reason Sarah Hazlitt and Nan Shepherd (and you and I) can walk thirty miles in a day, get a good night's sleep, and then—fully recovered—walk another thirty miles.

But walking for hour after hour is also the movement of escape. We cease to be human. The more we walk, the more of ourselves we lose. At every mile we discard another little bit of ourselves—our responsibilities and obligations are forgotten, our identity dissolves, our past and future fade. Even our names become meaningless. We are nothing more or less than a simple walking body, a fleshy frame with blisters on our feet, hunger in the base of our belly, thirst on our tongue.

The only parts of our body that dislike endless walking are our toenails. Which is why mine turned purple and dropped off after three months tramping the Himalayas. And why professional long-distance walkers have theirs surgically removed.

⁓

Beneath Shepherd's youthful face on the Scottish five-pound note is a line from her autobiographical novel, *The Quarry Wood*:

It's a grand thing to get leave to live.

What a strangely angled phrase that is. As if *to live* requires permission, consent.

But in a way, it does. It requires permission from ourselves. A permission that is inexplicably difficult and complicated to grant.

On my last day of wild camping, Claire turns to me. "I thought God had died. I thought my body was dying too. But God's here." She sweeps her arm across the horizon, where an opal sun is straining through the heavy white cloud. Then she knocks her fist against her chest. "This diseased old body is stronger than I thought." She thrusts her walking poles at me—and is gone, bounding over the heather like a mountain hare.

⌒

Later, as we pack up our tents, Claire tells me that she would like to make this place her own, as Shepherd did. She lives close enough to come here every weekend, but without a car this isn't possible. I've read the letters of Shepherd and her friends—they travelled the fifty miles by bus, often arriving after midnight on a Friday, then returning to Aberdeen on Sunday night having hiked all weekend. Shepherd never even bothered learning to drive.

"Why should all this only be available to people with cars?" Claire asks. Having spent hours trying to untangle bus and train timetables, I have no answer.

"If I could get here, this could be my chosen place too," she says, so quietly I can only just hear her. "My chosen landscape ..."

~

We all have our chosen landscapes, the places where we choose to live, holiday, walk. But many of us also have our *unchosen* landscapes—the places that have settled deep inside us, like my damp, green *cwm*. Shepherd's chosen and unchosen landscape were one and the same, and I envy her this. Because to know a landscape intimately provides a profound sense of connection, a feeling that we are rooted, that we belong.

Shepherd was rooted, deeply and firmly, in a way that now seems almost quaintly old-fashioned. Today so many of us are rootless: forced into exile, sent by large corporations to live in anonymous cities, or simply choosing to live nomadically. When Frieda Lawrence wrote in her memoir of "making homes and unmaking them . . . feeling so free and detached, no responsibility," she spoke for successive generations who recognised the endlessly reviving thrill of encountering new landscapes and cultures. For Frieda and Lawrence, to be dizzyingly adrift was to live richly and fully. Meanwhile, others like Gwen John cut themselves free of their childhood homes not for pleasure but out of existential necessity.

Today, thousands of travellers criss-cross the globe, guided by Google Maps and Instagram, their bucket lists and iPhones clamped beneath their arms. It's a phenomenon that goes beyond existential necessity, carrying with it a strong whiff of disconnection, of discontent. Reading Shepherd makes me ask myself whether it's time to accept the discipline and duties that come with living in and caring for a community and a landscape.

Such a complicated question. Because weren't our walking ancestors nomadic? Didn't they chase sunlight, warmth, water, wildlife? Isn't it possible that our need for constant change, for novel landscapes, is encoded in our genes?

Nan Shepherd is the antidote to all this restless travelling, to the women in this book who found fulfilment and autonomy in geographical freedom. Shepherd found everything she needed within fifty miles of the house where she lived all her life. When she became too frail to walk, she found joy in the view from her window: "I still rejoice in space and distance and the sky," she wrote to a friend.

⌒

Shepherd never severed her past, only leaving her childhood room for a nearby care home eleven months before she died. Here she wrote, with arresting optimism, "By all that is wonderful, it couldn't be better."[40]

6

In Search of the Body

Simone de Beauvoir

France. Forests. Fear. Sensualism. Embodiment.
The Body as Grasp on the World.

I took another walk yesterday and it was the most wonderful
of all. . . . When I find myself again lonely and quiet in
a lonely quiet country, it moves me deeply.

—SIMONE DE BEAUVOIR, letter to Nelson Algren, 1947

Such an odd thing, packing a rucksack. It's an act of austerity that liberates even as it frustrates. For every item to earn its place on my puny shoulders, it must be life-preserving in some way. I limit myself to 26.5 pounds, casting out the frivolous, the inessential. I check weather forecasts, tear spines from books, put things in—paints, camera lenses, walnuts—then throw them out. Every time I toss away an item, I feel a swift stab of anxiety followed by a ripple of lightness. So that even as I shunt the pack onto my back, I experience a sense of weightlessness. I have become disencumbered. Free. My life whittled down to the bone.

I've learnt to wash clothes as I go, soaping them in the shower and tying them to my rucksack so they dry as I walk. I've learnt to sketch, Gwen John–style, in miniature. And technology has made the rucksack infinitely lighter: maps, books, compass, flashlight, camera, all in a device that fits in the palm of my hand. Even so, it's an exercise in self-knowledge. To pack a rucksack is to know yourself.

⁓

Simone de Beauvoir's rucksack invariably contained a candle, an alarm clock, a copy of the local Guide Bleu, a Michelin map, and a felt-covered water bottle filled with red wine. It was a step up from the wicker basket she took on her first walks, after she arrived in Marseilles in 1931. She was twenty-three, had secured her first teaching post, and finally left home. Among the mountains, valleys, and cliffs of Provence, a passion for solitary rambles and "communion with nature" took hold of her. "I derived a satisfaction I had never known in all the rush and bustle of my Paris life," she wrote in her memoir.[1]

But the funny thing is, no one thinks of Beauvoir as a backpacking hillwalker. We think of her sitting in smoky Paris cafes, a string of pearls at her neck, a chic turban wrapped around her head, Jean-Paul Sartre philosophising at her side.

This is not *my* Simone de Beauvoir. My Beauvoir—the version I unearth from her letters, memoir, journals, and books, and in whose footsteps I walk—is a compelling, courageous, often reckless hiker. A lover of bare hills, forests, mountain ranges. A woman who walks as audaciously and rigorously as she thinks. A woman who shows us how walking can return us to our bodies. A woman who is nothing to do with Jean-Paul Sartre.

⁓

This is not to say that Beauvoir wasn't the quintessentially Parisian woman she appeared to be. She loved the city of her birth—its libraries, bookshops, cafes, jazz clubs, and apricot cocktails. She lived in Paris for most of her life, dying within a few steps of where she was born and raised. But, like so many of us, she needed both urban and wild in her divided life.

⌒

Having lived in London for over thirty years, I sympathise. I love the wilds more for living in the city. And I love the city more for spending time in the wilds. The one throws the other into stark relief, a delicate balancing act that Beauvoir managed with aplomb. But Paris Beauvoir is well-known and easily recognised—she's the one at the marble-topped cafe table, pen in one hand, glass of whisky in the other. The Beauvoir who piques and entrances me is rarely photographed (there's only one indistinct and grainy picture of her hiking) and rarely discussed. She's conspicuously absent from what writer Robert Macfarlane has called "the literature of the leg." She's never mentioned in books on walking, never quoted in anthologies of nature writing. Even a recent bestseller written by a French professor on philosophers and walking fails to mention her.[2] Instead, we read about the usual suspects—Rousseau, Nietzsche, Kant, Thoreau, etc., etc. We read of the remarkable results engendered by their walking: Rousseau, Thoreau, and Nietzsche are provoked into ideas of startling brilliance, Wordsworth composes dazzling lines of genius poetry, and so on.

Beauvoir never made grandiose claims about her walking. "I'm not doing much thinking, I'm blissful," she wrote to Sartre from one lengthy, mountainous hike. From the Italian Alps, she declared she "had not a thought in [her] head apart from flowers and beasts and stony tracks and wide horizons, the pleasurable sensation of possessing legs and lungs and a stomach."

It seems to me that feeling *bliss* and *pleasure* is a compelling enough reason for walking. And when I began researching her, I was convinced that Beauvoir walked only for this reason—to rest her febrile brain, to distract herself from the metaphysical anxieties that threatened to engulf her.

By the time I'd finished my investigations, I'd come to a different conclusion altogether. Her walking was infinitely more complicated and nuanced than I'd ever imagined.

Before she reached Marseilles with its miles and miles of hiking trails, Beauvoir had been suffering acutely from an onslaught of confused, oscillating emotions. "All my life I will preserve an uneasy memory of this period, of my fear that I might betray my youthful ideals," she wrote, thirty years later.[3] Riven with uncontrollable desire, unsure who she was, unable to write, desperately in love with the philandering Sartre but simultaneously needing to pull away from his influence, Beauvoir needed resetting. "I would like to learn how to be alone again," she confided to her notebook.[4]

Her new-found independence in a city where no one knew her provided the time, space, and means to travel, walk, and deliberately simplify her life—alone. Travel, she discovered, enabled her to lose herself: "Instantly past and future vanished, leaving nothing but a splendid immediacy." But it was walking in the hills and the calanques around Marseilles that really marked a new turn in her life. Beauvoir marched her emotional, hormonal, and metaphysical confusion into order, purging herself of her previous turmoil and exorcising the sexual urges that had been plaguing her to the point of distraction.

Every Thursday and Sunday she left her house at dawn, returning only after darkness. In an old dress and espadrilles, with a basket of buns and bananas over her arm, Beauvoir climbed every local peak, crossed every canyon, clambered in and out of every calanque. She refused to wear the "semi-official rig of rucksack, studded shoes, . . . and windcheater." She refused to accompany her fellow teachers or join a hiking club. Alone, she walked through dense mists and along lonely ridgelines, bracing herself against the unruly mistral wind, the stinging rain, and the scorching sun: "At first I limited myself to some five or six hours' walking; then I chose routes that would take nine to ten hours; in time I was doing over twenty-five miles a day."[5]

Her walks were plotted with military precision. She taught herself to map-read and navigate, meticulously planning every route. Her walks became "expeditions," each one "a work of art in itself."[6]

Beauvoir devotes pages and pages of her memoir to these "fanatical walking trips," explaining that they preserved her "from boredom, regret, and several sorts of depression." Elsewhere she says that time spent in nature gave her a "greater familiarity with myself." And in a letter to Sartre, she defends her arduous hikes as just "so healthy—all that fresh air and physical exercise."

⌣

As a child, Beauvoir had spent long, carefree holidays at the rural home of her grandparents. Here she had everything denied her in Paris: freedom, privacy, space, and nature. At the age of thirteen her love of nature took on "an almost mystical fervour," dramatically expanding her world: "I was no longer a vacant mind, an abstracted gaze, but the turbulent fragrance of the waving grain, the intimate smell of the heather moors, the dense heat of noon or the shiver of twilight; I was heavy; yet I was as vapour in the blue airs of summer and knew no bounds."

She spent long periods of time lying in the heather and gazing at the "shadowy blue undulations" of the massif near her grandparents' home, a mountain range called the Monédières.[7] Here, she felt the luminous presence of God. And the more she pressed herself to the grass and the earth, the closer she felt to him.[8]

⁓

Back in her parents' choked, balcony-less, toilet-less apartment, Beauvoir wasn't allowed to run or jump. She shared a room that was so tiny she and her sister had to take it in turns to stand between the two beds. Under the gimlet eye of her devoutly Catholic mother, her "wretched carcase" began an increasingly sedentary existence, buried more and more deeply in books and study. She developed an alarming and uncontrollable facial tic, while her awkward body spilled into lumps, bulges, and blotches.[9] Her father pronounced her "ugly," a memory she recalled over and over in later interviews and writings, as if continually confronting it might eventually erase it.

Beauvoir's parents had watched their money dwindle to almost nothing. "You girls must study hard to prepare yourselves to work all your lives," declared Beauvoir's father, after explaining there would be no dowries and therefore no husbands. According to Beauvoir, her bourgeois parents spent the rest of their lives hiding the humiliating and demeaning truth of their fallen circumstances.

At her Catholic girls' school, Beauvoir was intellectually brilliant but "entirely friendless," taunted for her make-do, ill-fitting clothes. At home she was vigilantly watched over by her mother, who opened her post, listened at her door, and banned all reading material she considered inappropriate. Merely reading about the stifling conditions of Beauvoir's Parisian upbringing makes me feel short of breath, as if a huge boulder is being lowered onto my chest.

Hardly surprising that she developed "a great longing for freedom," or that the prospect of "liberty and physical pleasure" dazzled her. Hardly surprising that her life became an obsessive quest for freedom.[10] Or that travel, walking, and backpacking—surely the most emancipating of all experiences—became such a significant part of her life.

~

In the two years before she discovered hiking, Beauvoir's world had turned on its axis. She had begun an intense love affair with Jean-Paul Sartre, "the genius who opened the world to me," who turned her life "upside down, inside out." The affair swept both of them away, as much for its sexual energy as its intellectual vigour. In her autobiographical novel *L'Invitée*, published in English as *She Came to Stay*, Françoise (a thinly veiled Beauvoir) explains, "We are really one. . . . [He was] as much a part of [my] life as of his. . . . There was but one life and at its core but one entity, which could be termed neither he nor I, but we. . . . Neither time nor distance could divide [us]." And so it would have been in real life.

Except that Sartre had a rapacious sexual appetite and a gluttonous need for beautiful young women. He suggested an open relationship: honesty was more important than fidelity in his existentialist world. Beauvoir agreed, thrilled by the affront to conventional bourgeois values their "pact" represented. And unaware of what it would entail (years of reading graphic letters detailing Sartre's numerous exploits, and the grooming of her own students for him), or of how much emotional tumult—anguish, jealousy, fear—Sartre's philandering would cause her.

As if emotional tumult weren't enough, a horrified Beauvoir also found herself in the merciless grip of physical desire. Having "surrendered" her virginity to Sartre "with glad abandon," she was now racked by her own bodily needs, which presented as "actual pain," "torture," "agony." She was seized with shame, repulsed by her "physical appetites" that cried out for anyone, regardless. Even the brush of an anonymous hand on the bus sparked fierce sexual urges that she felt unable to master.

At first she regarded her emotions and urges as mere weaknesses, and tried to *will* them away. Her attempts at subjugation failed. According to biographer Deirdre Bair, Beauvoir became a mess, so swamped with emotional pain she repeatedly drank herself into sobbing oblivion.[11] Her love for Sartre was unconditional, and the jealousy that gripped her was, Beauvoir said, "the most unpleasant emotion that had ever laid hold on me."[12]

Crushed between jealousy and thwarted desire, Beauvoir was rescued by her twice-weekly rural walks: "I ... subdued my rebellious body, and was physically at peace once more," she explained.[13]

Her alter ego in *L'Invitée*, Françoise, has the same redemptive experience after backpacking on "sun-baked roads and shadowy mountain tops," suddenly realising that "there were other things to love ... snow-capped peaks, sun-lit pines, roadside inns, people and stories." In the forests and hills, Françoise discovers simplicity, clarity, and joy—the very things Sartre had stolen from Beauvoir.[14]

⌒

On my first day in the calanques I spend an hour scrambling in and out of bleached-white inlets and peering into turquoise water so clear I can see the limestone rocks on the seabed. On slender crescents of sand, oiled bodies soak up the year's last rays of sunshine.

The trail is so busy I eventually tire of hiking in a line. Instead I slip inland to the scrubby woodlands where it feels more authentically Beauvoir, not only because it's deserted but because she often professed her love of trees and woodland. In her memoir she described standing motionless "day after day ... for hours at the foot of a tree." Trees, she wrote, made her "feel unique and ... needed."[15] Much later, in 1947, after suffering a series of crippling anxiety attacks, Beauvoir went to Scandinavia, where she claimed the forests restored and revived her.

But trees don't occupy my thoughts for long, because I've read something else about Beauvoir that is gnawing away at me. She was always the last chosen for any team game or sporting contest at school, and considered herself without grace or athletic ability. "I couldn't do anything with my body," she wrote in despair. "I couldn't even swim or ride a bicycle."[16] Reading this had thrown me back to a similarly scarring experience, one I thought I'd buried but now blasts from my memory as brightly saturated as if it were yesterday.

After leaving our Welsh village, I arrived at secondary school in an English town, having never played a game of netball or hockey, having never kicked, batted, or thrown a ball. Nor could I swim or ride a bicycle. In my first games lesson, a tennis racket was thrust into my hand. I struggled agonisingly with it, twisting my wrist this way and that, swiping it through the air. The racket leapt and danced, like a cat struggling to escape. A ball was flung at me. I chased after it, trying to scoop it onto the strings of my racket. In a single feline movement, both ball and racket escaped, skittering across the court. As girls leapt from their path, Miss Monk blew furiously into her tin whistle. She instructed the girls to form a circle round me, and demanded that I "serve the ball." Hot and confused, I swung and tossed. The ball sailed out of the court. A group of girls giggled. The racket felt clumsy and unfamiliar in my hand, but for some reason I continued swinging it. Until Miss Monk, her face shut-tight and red with outrage, screamed at me: "That is exactly how *not* to serve."

This went on for years. I was always the example of how *not* to catch, how *not* to throw, how *not* to sidestep. Sports teachers told me, repeatedly, that I was hopelessly uncoordinated. No one wanted me on their team. Only my friend Tamara stood beside me every Wednesday afternoon, in the dwindling, demeaning pool of sporting undesirables. Later, Tamara won an open exhibition to Oxford University. Beauvoir faced down her sporting mortification in the same way, devoting her formidable energy to becoming a brilliant scholar.

But there's only one top-of-the-class spot. And in my class Tamara, with intellectual justification, had taken it. So I pursued a strategy that avoided ignominy altogether: at every games or PE lesson I smoked cigarettes in the boys' toilet, got caught, did it again, and stood for punitive hours outside the headmaster's office. Eventually I began bunking off entire days, pretending I was too cool for school. By becoming the class renegade, I maintained a modicum of self-esteem, my humiliation hardening into rebellious anger.

Being singled out as physically incompetent, weak, and flawed at the very time I was going through the disorienting years of puberty altered the relationship I had with my body. Our bodies are the prism through which we experience the world: from then on I felt as if my control over life was tenuous and frail, that I would never be fully independent. Somehow, my own body had betrayed me.

⁓

When I took up hiking—in my early twenties, the same age that Beauvoir began distance walking—it was a profoundly affirmative experience, reconnecting me with a body that had become little more than a source of shame and indignity.

Suddenly I could outwalk other people. My legs ceased being flimsy and unreliable. They became a ferocious pair of pistons, and a source of deep inner pride. I couldn't catch a ball, but I could walk—for hours and hours. Slowly, I began to feel that my body wasn't an alien, ungovernable lump of fat and bone. I realised that my body could *become*. Emboldened, I learnt to ski and swim. I learnt how to hold a tennis racket and a Ping-Pong paddle. I ran, often for miles and miles. I joined a gym and lifted weights. I discovered yoga. My body was me. The world began to feel different. And for the first time, I liked who I was.

Beauvoir went through a similar journey, ignited by a throwaway comment from an early crush: "How fast you walk! I love that," he told her.[17] Beauvoir—who never forgot this compliment—began to see herself as a walker, "just like a man."[18] From here it was a short step to strenuous hiking. "I had never practiced any sport, and therefore took all the more pleasure in driving my body to the very limit of its endurance," she explained in her memoir.

Scrambling, climbing, jumping, and lugging a heavy back-pack were a means of obliterating the clumsy, gawky girl Beauvoir had been. Week by week, she began the process of reconstructing herself as physically strong, athletic, graceful. Climbing requires strength, agility, and balance, while hiking for hour upon hour requires exceptional physical and mental stamina. Beauvoir had these in spades. No wonder she bragged about her walking feats. Walking through spaces usually pos-sessed by men was proof of her own physical presence, proof of her autonomy and resilience. But it was also proof that she could recast herself. Later, she wrote of her time in Marseilles, "I felt a certain self-satisfaction. . . . I no longer despised myself."[19]

Little wonder that her year of fanatical walking saw a "truly astonishing change in her personality."[20]

⌒

Walking embeds us in the landscape. It embodies us, transforming the relationship we have both with the physical world and with our own bodies. Sartre didn't agree. For Sartre, the body was nothing. If anything it was an impediment. He once described physical life as "the nothingness of the flesh." Biographers claim he disliked and distrusted his own body. For him neither landscape nor nature had a splinter of meaning.

This is how I see it: every time Beauvoir walked wild, another little bit of her broke free from Sartre.

⌒

At the train station in Marseilles I loiter, light-headed, at the top of the long flight of stone steps leading into the city. Beauvoir stood in the very same spot, surveying the hundreds of red rooftops, the scrum of fishing boats, the miles of blue sea—and tasting freedom, "alone, empty-handed, cut off from my past and everything I loved."[21]

A Japanese freight-train driver helps me buy a ticket to Cassis, then spends the journey regaling me with stories of the 262-foot-long trains he drives through the French countryside in the black of night. Wild boars and cows wander onto the tracks, he tells me. Once he hit a boar and tried to scrape its flattened body from the tracks, thinking it would make a good supper. He carries with him a large silver key that opens the door of every train driver's cabin in France. He shows it to me and when I look surprised he gets up, goes to the driver's door, and unlocks it. I watch him chatting with the driver. Then he backs out, relocks the door, and starts using his magic key to open strange metal boxes beneath my seat. When the train pulls into Cassis, my mind is full of mysterious keys and mile-long freight trains trundling through the nocturnal silence of Provence, smashing into boars, foxes, beloved cows.

From Cassis, I climb the copper-coloured cliffs and walk east to La Ciotat. This was Beauvoir's first walk after arriving in Marseilles, and she loved it so much that as soon as she reached the end, she wanted to do it all over again. To my right is the sea, a dim rippling pewter. To my left stretch acres of scrub beaten flat by the mistral—pine, juniper, rosemary, lavender. I walk through an orgy of perfume, snapping at dead pieces of juniper wood to release its spicy gin-ish fragrance, splitting twigs of pine and sniffing their sharp, pitchy scent. I rub at the coarse leaves of rosemary and lavender, so that my hands are richly perfumed. Every time I hold them to my nose, I feel a shock of satisfaction.

I take off my boots, imagining myself in thin-soled espadrilles. The ground feels soft and rutted beneath my bare feet. The wind rushes from the sea, tasting of salt and vaguely of kelp. The clean scent of rosemary lodges in my nose. Branches of broom and pine prickle and tickle the bare skin of my arms. My ears are full of seagull, breeze, the clicking bones of my feet. With a jolt, I feel my body spring awake.

We forget that to live fully is to live through all our senses, that the deadening of the senses becomes the deadening of the soul. It took me years to recognise this. For three decades I swung, irreconcilably, between longing for the calm solitude of the country and yearning for the whirling energy of the city. Too long in London and something inside me strained and snapped. My mood altered, becoming by turns fractious and restless, then low and weary. For ages I attributed these inexplicable tilts of temper to time of the month, vitamin deficiencies, lack of sleep, work trials, stress. Or anything else I could think of. Not until my late thirties did I understand why, every few weeks, the city that I loved could turn so swiftly to a place of pathological oppression. The thronging, surging drifts of people—pressed into lifts, tucked into every cubic inch of every train, jostling the sidewalks—lost their thrill. The miles and miles of concrete seemed to lead not out of the city but always back into it, like some nightmarish labyrinth. Everywhere I went, diesel collected in my throat so that I could taste nothing else. I couldn't get the ceaseless whine of aeroplanes out of my head. I drifted obsessively towards nature books. My tired gaze lingered on window boxes or moss grouted greenly between the city's bricks. I spent hours looking in the fridge. I ate constantly.

Eventually I self-diagnosed my constellation of symptoms: I was suffering from sensory displacement. A hankering for the sights, sounds, smells, tastes, and textures of wild green places. Because only there and then did I feel a stillness, a nowness. Sitting amid greenery was OK, but walking was better. Long days cramped double over a desk left my feet numbed, my legs thick and heavy, my spine as stiff as a beam. I needed to feel joined-up again. I needed to feel embodied and alive. Which is exactly how I feel striding along the Route des Crêtes.

Beauvoir's biographer believes it was here, in the wild environs of Marseilles, that Beauvoir finally learnt to live "in the present."[22] By the time I descend into the town of La Ciotat—sun-dazed, windblown, euphoric—I have forgotten every "metaphysical anxiety" I ever had.[23] I am utterly in the present.

⌣

Beauvoir's expeditions began to follow a pattern. After a particularly bruising experience she would pack her rucksack and disappear to the country to outwalk her distress.

When her first novel was unexpectedly rejected, she took to her bed, ill, ashamed and seething at the editor's suggestion that publishing a book about modern women would damage the company's reputation. Sartre cheerfully took her manuscript to a second publisher. But they too rejected it, claiming, "The novel is lacking in any originality. . . . The social picture you create has been painted countless times already."[24]

Beauvoir was deeply wounded: "Two rejections were enough insult, enough humiliation. . . . I saw myself as a failure . . . unworthy." After a night on the sleeper train, she hopped off in the Alps and "started out at once, over hill and dale," walking for nine continuous hours. Over the ensuing days she climbed "every single peak between Chamonix and Tigne." Her depression lifted and, rejuvenated, she started working on a new novel. Published in 1943, *L'Invitée* made Beauvoir the published writer she had always yearned to be.

⌒

Beauvoir took huge pride in her walking, writing to Sartre that she climbed alone for 3,051 metres "to where there was just snow and rock. . . . I came back not tired in the least." She bragged of sleeping "1,700 metres up in a windswept mountain hut," and walking "30 km along the Dordogne gorges." In another letter to Sartre she wrote, "I'm very proud of myself because, in spite of certain female frailties, I did 35 km between 11 in the morning and 8 in the evening without feeling tired." She crowed of walking thirty to thirty-five kilometres a day "only in the mornings and in the evenings after four." Her rest day consisted of a mere seven and a half hours of walking and 1,200 metres of climbing. In between all the (justified) boasting, she alluded, casually, to the sunburn, blisters, scratches, and cuts. Her badges of honour. Her battle wounds. A bemused Sartre wondered why she possessed this "strange mania for gobbling up kilometres."

Years later, after she'd stopped her indefatigable walking, Beauvoir continued to talk of her past prowess. "I could walk about 30 miles a day, you know," she wrote to her lover, Nelson Algren, in 1948. But it was the memories of her Marseilles walks that lingered longest. She wrote to Algren that "twice a week I went to the mountains all around and walked crazily for hours. . . . [It was] the place where I learnt to live by myself, to support myself, not to be dependent on anyone in any way."

How we experience our bodies is crucial to our sense of freedom and to our feelings of empowerment. To understand our bodies' capabilities, the way in which our limbs, nose, feet engage with the physicality of a place, is to understand who we are and our place in the world. Beauvoir was deeply aware of this: in *The Second Sex* she describes a strong, athletic body as "a hold on the world." It was something very few women possessed, she added. Lured by the power of the male gaze, women saw themselves as objects valued for their appearance, and in concentrating so exclusively on how they *looked*, they alienated themselves from their bodies—an alienation that came at a very high price. Enfeebled (by high heels, impractical clothing, weakened limbs, elaborate hairstyles, lack of confidence), women reduced their hold on the world, confining themselves still further.

I like this idea, which I pare right back and paraphrase:

From outer strength comes inner freedom.

It's the reason I lift weights every day. I want to be able to carry a backpack when I'm eighty, but I also want the emotional strength that accompanies muscle and sinew.

⌒

I've spent an hour scrambling uphill, much of it through tumbling water. It's November and the lean, rocky track that twists up through the white cliffs and crags of the Luberon massif in southern France is now a series of waterfalls. Every now and then my boot dislodges a wet stone and a small avalanche rattles down the mountain. The streaming path is shaded by a soaring rock face riven with tiny cracks, home to arthritic oak trees, scrawny, unkempt pines, fat cushions of moss in hues of crème de menthe.

The path opens, the pale November sun seeps in, the stream bed becomes a narrow, flinty gash. Scrappy shrubs of rosemary and juniper replace the ferns and moss. Thyme and grey-leaved euphorbias with crimson stems sprout from the limestone. Small caves are bitten from the cliffs, often with rock walls at their mouths as if someone has been here, making troglodyte shelters.

Beauvoir walked here almost ninety years ago, recalling in her memoir that "alone again, I got lost in a mountain ravine on the Luberon range." Buoyed by her pluck, I'd set off early with a very rudimentary map and a vague idea of crossing the massif, of testing my body, Beauvoir-style.

I climb out of the gorge, breathless with exertion. The signs, painted yellow dashes, have disappeared, but the track continues to curl up towards the ridgeline. The limestone crags above me are ribboned with ochre, all of it turning honey-coloured in the light. There's silence but for the splash of water and I realise that, although it's a sunny Saturday, there is no one here but me.

At first I find this an exhilarating thought. But then my path narrows, turns northwards. And all of a sudden I'm on a ledge, with a sheer, plunging drop to my left. I pause, catch hold of a pine branch, take a long breath. I summon Beauvoir, her swagger, all those words of bluster and bravado: "I had made it a rule never to worry about anything prematurely. . . . I regarded [fear] as mere weakness and made myself subdue it." Nothing defeated her.

With her words milling in my head, I pack away my walking poles, tighten my backpack, crouch low, and move slowly across the ledge. Never looking down. Never looking up. *Subduing my fear.* With relief I arrive at the other side, where the path widens. But at the next corner it shrinks again and the gorge comes gapingly back into view. Worse, my path is blocked by a colossal boulder, which has to be climbed. There's no way round. I'm almost at the top of the ridgeline. If I can just pull myself up this vast grey rock, the path might start descending. Perhaps into a sunlit valley. The truth is, I have no idea what's beyond the ridge. On my map it appears to be uninhabited forest descending for one and a half miles to a small road. I stare up at the boulder: sun-smoothed, blank. Nothing to hold on to. There's a small hole where I could put a foot. But then I'd have to grip the upper rim of the stone—which is the height of my head—and haul myself up. And if I misjudge or my hands slip, I'll stumble back, possibly toppling into the gorge several hundred feet below me.

On the other hand, if I don't scale the boulder, I'll have to crawl back along the sweat-inducing ledge. I stare at the rock. A small voice in my head begins hurling questions at me: You don't even know where this track goes . . . what if the ledges are narrower, more perilous, on the other side? What if you break a leg? It's true. I'm miles from anywhere. Slowly I turn back, a tear of disappointment prickling at the back of my eye. But that's all it is—disappointment. And a recognition of my responsibilities. It's survival, not apocalyptic defeat.

Besides, Beauvoir *did* occasionally feel fear. At one point she was followed by a dog that became dehydrated to the point of frenzy, exhibiting horrifying symptoms of rabid delirium. On another occasion, she had "painfully struggled up a series of steep gorges" expecting to reach a plateau, but eventually coming to a wall of rock. Forced to retrace her steps, she came to a deep fault line which she couldn't jump. Terrified of dying in that lonely place, she began shouting for help. For fifteen minutes she shouted and yelled. "The silence was appalling," she recalled. Eventually she mustered her courage and climbed in and out of the fault line.

I felt relief reading about her fear, because there was something so dogged, almost inhuman, about how she walked. "There were certain things, such as accidents . . . or rape, which simply *could not happen* to me," she wrote. Where did that certitude come from? Even when unpleasant incidents did happen, they left her unfazed. On another occasion, hiking alone high in the French Alps, she stumbled, lost her footing, and plummeted into a ravine. As she fell she assumed this was the end—death. She survived with a few cuts, but was astonished at her own lack of emotional reaction. Picking up her rucksack—which had hurtled down ahead of her—she casually hitched a lift back to her hotel.

Despite the endless warnings of rapists on the loose, Beauvoir was never attacked while hiking. But she often thumbed a lift to get to and from her start and finish points. In the confines of cars and trucks, she had several terrifying experiences. Once she fought off a large truck driver who beat her up and threw her into a gravel ditch. On another occasion, a travelling salesman left her flat in the middle of the road after she refused to "roll with him in the ditch." Later, two men invited her into their car and then drove towards a deserted hill, forcing her to threaten to leap from their moving vehicle. What on earth was Beauvoir thinking? "Far from teaching me a lesson," she wrote, these incidents "strengthened my presumption: with a little alertness and brisk self-assurance, I thought, one could get out of any jam." In her memoir, she recognised this as an "illusion," but had no regrets: "It supplied me with a touch of audacity."

⁓

I'm so determined to develop a modicum of Beauvoir's audacity that I retrace my steps—slipping and sliding down the gorge, splashing through hurtling water—and immediately begin hunting for another route. It's only half past two; Beauvoir's hiking days started at 6:30 AM and never ended before 7:00 PM. I find a trail sign pointing into the forest. It's vaguely in the direction of where I'm staying, so I take it. The path is wide and sunken, perhaps the original drovers' route connecting the villages of the Luberon. I have a sudden urge to see a fellow human, and walking on a wide track carries the possibility of a passing dog walker or hunter. The path pushes deeper into the forest, curving round the base of the massif. Trees crowd in, their twisted boughs bearded with long, pale lichen. The light drains away. The air smells dankly of raw mushrooms and rotting leaves. I walk on. And on. Thinking about Beauvoir, about her frenzied, fearless hiking, her casual disregard for risk.

This wasn't the first time she'd displayed an appetite for danger. At the age of nineteen she began hanging out in cheap Parisian bars, ordering a whisky or a gin fizz and drinking it alone, propped at the bar. From there she moved to nightclubs, where she and a friend allowed men to buy them drinks, to drive them through Paris's sleaziest red-light districts. When she tired of picking up men, she staged mock fights in bars, until the proprietors threw her out. She began going alone to sleazier and sleazier parts of Paris, walking the streets late at night, allowing men to pick her up, laughing when she was flashed at, drunkenly vomiting on the metro. One night she and a friend ended up in the rooms of two men who tried to assault them. The two girls fought back and fled. So why did she do it? Why go out hitch-hiking alone? Why climb remote gorges in espadrilles?

Even Beauvoir was bewildered by her urge to self-destruct, asking, "How does it come about that I like these things, have such an incongruous passion for them; and why does this passion have such a strong hold over me?"[25]

Let's put it another way: When we behave with reckless abandon, exposing ourselves to pain and damage, possibly death, are we unconsciously tempting fate or purposely flirting with danger?

⁓

Beauvoir's biographer, Deirdre Bair, attributes her sexual risk-taking behaviour to the fact that "she had seldom been touched by anyone in her family." Her father shrank from her, even when contact was accidental. Her mother hadn't hugged her since she was two years old. But can this really explain Beauvoir's proclivity for hitching rides, or sleeping on benches? It seems to me that Beauvoir needed to engage with danger, that encountering physical danger made her feel more deeply and physically alive *in her body*. And by confronting her fear she felt stronger, more akin to a man with all his incumbent freedoms.

There's an extraordinary chapter in *The Second Sex* in which Beauvoir complains that the sports open to women don't "teach about the world and about one's self . . . as does an unruly fight or an impulsive rock climb. . . . Most girls . . . only submit to their bodies passively . . . they are banned from exploring, daring, pushing back the limits of the possible." Since she is not allowed to "learn the lessons of violence," a woman's hold on the world weakens. She is disempowered and diminished, made "weak, futile, passive and docile." If, says Beauvoir, women "could swim, scale rocks, pilot a plane, battle the elements, take risks and venture out," they wouldn't feel "timidity towards the world." They would be less bound, like boys who learn how to impose themselves on the world through an "apprenticeship in violence" that nurtures their "will for self-affirmation."[26]

As Beauvoir climbed mountains, scrambled into ravines, thumbed lifts, and fought off men, she was giving herself the physical education she had been deprived of, testing both her body and her resolve, shaking off the vestiges of her own timidity.

⌒

After leaving Marseilles, Beauvoir began inviting friends to join her on walks. In Alsace, Greece, and the Atlas Mountains of Morocco she walked with Sartre, despite his claims of an allergy to chlorophyll. In Normandy and the Alpes-de-Haute-Provence she walked with Olga Kosakiewicz, a student of hers who became her lover. She hiked in the Alps with a male friend who also became her lover during the hike (and later married Olga). She took another student (the sixteen-year-old Bianca

Bienenfeld) hiking in the Morvan, where their relationship was consummated.

Beauvoir still needed to walk alone. After nearly dying of pleurisy (although at least one biographer believes the real diagnosis was jealousy),[27] she was off work for weeks. Ignoring her doctor's order to rest, she took the train to Toulon and then to Bormes-les-Mimosas, where she walked and climbed twelve and a half miles a day, despite being bone-thin and wheezing constantly. In the Haute-Loire, she walked "solidly for three weeks," sleeping in barns and remote mountain huts, on park benches and beneath chestnut trees. Tramping through mountain gorges and over high upland plateaus, she picnicked on hard-boiled eggs and sausages.

Beauvoir walked with a military determination, proving to herself that she was entirely self-reliant, that she could withstand loneliness and separation, heat, cold, and pain. Her knee swelled up, agonisingly, from overuse. She burnt the soles of her feet and had to wear ankle socks inside her espadrilles. On one occasion she was accompanied by her younger sister, Hélène. But when Hélène fell ill, Beauvoir callously left her in a pharmacy and carried on, only returning to collect her when she'd completed her grand randonnée several hours later.

Over and over she tested herself, each test another cut in a journey of cutting loose, of freeing herself, of becoming Beauvoir.

⁓

In the summer of 1939, still refusing to believe war was imminent, Beauvoir took what was to be her last hike for seven years.

"It can't happen to me; not a war, not to me," she whispered, as she packed her rucksack and set off alone for Provence. It was to be the "most delightful" of all her walking tours. A friend joined her for two days of nine-hour tramps but then collapsed with delirium. Beauvoir left him, ill and shivering, and continued alone. She marched over the mountain pass between France and Italy at Col de Larche, bumping into soldiers on manoeuvre. The place was so overrun with soldiers she had to share a bed with the wife of the local policeman. She remained impervious, walking without "a thought in my head."

As the war unfolded, Beauvoir changed, writing in her memoir, "I became a different person." She became less certain, less judgemental, more aware of the ambiguities and ambivalence of life. It was a change that affected not only how she thought but also how she walked.

～

Beauvoir was deeply affected by the war, writing to Sartre in early 1946, "I feel in some way out of things, as though in another life: I don't recognise either myself or the world." She felt unable to connect her memories of the past with the present, as if her life had snapped irretrievably in two. The bleak uncertainty that had propelled Nan Shepherd to spend hours in the Cairngorms and then write *The Living Mountain* had also propelled Beauvoir into feverish writing. But unlike Shepherd, Beauvoir was now famous. Her debut novel, *L'Invitée*, was a literary sensation. By 1943 the names of Beauvoir and Sartre were on everyone's lips. The pair could no longer work anonymously in cafes.

For seven years Beauvoir had existed without the solitude and vigorous hikes she held so dear. She had new clothes made and moved into a hotel room with a view of the River Seine. But most of all she partied hard, smoked heavily, and drank: herculean quantities of cheap, gut-dissolving whisky and terrible wine.

⌒

Finally, in the summer of 1946, Beauvoir left Paris for Milan and travelled north, alone, to the Dolomites. She'd planned a three-week route to help recover her shattered equilibrium. For months she had been tormented by thoughts of Sartre's most recent lover, who was proving a formidable rival. She knew that her own relationship with the sex-addicted Sartre was slowly unravelling. Their "pact" was fraying at the edges: "In place of two free persons, a victim and torturer confront each other," she wrote.[28] She was the victim, he the torturer.

Beauvoir was thirty-eight, but she felt old and decrepit. Agonising headaches, nightmares and shaking hands, stomach upsets, blurred vision and attacks of panic and anxiety combined to make her dwell obsessively on her health and mortality. Lectures made her nervous for days in advance, and she would sweat visibly at the lectern. Friends described her as "in a bad way." Carole Seymour-Jones, in her 2008 biography, speculates that Beauvoir had recently been date-raped by the writer Arthur Koestler.[29] In the Dolomites Beauvoir intended to nourish her stricken mind and her ravaged body.

She spent her first night in the town of Merano, where she lay on her bed thrilling at the prospect of three weeks of solitary walking, but also mulling over all that had passed since her last walk. Her eyes misted with tears: "It had been a long time since I had contemplated several weeks of mountains and silence . . . unhappiness and dangers that I now knew about added to my joy a dimension of pathos."

Her Dolomite hike was exhilarating: "From peak to peak, from one mountain hut to the next, across alps and rocks, I walked. Once more I smelled the grass, heard the noise of pebbles rolling down the screes, experienced again the gasping effort of the long climb, the ecstasy of relief when the haversack slips from the shoulders that lean back against the earth, the early departures under the pale sky, the pleasure of following the curve of the day from dawn to dusk."[30] But at some point during this majestic walk—which she later described as one of the hardest and most beautiful of her life—Beauvoir lost her walking confidence. Even as she hiked, she knew this was to be her last long journey on foot.

When she returned to Paris, the sculptor Giacometti found her looking "wild" and sobbing in a Paris bar. She had decided she was too old for such long and strenuous routes. Perhaps her long years of hard drinking, smoking, and war rations meant she could no longer pleasurably walk the daily twenty-five miles she set herself.

Even so, it's odd to hear Beauvoir expressing the defeatism she derides in *The Second Sex*. Is it possible that she no longer felt the need to test her mettle? Or had she simply come to terms with knowing that—like her alter ego Françoise—"she would never be the type of woman who had absolute mastery over her body"?[31]

Either way, she returned from the Dolomites to start work on the most significant book of her life.

⌒

And yet this wasn't her last hike. A year later, confused and depressed, she flew alone to Corsica where she walked doggedly through a landscape "lonely and with the smell of dried maquis everywhere." After a few days, she returned home "very ugly . . . sunburned, wild-haired, scratched and shabby." Most importantly, she returned having made an important decision: to stay with her new lover, the American writer Nelson Algren. Slowly, she was beginning to snip herself free of Sartre, to creep out from beneath his greedy black shadow.

Eighteen months later (during which time she had been relentlessly sedentary, researching and writing *The Second Sex*), the fitness and good health that characterised her pre-war hiking years had evaporated: "I was fat, with a huge stomach from too much drink and pills and not enough food," she recalled. Corsica really was her last solo hiking expedition.

⌒

At first I struggle to understand the ease and stoicism with which a still-young Beauvoir resigned her hiking life. It seems a failure of sorts. A failure to persevere. A failure to whip her body back into shape.

But here's the point about failing: it doesn't mean failure. Failing is merely another step in a trajectory of becoming. We fail. We dream again. We try again. We fail again. Or not.

⌒

Besides, Beauvoir wasn't quite ready to hang up her espadrilles altogether. Her two final walks were the most stupidly reckless of all. In 1953, when Beauvoir was forty-five, she and her new lover, Claude Lanzmann (who was twenty-seven), took a holiday in the Alps. Here, despite being out of training, Beauvoir plotted an ambitious eight-hour hike involving the ascent and descent of a daunting sweep of peaks, including the Mönch, the Eiger, and the Jungfrau. She refers fleetingly to this hike in her memoir, writing with her usual pride, "We squeezed a delicious sense of adventure from our fear . . . saw the sun rise on the Eiger. And then we walked: I still could walk. Wearing espadrilles we would walk for seven miles at a stretch across the glacier snows."

Lanzmann's memoir tells a different story.

"We were both excited," he recalled, "and set off at a fast clip wearing espadrilles, with no protective creams or potions for our lips or faces, no cover for our exposed heads." Lanzmann was suffering from an outbreak of boils, one of which (a "monstrous abscess") had exploded the night before, so that Beauvoir had spent a sleepless night mopping up pus.

Two-thirds of the way through their hike, a second boil on his knee erupted. "The pain was excruciating, the boil swelled and expanded quickly and two heads appeared; we were miles from anywhere and had no medication, no first-aid kit. . . . Sunburn exacerbated the fever from the carbuncle, I moved painfully, limping as I walked." Beauvoir, who was "red as a beetroot, sunburnt and sweating, shuffled like a sleepwalker, her eyes glazed." Dusk fell suddenly, and they lost their way, only making it to the mountain shelter at midnight. Here, a group of "well-equipped Swiss climbers" castigated the pair and provided painkillers, food, and soothing creams. By this point, Lanzmann's temperature was almost 104 degrees Fahrenheit and the abscess had "burst in a liberating geyser." He ended up in the hospital, quipping in his memoir, "Since then, a passion for high mountains has run in my veins."

Indeed, the passion was so strong that he and Beauvoir returned to the Alps a year later for a last escapade, one that Beauvoir made no reference to in either her memoirs or her letters to Sartre. Again, the details of this truly disastrous hike—Beauvoir's walking swan song—are recounted by Lanzmann.

In blindingly bright snow, the pair set off at sunrise to hike over the Matterhorn, from Zermatt to the Theodul Pass. As before they carried neither sunglasses, hats, nor sun lotion. As before, they walked in espadrilles, with Lanzmann (in skimpy shorts) weeping "with love" for Beauvoir's "headstrong courage, her steady pace."[32] So far so good.

But then Lanzmann grew hot and decided to strip off his shirt, exposing his skin to the blazing elements. The climb took longer than expected and they arrived late at the mountain hut, "famished, red as peonies, bathed in sweat." Instead of pressing on or bedding down for the night, they indulged in a long, drunken lunch, polishing off at least one bottle of wine. Several hours later, they continued hiking to the pass, where they planned to catch the last cable car down the Italian side of the mountain. With the light fading rapidly and overcome by fatigue, they decided that Beauvoir should shelter behind a rock while Lanzmann pranced—in his espadrilles—across glaciers normally traversed using ropes and crampons. Lanzmann then had to bribe three Italian soldiers, who put on skis and helmet lamps and headed back up the mountain with a sledge covered in blankets. Beauvoir was rescued, but it was a feverish Lanzmann who was ambulanced to the hospital, where he spent three days being treated for second-degree burns to his back and shoulders.

From this point on, Beauvoir confined her walks to cities or took short country strolls. The physical mastery she had worked (and walked) so hard for had finally deserted her.[33] Instead she bought herself a car which she drove with considerable brio, much pleasure, and a fair bit of recklessness.

⌣

My brain struggles with this, too . . . She happily swapped hiking for driving? Really? But I think there's another reason Beauvoir doesn't waste time lamenting the loss of her hiking pins. After the hardships and losses of the war, she and Sartre were in thrall to a brave new future of technology and science and radical politics. The motor car—with its gleam of modernity, its uncompromising promise of freedom and adventure— offered hope and possibility.

For Beauvoir, driving was a new (and tantalisingly dangerous) route to self-determination, another form of freedom to be explored. How was she to know that once we master driving, many of us cease to walk? That our muscles soften, our arteries harden, our hearts shrink?

⌣

When Sartre died, something odd happened. Beauvoir lost all use of her legs. They crumpled beneath her, like tissue paper. With her legs limp, broken, disarticulated, she could not walk. She learnt to shuffle. A year later, when her first biographer arrived to interview her, Beauvoir was seventy-three and shuffling with slow, painful deliberation. Her skin was a jaundiced yellow from cirrhosis of the liver, the disease that would kill her.[34]

They didn't know what we know—that, eventually, too much pain and too much alcohol strip away our existential freedom.

While I've been thinking about Beauvoir I notice the forest around me has altered, very subtly. The shadows have drawn tighter and the air has cooled, as if there's ice at the back of it. The trees are taller, denser here, their knuckled branches woven into a thick hairnet of yellowing leaves. Every now and then a shaft of dusty light penetrates the canopy—a strange, ancient light, grainy, as if it's tumbled out of a musty Bible. I pass through the shaft and sense darkness pressing in on me. The silence is thick and mildewed—no birdsong, just the occasional crack of an acorn beneath my boot. Why is it so silent?

Suddenly I feel uneasy. Afraid. Infinitely more afraid than I was in the gorge. I feel—inexplicably—as if I'm the only person on earth. It's an eerie, isolated feeling, as sharp as hunger. I walk deeper into the hunched gloom and the silence starts to seethe in my ears. As if the forest is breathing. As if something is softly pulsing in the tangle of branches and brambles. My (utterly irrational) fear spirals out of control.

I turn and do as my body begs: I run. My backpack rattles up and down. My booted feet stumble, as heavy and clumsy as parcels. I run and run until I reach a road, a house, a plume of blue smoke coiling from a chimney. A car passes and I wave with febrile ebullience. Never have I been so pleased to see sunlight on tarmac, a car, another human being. As my breath slows and my heartbeat returns to normal, I berate myself for my cowardice, my *failure*. Why did I run out of the forest when I was on a perfectly good track? How had I failed—as Elizabeth Austen so eloquently expressed it—to keep the voices in my head at a "manageable pitch of hysteria"?[35]

I get back to my room and riffle through my notes, unsure what I'm looking for. I vaguely remember a hike in which Beauvoir described walking over the brow of a hill to find it utterly deserted, with the light draining away: "as though I had brushed the edge of that ungraspable emptiness." The feeling induced sudden panic in her, the same panic she'd felt at fourteen when she realised there was no God. She'd hurried to an inn, desperate to hear another human voice. I feel better remembering this. Less cowardly. Less alone.

But it's Shepherd who helps me most. On one memorable occasion she disarmed her fear, transmuting it into another emotion altogether. She and a friend had stripped and waded into the cold, limpid waters of Loch Avon, where Shepherd looked down and "at my feet there opened a gulf of brightness so profound that the mind stopped. . . . My spirit was as naked as my body. It was one of the most defenceless moments of my life." This is a significant epiphany for Shepherd, an "unheralded moment of revelation" on her journey into being.

Shepherd knew men had drowned in water like this, assuming it to be shallow because of its extraordinary clarity. Initially she refused to ascribe her *defencelessness* to fear: "I do not think I was in much danger ... nor was fear the emotion with which I stared into the pool." And yet, in her next sentence, she writes of the "exhilaration" of fear: "Fear itself, so impersonal, so keenly apprehended, enlarged rather than constricted the spirit."

Shepherd couldn't swim.[36] To find herself perched on the very lip of a submerged precipice of inordinate and dazzling clarity (she could see every stone at the bottom of its one hundred feet) must have been as terrifying as it was surprising as it was beautiful. But instead of becoming paralysed by fear, she transformed it into another means of experiencing the richness of life. Could I do this? Could I return to that sepulchral forest and bend my fear into something *enlarging*?

⌐

Apparently fear of forests is a genuine phobia—when it occurs during the day, it's known as *hylophobia* or *xylophobia*, and when it happens at night, it's known as *nyctohylophobia*. Some people suffer from such severe hylophobia they can't look at a picture of woodland without becoming panicked. And yet endless studies suggest that walking in woodland is calming, de-stressing. The phytoncides, the geosmin ... if it's all so good for our bodies and brains, why did I tear out of a forest as if there were fire beneath my boots? Was it the dying light that made me feel so peculiarly alone? Or an acute attack of fear of the unknown, because I didn't know where the path led? Studies blame hylophobia on fairy tales and horror films where forests often act as a metaphor for the wild, the untameable, the ungovernable.

Once upon a time, forests were also places of death, primarily from wild animals. They were home to the dispossessed: outcasts, misfits, vagrants, and bandits. At the same time, forests were places of human life: woodcutters, charcoal burners, hunters, people moving on foot from place to place. Today most of our forests and woodlands are neither places of death nor places of life (other than nature of course): they are recreational, abandoned, or entirely commercial.

And yet there is something unnerving about dense forests: the paucity of light, the scarcity of waymarkers, the silence, the feeling of being hemmed in, the horror of being unable to escape. A thick forest is devoid of what Shepherd called "the liberation of space." Which is why a path is so crucial, so imbued with significance, leading us from dark to light, from wilderness to civilisation, from danger to safety.

I post a picture of the Luberon forest online and throw out the question: "How do you feel about forest walks?" Replies fire back: "I am terrified of forests"; "I'd only walk in a forest with other people"; "I might walk with a pack of dogs, but never alone"; "More than petrified." One plucky friend says, "I love the thrill of forest fear."

And yet all those forest-fuelled fairy tales are stories of survival (often but not always thanks to the male hunter or the handsome prince): Snow White, Little Red Riding Hood,

Hansel and Gretel return unscathed. An evolutionary psychologist explains that fears of forests, snakes, and spiders are leftovers from our ancestors ten thousand years ago, when forests were home to wolves, when snakes and spiders killed. "We're living in the twenty-first century with brains stuck in the Stone Age," he says.[37] It's known as *evolutionary mismatch*—when our ancestrally conditioned brains send instructions that are utterly irrelevant to the modern world we live in.

Our distant ancestors didn't come from forests but from warm, open land where they hunted, using their eyes rather than their ears or noses. Their acute vision reigned supreme. But what use are a keen pair of eyes in a dark forest? As Peter Wohlleben points out in his forest guide, "By nature, humans are not comfortable living in the forest."[38]

So how do we learn to fall in love with the "last reasonably intact ecosystem we have"?[39]

⌒

In the middle of the night, my eyes snap open. A memory whirls into my head . . . threads of a recent conversation . . . atrocities in the Luberon. The massacre of Mérindol, a series of horrific attacks that took place in a single week, killing three thousand people. In these very mountains. I open up my laptop and start tapping in words, names, places. Two hours later and the sky outside is turning faintly, opaquely blue. I've pieced together details of an unspeakably gruesome atrocity, five centuries ago, involving twelve villages circling the area where I'd walked. The track I fled was the original road running between the village that led the massacre and the villages that were razed to the ground, their inhabitants brutally murdered, raped, burnt. These villages were the homes of early Protestants, known as the Vaudois or Waldensians, who quietly followed the teachings of a man called Peter Waldo. The Waldensians were dangerously radical for their time, preaching non-violence, translating the Bible from Latin into Provençal, and allowing laypeople and women to preach.[40]

Predictably, the pope declared them heretics. And in the week of April 15, 1545, acting on papal orders, Baron Jean Maynier—his portrait shows a man with thin, flattened lips and hooded eyes, wrapped in animal pelts—led an army from the village of Oppède in the Luberon. Moving from village to village, they destroyed entire communities. Reports from onlookers were so repugnant that Maynier and his lawyer later served prison sentences for their crimes. A few villagers escaped into the mountains, hiding out in caves until they starved to death.

I don't normally believe in hauntings. Or the supernatural. But had the massacre of Mérindol left a ghostly imprint in those birdless, lightless woods? Can an atrocity leave a chill claw of air lurking in its wake?

I decide to return, to tackle the path from the other end. To go earlier in the day, when the light is cleaner, sharper. To test my own fortitude, Beauvoir-style. To test my own *hold on the world*.

⌇

In *The Second Sex*, Beauvoir argues that the body is "a situation" through which we experience the world and, ultimately, find freedom. She also suggests that the female body comes with disadvantages that make it potentially more difficult to find that freedom. But her conclusion is clear: it is up to each woman to determine whether her body is to be a source of oppression, or of liberation. In other words, it is not our biology that handicaps us but how we *perceive* our biology. And yes, how we perceive our biology is shaped overwhelmingly by a society in which women are lured into seeing themselves as "objects," alienated from their own bodies.

There's a slither of silver lining—the additional complexity women live with can be enriching, Beauvoir adds. Particularly in the countryside, where women are more receptive, better able to connect deeply to nature: "Her interior life develops more deeply. . . . Her openness can engender a precious faculty of receptivity. . . . That is why she will devote a special love to Nature."

Here, away from the covetous eyes of men and the critical eyes of "mothers," women can also define their bodies as they wish. Freedom, she suggests, needs unpeopled space in which to flex its muscles, well away from the public gaze.

Towards the end of this section, Beauvoir has a line that seems to speak directly to me in my hour of ludicrous fear. I commit it to memory, so that I can take it to the haunted forest with me: "From her subjugation, her impoverishment, and the depths of her refusal, the girl can extract the most daring courage."[41]

Which is to say, our fear can become the engine of our own transformation.

The sky is a pellucid blue with thin, trailing clouds, like back-combed lambs' tails. On the horizon the highest peaks of the Vaucluse Mountains are trimmed with glimmering snow. The weather bodes well for a return to the forest track which so spooked me. This time I've prepared thoroughly, checking the route and the distance. But I've also buried myself in facts and data, reading the latest research on trees and forests. I've read about the astonishing mycorrhizal webs that connect plants and trees.[42] I've discovered that trees have extraordinary parental instincts, nurturing their young in ways that are barely believable. I've studied reports of people whose blood pressure miraculously falls when they walk in woodland, and read accounts of remarkable experiments in which pine-tree extracts shrink cancerous tumours.[43] By the time I set off, all ideas of the forest are utterly recast. Any phantom massacres are wholly eclipsed by what I've learnt. I'm also chanting the word *Waldeinsamkeit*, a German word which roughly translates as finding peace alone in the woods. *Waldeinsamkeit . . . Waldeinsamkeit . . . Waldeinsamkeit . . .*

I enter the forest and follow the narrow, twisty path of limestone rocks. The path climbs, then dips. Oak trees, larch trees, saplings of ash, cherry, birch, and maple jostle for light. The canopy closes in. The air cools. Birdsong fades. My heart gives an involuntary jolt, but I ignore it. Instead I poke and prod at black fungi the size of saucers and gleaming like wet liquorice. I rake my fingers through freshly turned earth—the work of wild boars—and hold it to my nose. I inspect the smoke-green lichen that drips from every deadened branch. I rapture over rotting stumps circled by beautiful fungal ruffs in pastel stripes of pale orange, cinnamon, and pigeon grey. My new understanding of forests and trees, of the earth beneath them, is changing how I walk, how I look, what I see.

As the forest becomes darker I ignore my trepidation because I know *why* the canopy closes up: the less light that percolates through, the sturdier and healthier saplings become. According to Peter Wohlleben, "baby trees" in densely canopied areas are often wider than they are tall. They're waiting, building up their strength and energy, ready to replace a larger parent tree when it dies. I peer at saplings, checking the width of their branches and comparing it to their height. I look at the fretted boughs above, knowing they protect their offspring from too much heat and light. I know, too, that they scrap for sun. Just as their roots are scrapping for water, sharing nutrients, feeding their tree-families. I check the moisture content of the clotted, red soil, relieved at how damp it is—which means none of these trees are crying from acute thirst (another arboreal revelation).[44]

I skip on through the forest, energised by this kaleidoscope of colour, scent, knowledge, when all at once I recognise where I am. I've reached the length of track from which I previously fled, terrified. I pause and listen. Silence. Unbroken silence. The air feels oddly stiffened. Braced. There's a stillness too, as if the breeze is staying away. Except this time I know the nearest village is only a mile away, that I can be there in twenty minutes, that the path winds into light and open space. I walk on, a little faster, wondering what these trees have seen, if memories can be held in trunks, branches, bark, in the fifty thousand fungi that teem in the damp humus beneath my feet. Because I've learnt this too: that trees can count, that trees remember, that trees recognise the chewing of a caterpillar.

When I reach the next village, I feel dizzy and slightly mad with freedom. I turn around and walk straight back—into that cathedral of trees—without a single fibrillation of anxiety.

⌒

Frieda and Lawrence believed that "as knowledge increases wonder decreases." Nan Shepherd disagreed, countering that "knowledge does not dispel mystery." Shepherd was right. How can our new-found understanding of forests, trees, soil, fungus, insects, do anything but kindle our curiosity? Astonish us? Endear us to things that once repelled or intimidated us?

And yet wonder—or awe—is still an experience associated more with "the great and sublime in nature": mountains, waterfalls, vast skies.[45] But the emerging science of woodland shows us that forests—with all their invisible miracles—are also sources of wonder. The science of awe (yes, there is such a thing) attests to this. Looking at something we've never seen before can induce awe, says psychologist Amie Gordon.[46] Wonder is often a result of the profoundly unexpected. And what could be more unexpected than the discovery that soil contains antidepressant bacteria, that trees live in families, that birch trees use their drooping branches to beat back their neighbours?

In the eloquence of knowledge and detail we can shake off crushing fear and find another layer of freedom. Although I'm not sure we ever shake it off entirely. Perhaps we merely accommodate it in the mesmerising messiness of our lives. Perhaps we need to recognise that fear, even imagined fear, is a vital part of the fullness of life.

⌒

Something else had helped blunt my fear, helped me cautiously welcome it into my life. I discovered that every woman walker (without exception) felt paralysing terror at some point. Even the global adventurer Rosie Swale (apparently one of "the most courageous, gutsy women" in the world, whose encounters include Siberian wolves and unexpected axemen), wrote of feeling "full of fear" and "horror" when she became lost in a forest on her 1,375-mile winter walk round Wales.[47]

Fear is not gendered. Male walkers simply omitted it from their accounts. John Hillaby, one of Europe's most celebrated long-distance walkers (and a fellow sufferer of vertigo) lets us into this secret in a casual, throwaway line at the end of his 1972 hiking account *Journey through Europe*. "Fear is something most people prefer to say little or nothing about, and on this I'm with the majority," he reveals. He doesn't mean *people*, obviously. Because women are quite open on the subject.

But then Hillaby's tone changes: "It would be glossing over a chronic factor . . . if I didn't admit plainly that I was often afraid."

I'll confess—I danced when I read that thunderbolt of a line. We are all afraid at some point. It's just that some of us pretend otherwise.[48]

⌒

One day, I pack a sandwich and a flask and head off for a day hike through the mountains and forests of the massif. The sky is a crystalline blue. The trees are on fire—gold, scarlet, bronze—and the smell of wood smoke is heavy in the air. The distant mountains are a diaphanous slate blue, hung with shreds of pale cloud.

I walk to the loosely flinted track that winds through the forests and limestone cliffs to the next village. As I get closer, I hear dogs baying, sleigh bells, gunshot. I ask a farmer, who's clipping at rows of skeletal vines, whether it's safe to go into the mountains.

He points at his chest and I notice he's wearing a bulletproof vest. He explains, in rapid French, that I can go into the forest today only if I too am wearing a bulletproof jacket. The local hunters scout for wild boars with packs of dogs that wear bells round their necks, he explains. So if I insist on going:

1. I could get torn apart by frenzied, murderous dogs.
2. I could get charged by a terrified wild boar (which will eat me if I bleed in the process).
3. I could get shot at by overexcited, bloodthirsty hunters (all men, he tells me, *pas de femmes*).

He points again at his bulletproof vest. It strikes me that if he's worried about a bullet while tidying his vines in the valley, it would be reckless to go wandering into the woods. I walk just far enough to see the hunters' parked trucks at the foot of the mountain. Two trucks. So two men have rendered a vast tract of wilderness inaccessible for everyone else . . . Isn't this how the wilderness was first appropriated? How women were

denied access, kept out, ushered back into the circumscribed
confines of their houses?

⌣

A few months before her death, Beauvoir was back in her beloved Alps, driving through the Austrian Tyrol. The previous year
she had explored—by car—Niagara Falls, the Hudson River, and
Maine's Acadia National Park. She may be more associated with
the cafes of Paris, but wild landscapes were a lifelong part of her
becoming. Her strenuous, exuberant walking, whether rural or urban, played a crucial role in who she was, helping her re-engage
with her own body after a childhood of Catholic piety had rendered her "a pure disembodied spirit."[49] "To lose confidence in
one's body is to lose confidence in one's self," she famously said.[50]

When she was fifty-five, Beauvoir had what—in contemporary parlance—might be called "a moment." She thought
about her death, mourning the future passing of all her experiences, all the places she'd seen: "The arena of Huelva, the
candomblé in Bahia, the dunes of El-Oued, Wabansia Avenue,
the dawns in Provence, Tiryns . . . a sulphur sky over a sea of
clouds, the purple holly, the white nights of Leningrad, the
bells of the Liberation, an orange moon over the Piraeus, a red
sun rising over the desert."[51]

Her prose, with its wistful air of melancholy, suggests she
was on the cusp of death. In fact she had another twenty-three
years to live. But these words (which were later read at her fu-
neral) also reflect her talent for conjuring the exuberance of life
lived *outside* the home. It was a talent she shared with Shepherd,

whose equally heady and intoxicating words rush and tumble from the page, pulsing with promise and possibility, reminding us of "the single wonder of life,"[52] of life exploding "sticky and rich and smelling oh so good."[53]

In the art and craft of their prose, both Beauvoir and Shepherd show us how to turn our bodies into sensual sources of freedom and delight, how to live *through* our bodies. But they also remind us of our relationship to the living world—our common home. They show us not only how to *become*, but how to *belong*.

⌒

I finish writing this chapter in the Luberon, where every morning and evening I tramp through a deserted woodland. I've set myself a final goal: to walk the two-mile route as night falls. At the end of three weeks—by which time I know my route intimately—I'm comfortable walking alone at twilight. At the end of four weeks, I'm walking in semi-darkness. A year before I couldn't have countenanced, let alone executed, such a thing: the thought of being alone, in a darkened forest, terrified me.

On my final evening, the sun sinks behind the hills in a burst of fuchsia pink, lilac, gold. The moon appears, a cratered wafer of ice in a blue-black sky. I walk through the trees, listening to the chitterings and scufflings of countless invisible creatures, breathing in the scent of pine needles, sap, earth. I take off my shoes and feel the soft soil on the soles of my feet. A zigzag breeze picks at my hair. I feel slightly unmoored, as if I've unexpectedly lost and found a part of myself. As if I've taken off an old dressing gown and discovered myself in sparkling evening dress instead of dirty pyjamas.

I've sloughed off a skin of fear and anxiety, I decide. Fear and anxiety endowed to me by distant ancestors, cultivated and fermented by society, amplified during motherhood. But no longer necessary. Fear and anxiety that have confined and restrained me for too long.

⌒

Remember this: a self is not a thing, but a becoming—on and on until we die.

7

In Search of Space

Georgia O'Keeffe

Texas. New Mexico. Desert and Plains.
Birds. Darkness. Wind. Creativity. Fear Not.
Emma Gatewood. Notions of Home.

The air just makes you feel free—free from everything . . .
I don't seem to be wanting people—just space.

—GEORGIA O'KEEFFE, letter to Alfred Stieglitz,
October 9, 1916

There was a time in my life when I became obsessed with the desert. I was debilitatingly stressed, working full-time in a demanding job, pregnant with my third child, juggling a toddler, a preschooler, and a career that was ablaze in the dot-com frenzy of the new millennium. I hung on by my (bitten) fingernails. But beneath it all I was quietly imploding. The countryside had always been my place of refuge, except that now I was too tired, too busy, too constrained to be anywhere other than where I lived and worked—London. But that didn't matter because trees, greenery, even flowers had become excessively cluttered for me. I had no emotional space to accommodate their intricacies. It was the desert I longed for. I began thinking and dreaming of its empty, undulating dunes, unbroken by tree or building. Sand and sky were all I could hold in my mind's eye. For a few weeks the desert took hold of my imagination, returning me to sleep at night and calming me during those precipitous days when everything threatened to unravel.

At first I took this as a sign that I needed to visit a desert. But then a paragraph from the diary of Dutch writer Etty

Hillesum convinced me that my desert fantasies weren't so much a desire to go to the Sahara as an unyielding need to pare back the clutter of my life.

> A lot of unimportant inner litter and bits and pieces have to be swept out first.... So let this be the aim ... to turn one's innermost being into a vast empty plain, with none of that treacherous undergrowth to impede the view. So that something of "God" can enter you, and something of "Love," too ... the love you can apply to small, everyday things.[1]

⌒

When the chronic stress passed, so did my longings for emptiness. By then I had uncluttered a large chunk of my life, giving up full-time work so I could raise our children with a little more serenity and steadiness. I forgot about my desert cravings.

But reading Georgia O'Keeffe's letters, those anxious, fraying days floated back to me. Because O'Keeffe was a woman who found solace and fullness in emptiness. She needed topographical emptiness in order to turn her *innermost being into a vast empty plain*. She loved *small, everyday things*, like pebbles, bones, and feathers, claiming they spoke to her of "the wideness and wonder of the world." But she loved them with greater passion when she had space around her. She purged her inner clutter with outdoor space. And a part of me understood it.

⌒

O'Keeffe's life is one of tentatively finding herself, then losing herself, then finding and reinventing herself all over again. It's a journey played out in her art, in the hundreds of photographs of her, and in the thousands of letters she wrote. But above all, it's a journey through bare, windswept, ungovernable space.

Despite my desert fantasies, I'd never actually been anywhere as exposed and immense as the Texas Panhandle, where O'Keeffe's career as an artist took shape. I looked on the internet at images of the West Texas plains: stark, barren, completely alien. The thought of so much emptiness terrified me. How would I make sense of a landscape utterly denuded of streams, hedges, fields, hills, and woods?

Decades back, Matthew and I walked over the (minuscule) Wiltshire plains. We left early, with much relief, because fighter planes kept swooping an inch above our scalps, and when the rain came there was nowhere to shelter. We'd felt disconcertingly exposed and vulnerable. Safely on our London-bound train we decided that *plains* were too open to the sky, too lateral. Besides, they were dull and monotonous to look at—there was nothing for the eye to penetrate. All that nothingness.

⌒

I was in the middle of planning my pilgrimage to O'Keeffe-land when I met an American called Bob who wore boots with heels and told me I was "mad" for thinking I could tackle Texas on foot. "No one walks in Texas," he said. "It's the land of the car."

He told me that Amarillo (O'Keeffe's first Texas home) was the ugliest city in America and that I'd be plain dumb to go there without a getaway car. Finally he said my plan of taking a public bus from Amarillo to Santa Fe was the dumbest idea of all. "The Greyhound is for junkies and homeless people," he said. "They'll have guns and you'll need one too."

O'Keeffe had taken a train from Amarillo to Santa Fe, but trains no longer ran this route, so I'd happily opted for the bus, knowing Beauvoir took the bus when she travelled across the US in 1947.

But Bob's words terrified me. I didn't want to drive in a hermetically sealed car. Nor did I want to carry a gun or get shot on a bus. I became convinced that not only would I dislike the unwalkable Texas plains and New Mexico desert, but that I wouldn't *find* O'Keeffe. And if I didn't *find* her, how could I understand her long struggle for freedom—a drama that had unfolded often on foot and invariably against an expansive backdrop of red dust and empty sky? Suddenly my trip seemed ludicrous, naive, badly planned.

And how on earth had O'Keeffe fallen so tumultuously in love with the ugliest city in America?

⌒

Big-heeled Bob was—partially—right. As my trip planning progressed, I discovered the log cabin I'd rented was twenty miles from the Amarillo airport, an airport without a bus stop, train station, or taxi rank. It was also fifteen miles from the nearest gas station, shop, or cafe. In a sudden whirl of nerves,

I rented a car and begged Matthew to come with me, to share the inevitable shock of displacement as I swapped oh-so-tiny England with a land too big to walk.

O'Keeffe always maintained that she didn't have huge talent or a "great gift," just a capacity for hard work and "a kind of nerve . . . mostly a lot of nerve." On the rough, lonely plains of West Texas, O'Keeffe began the long, arduous process of building her "nerve."

The irony isn't lost on me—I, too, must reclaim my nerve.

⌒

On August 15, 1912, the *Amarillo Daily News* announced the arrival of Miss Georgia O'Keeffe, drawing teacher, at the newly opened high school. She was twenty-four, and desperate to escape her latest family home—a boarding house in Charlottesville, Virginia, where her TB-infected mother was illegally renting out rooms and where a "destitute and shabby" O'Keeffe had been serving meals. Her father, humiliated and demeaned by a series of business failures, had disappeared to try his luck elsewhere.

In the previous decade, the O'Keeffe family had tumbled from being wealthy, respected landowners in possession of a 640-acre farm in Sun Prairie, Wisconsin, to being penurious outsiders, unable to pay for the education of their seven children, and unable to afford the clothes, carriages, and trappings of their earlier life.

O'Keeffe had given up her artistic dreams after two gruelling years working in Chicago as a commercial illustrator. She knew her mother might die—the white plague was frighteningly infectious and had already killed three of her uncles, the last of whom had been nursed by her mother. She also knew that she had to earn her own living. Despite attending several art schools, winning awards and prizes, she didn't have a teaching qualification. When she arrived in Amarillo, the *Daily News* mistakenly described her as "having the highest degree known to her profession." To avoid being found out, O'Keeffe kept away from her fellow teaching staff and took a room at a cheap hotel beloved by cowboys.

Raised on stories of the Wild West, she had the myth of endeavour, renewal and liberty in her blood. "I was very excited about going where Billy the Kid had been," she recalled. By choosing the Texas Panhandle (one of the last settled regions in the United States), she gave herself a tacit permission to *be* wild, to break free of the traditions and encumbrances of conventional America, to become an outlaw and fugitive—much like Billy the Kid himself. Already O'Keeffe knew she was in man-land, writing of her longing to "be a man" so she could "go hunting for that big loneness—away from folks." She understood the landscape as belonging to men, connecting the physical freedom and solitude it offered with masculinity and autonomy.

She yearned for the same independence. "I wouldn't ask the men of my family for anything," she wrote defiantly. Walking in territory she associated with cowboys and buffalo hunters made her feel closer to independence. But it also intimidated her—she complained of not having "the courage to go as far as [she wanted] to alone," a fear she battled all her life.

O'Keeffe was instantly thrilled by the High Plains, the Llano Estacado. "I had nothing but to walk into nowhere and the wide sunset," she recalled. "The plains are wonderful—mellow-looking—dry grass—the quiet and the bigness like that is marvelous."[2] She loved the erratic weather, the ferocious winds, the land that stretched, flat and empty, into infinity. Her letters pulse with excitement: in seventeen months of letter writing she describes the landscape as "wonderful" fifty times. In a single letter, she states nine times how much she "likes" it, "loves" it, and is "crazy about it."[3]

O'Keeffe had always enjoyed taking walks, but in West Texas her walking subtly changed, becoming part of her sense of self rather than merely a pastime. In winter she stuffed newspapers under her coat to keep out the glacial winds. In the crackling summer heat, she returned home coated in thick red dust "the color of the road." "Oh, the sun was hot, and the wind was hard, and you got cold in the winter. I was just crazy about all of it," she recalled.[4]

Later, she described the plains as "the only place that I ever felt I really belonged. . . . That was my country—terrible winds and a wonderful emptiness." Again and again she spoke of being restored by the "emptiness," revived by the "nothingness." Even in her nineties, when asked for her favourite place after her much-loved home—Ghost Ranch in New Mexico—she immediately replied, "Amarillo, Texas." Not Bermuda or Hawaii or Japan or any of the exotic places she'd visited and adored, but that savagely austere, waterless, treeless landscape where she first saw the curvature of the earth.

⌒

How does walking stop being something you *do* and become part of who you *are*?

Impatient for an answer, I leap out of bed, jet-lagged and disoriented. A sheet of paper on the kitchen table warns of winds that travel at forty miles an hour, rattlesnakes, poisonous centipedes, fanged flies that sting, roaming coyotes, lightning strikes, and tornados. An extra paragraph in bold lists the number of people who die here annually from dehydration, falls, flash floods. A scroll of emergency telephone numbers follows. Finally, capital letters warn us not to walk near the cliffs. They are fragile, crumbling, DANGEROUS.

Outside, the sky is inky blue and vast, so vast the breath catches in my throat. In the corner of the sky hangs a fingernail moon, silver, ice-thin, minuscule in an ocean of darkness. I walk east down the track, towards a thread of pale light. The stillness and silence remind me of the Cairngorms. But the measureless space, the immense dome of sky, are like nothing I've ever experienced. As my eyes grow accustomed to the dark, I make out stunted, knotty bushes, barbed wire, sleeping cattle with long, curved horns.

A soft whooping call—an owl?—blows across the plains. A coyote howls. A dog barks. Then silence again. I have a strange sense of being on the very rim of the earth. Of being so microscopically small the sky could suck me in with a single breath. I follow the mud-beaten path that leads from our cabin. The sun begins to rise. And suddenly the long hem of the sky is on fire, ribbons of orange, lavender, rose. Within minutes the sun is up, flooding the world with pearly pink light. Before me, the flat land with its bleached buffalo grass unrolls on and on, cut from the huge bowl of sky by the narrowest and straightest of lines.

In first light, everything is round. I feel as if I'm wobbling on a colossal ball, as if I'm the only person alive, as if I'm in the centre of the universe. Even as I balance on its lip, I have this odd feeling of being in the middle of the world. But I also feel ant-small. Dwarfed.

There's nothing to impede my line of sight, nothing for my eyes to latch on to—no hills or mountains, no buildings or trees. Just me and land and sky. The space hums, limitless and terrifying, but I also feel contained by it. As if all its emptiness is holding me, wrapping itself around me so that I am its beating heart.

My hand gropes at my pocket, but I resist the urge to whip out my phone. I want to absorb this place, to understand how it orients and disorients me at the same time.

⌒

I'd read an essay on the plane about the way certain landscapes plunge us into states of topographical sensory deprivation. The writer had speculated that for people with keen imaginations, being in topographical sensory deprivation is a potent means of being thrown back inside themselves, into the life of the mind. The empty landscape becomes a sort of incubator for thought or artistic expression.[5] Put simply, if there's nothing outside, our eye turns inwards. It's certainly true that O'Keeffe was propelled into making extraordinary paintings that came "from inside my own head" during her Texas years.

But this theory underplays how much the landscape spoke to her. She spent much of her life paring things back, always reducing and simplifying the struts of her life. She wore only black and white. She kept her face bare of make-up and her hair free of styling and colouring. Her homes contained very little furniture: she liked the walls bare and the chairs covered in plain white slips; she insisted curators hang her art on plain white walls. "I like to have things as sparse as possible," she once said.[6]

As I walk back to the cabin, blue clouds are massing softly in the sky. With nothing to hold my gaze, the firmament takes on a new significance. I notice how the clouds have shapes and forms and twists at the end like knotted handkerchiefs or rabbits' tails. Some are smudges, drifting and meandering. Others are dense and billowing. Beyond them float wisps of cirrus, like shreds of cotton candy. As I stare into the sky, I feel lightened in some way. As if a slip of cloud has eased itself between the sole of my boot and the earth.

But here's the other thing about boundless space: we appreciate it more—its scale and solitude—after being somewhere closed, small, busy (including our own mercilessly revolving minds). At these moments the openness and bigness of plains or oceans can shift how we feel and how we think.

O'Keeffe hunted down space, responding to it most viscerally at times of her life when she felt crushed or oppressed. Long walks beside the ocean, over the plains, or through the desert helped her recover from repeated setbacks, as well as proving a fertile source of ideas and inspiration.

Eventually she began painting space in such a way that it became an object. Using paint she hardened and solidified the space, while also softening the ostensible subject matter of her canvas. By giving distance the same significance, she transformed emptiness, nothingness, into a "thing." Beneath the deft strokes of her paintbrush, emptiness became a presence.[7]

Forty years later, long after she'd left Texas, she was still trying to capture its endless horizons, its livid light, its imposing emptiness.[8]

⌣

I return from my dawn stroll with skin nipped pink by the frosty air and ears echoing with the eerie baying of coyotes.

I'd expected to feel overwhelmed by the flat, dusty plains. Instead I feel very calm. If I hadn't reached an electronically gated community, I'd have continued walking into the *nothingness*. On and on, into that ocean of sky.

⌣

I can see how O'Keeffe reinvented both herself and her art here. The plains feel curiously bereft of past and present, like a clean, blank canvas. All that space to blossom into. Emptiness does that—if it doesn't dwarf you, if the earth's callous indifference doesn't crush you, that is.

O'Keeffe never understood why she loved this infertile, hostile place as much as she did. She thought she was abnormal, writing to her friend, "There is nothing here—so maybe there is something wrong with me that I am liking it so much."[9]

Eighteen months on and she was still trying to understand why she responded so rawly to the landscape, writing, "I wonder why I like it—isn't it queer that I like it here—like it so much."[10]

⌒

I like it too, but for quite prosaic reasons: on the plains I feel safe. When we can see for miles and miles—and all those miles are empty and the sky is limitless and the light is abundant— we don't think about what, or who, might lie round the corner or over the hill or through the trees. O'Keeffe didn't even concern herself with the weather. After all, she could "see it coming for a week."

This sense of being cut loose from fear is amplified by the silence. And for the same reason: silence is liberty, because it implies we are safely alone. When the coyote howl is very faint, we know it's far away.

As O'Keeffe once said, after a solitary midnight ramble, there was "nothing to be afraid of—because there is nothing out there."

⌒

O'Keeffe proved a popular and impassioned teacher, returning to Texas in 1916 to live and teach in Canyon, a small town twenty miles from Amarillo. In the intervening time her life had turned on its axis: a friend had shown O'Keeffe's charcoal drawings to the celebrated photographer and gallery owner Alfred Stieglitz, prompting him to exhibit them in his famed New York gallery, 291.

Emboldened, O'Keeffe began painting again, inspired by both the solitude and landscape of the High Plains and the Palo Duro Canyon. Lying eight hundred feet below the arid, windblown plains, the canyon is a sixty-mile fissure. O'Keeffe called it "a slit." This rich and fragile tangle of history, geology, geography, wildlife, and culture was eroded, widened, and flattened by rushing water and scourging winds, which carved out a landscape of layered escarpments and sculpted peaks, spires, serrations, and fantastic formations that look like huge, tilting mushrooms. Two hundred and forty-six million years of geologic history have left a striated landscape of sandstone, shale, clay, and gypsum—an ephemeral mosaic of crimson, tangerine, pearl grey, ochre, pink, crystalline white.

O'Keeffe found it intoxicating, eulogising its scale and magnitude, its "big hills," its "long drops," its "thick-trunked scrubby cedars," and its colours. "I love it," she wrote. "I want it all . . . it makes me almost crazy." Here she lost all vestiges of feminine restraint, climbing and scrambling its red cliffs so frequently that she took to visiting in "high-heeled slippers" to force herself *not* to climb.[11]

She began painting the canyon repeatedly, simplifying and abstracting its shapes, lines, and colours with a growing sense of confidence and playfulness. Its colours ("lavender and pink and red and blue"), its lines (the "tremendous line" where earth and sky met), and its shapes were bolder and more dramatic than any other landscape she'd encountered. Here, she produced some of the most audacious and inventive paintings of her sixty-year career.

~

O'Keeffe followed cattle tracks, but Matthew and I take a rocky, twisting path to the floor of the "slit." The pale air is charged with ice and frost, and as the sun swings slowly from the east, the colours of the canyon change, brightening then dimming, then shimmering with moving light so that the fissure itself seems to expand then shrink, widen then narrow.

The air feels very still—as if it's freighted with the past, with its thousands of years of converging history. For twelve thousand years Native Americans lived here—hunters, gatherers, farmers who took what they needed and left the gorge and its life essentially as they found it. Since O'Keeffe's time, much of the million-year-old canyon has been dramatically altered. A tidy tarmac road loops into it. An open-air theatre, public toilets, burger bars, car parks, and holiday cabins have been built within its cliffs. The Native Americans and the bison have gone.

We peer at our map, trying to locate the river lined with cottonwood trees where O'Keeffe often walked. A man and a woman, weighed down beneath cameras, binoculars, and backpacks, offer to show us a path, saying they're going that way. Matthew and I exchange a look, the same thought running through our heads: that to follow is not to roam, that to follow changes everything utterly. But we nod, wordlessly agreeing that to follow has some advantages in unknown spaces.

We trail David and Sarah to a riverbed where reeds and purple-eyed grasses grow in clots. The cottonwood trees are white skeletons, their ghost-pale branches spiking at the sky. David and Sarah toss us their binoculars, motioning into the undergrowth. We aim the binoculars blindly, but before we see anything we hear flutes of birdsong, rising and falling in silvery waves. From the trees above bursts an a cappella of birdcall:

shrill chirps, jeers, hammer peckings, rawkings, cooings. The shrubbery and trees are alive with tiny birds.

As we listen, our ears bent into the sandy half silence, we become aware of other sounds . . . soft, lisping sounds, the frenzied flutter of wings, the shushing of leaves.

When we finally focus the binocular lenses, we see birds with striped heads, birds with bright yellow streaks beneath their wings, birds with darting, scarlet eyes, birds with dark, punkish crests, birds with buttery beaks and amber underwings and mottled markings in softest grey. We squint excitedly, nudging each other like children.

One by one the birds fly away. Sarah reels off a litany of names: the black-crested titmouse, the white-winged dove, the hermit thrush, the spotted towhee, the white-crowned sparrow, the dark-eyed junco. And in that moment I am eight again, entranced and poring over my pressed wild flowers, chanting their names in a single-pitch incantation: ragged robin, white campion, stitchwort, cow parsley, purple vetch, bird's-foot trefoil, foxglove, rosebay willowherb, celandine.

A sudden trill of amplified birdsong makes me jump. David laughs and tells us it's an app. "I'm calling 'em in," he says, increasing the volume so that birdsong blasts from his phone. Within seconds, a bird chirps its muted reply. David replays his phone, and the bird chirps again, then hops out from beneath the undergrowth.

"It's cruel," I whisper to Matthew. "To trick the bird like that . . ." I feel a tiny ball of irritation swelling inside me. Why the constant need to exert our mastery over nature, over something smaller than the palm of our hand?

But Matthew sees it differently. "He's getting it back for us, because he wants us to love birding like he does."

Sarah has her phone held in the air. "I'm recording its song," she explains, as if she's sensed my discomfort. "We upload everything to a database so the birds can be tracked." David photographs the bird, first with his camera (telephoto lens the length of my arm) and then with his phone.

All day we follow David and Sarah, watching roadrunners and Chihuahuan ravens, red-tailed hawks and scarlet cardinals, finches and fox sparrows. There are 219 bird varieties in the Palo Duro Canyon and we are utterly captivated, by the delicacy of their markings, by the brightness of their eyes, by the symphony of their song—by their sheer abundance. This is completely unlike our usual walking. Slowly, and with our sharpened ears leading the way, we follow the flight, flutter, and song of tiny birds. At one point we follow the scarlet streak of a cardinal. Later we pursue a wheeling, coiling hawk, the sun flashing from its red-tipped wings.

But David keeps playing his birdsong app, luring out fat little birds from beneath the sagebrush, and making roadrunners turn in frantic circles. It seems to me that the lured-out birds are confused—I see it in the perplexed tilt of their tiny heads, in the curious luminosity of their eyes.

"Don't be so anthropomorphic," whispers Matthew.

That night I try to stop thinking about David and his birdsong app, but I can't. There was something about his need for control that nauseated me. Half-remembered words from Simone de Beauvoir keep swarming in my head, droning in my ears like mosquitos . . . "Nature . . . the kingdom [man] bends to his will."[12]

"Why are you going on about it?" asks Matthew, irritated. "He's helping save them. Have you forgotten Malta?" Two years earlier we'd hiked in Malta and Gozo, observing with horror the camouflaged clifftop cabins where overweight men sat shooting migrating birds as they flew past. Sixty years earlier, Clara Vyvyan had written, sickeningly, of her encounter with a grinning Greek man proudly swinging braces of shot kestrels, his neck adorned with strings of dead songbirds.

As I frown into the darkness, it strikes me that I walk differently now—with heightened emotions, with a thin sense of loss. The freedom and pleasure I've walked with for decades carry a new undertow of anger, sadness, guilt, hunger, ebbing and flowing according to circumstance. I need to walk, to be in wild landscapes, but a part of me now tips readily into rage, or a melancholy feeling of impending loss, or a delighted, greedy determination to walk everywhere, smell everything, touch every leaf, petal, blade of grass—while I can, while it exists.

O'Keeffe had similar feelings, talking of the "wonderful" blue sky "that will always be there after all man's destruction is finished." But here's the difference: she believed the blue sky would continue into eternity. We no longer have this certainty. We have only a frail, fragile hope.

"Sarah carries a knife when she's birding alone," I add, suddenly remembering big-heeled Bob's exhortation to buy a gun. "D'you think I should get a knife? I mean like a penknife?"

Matthew's not listening. He's staring intently at the ceiling. "What was that little bird called, the tiny one with the blue crest? I can't get its song out of my head. How can something so small sing with so much . . . bravado, beauty . . . virtuosity?"

I think of Nan Shepherd, laughing out loud as swifts whistled through the windless Scottish air, making her feel as if she "had been dancing for a long time."[13] Later I come across a report from King's College London which finds that hearing birdsong provides city dwellers with an emotional boost that persists for up to four hours.[14]

One tiny bird. One short song. Four hours of happiness.

⌒

Stieglitz lured O'Keeffe from her wonderful Texas wilderness with his own loud and dominant song. He enticed her to New York with his flattering attention, expressed through letters that often ran to dozens of pages. How gratifying that must have been: the country's most prestigious gallery owner, a feted and brilliant photographer, begging for your presence, affirming and feeding your deepest and most secret artistic desires. How could O'Keeffe fail to be flattered into submission?

And then he started observing her, posing her, photographing her. Flattening her where once he had flattered her. Compulsively. Masterfully. No app required.

⌒

Reading the letters that raced between O'Keeffe and Stieglitz in their early years of epistolary courtship is a peculiarly voyeuristic experience.[15] In one missive, Stieglitz recalls the night she "gave" him "[her] virginity," describing her "on the floor afterwards naked with a bandage on—a wounded bird."

If the bird in flight is a powerful symbol of freedom, so the grounded bird is its antithesis.

Not only was she a wounded "bird"—his more usual term of endearment for her was "child": she was his "Dearest Grandest Child," "child-woman," and "great little girl." Stieglitz was the same age as O'Keeffe's mother, but this hardly justifies the way he infantilised her, or her complicit encouragement of it— an encouragement explained in part by her experience of the plains, which she pressed on him in her hundreds of letters.

It's odd, this feeling of smallness out on the plains, the loss of self it induces. O'Keeffe referred to it again and again, because even when the landscape staggered, baffled, and exhilarated her, it also made her "want to breathe so deep that I'll break." She revelled in the ability of vastness to blot her into insignificance. "I seem to feel lost out there" and "little," she wrote, calling herself "just a little girl" often in the same breath as she asserted her need to be "independent" and "free of everyone." Despite being nearly thirty, she gloried in returning from walking the plains like "a very wobbly little girl," writing excitedly to Stieglitz, "It's great to be little—I like it." Her emotional vulnerability in the face of land and sky spurred Stieglitz's paternalistic fantasies in which O'Keeffe starred as both a courageous abstract painter and an incompetent child in need of tutelage and protection.

We tend to think of O'Keeffe as the spirited, testy woman she became in New Mexico, but her early correspondence shows a very different woman, tasting freedom in a complicated swill of fear, bewilderment, and intoxication. She never again wrote so exuberantly of feeling free. But the fear and bewilderment had much farther to run.

⌒

While I'm rambling around on the plains, I think about O'Keeffe's sudden enthusiasm for being "little." I feel a version of it myself, for there's something curiously emancipating about feeling so antlike, so punishingly small.

Emily Brontë, an enthusiastic walker of the moors, identified her greatest source of happiness as being outside at night, with the moon shining and the wind blowing:

When I am not and none beside
Nor earth nor sea nor cloudless sky
But only spirit wandering wide
Through infinite immensity

After a lifetime of walking, the writer Katharine Trevelyan put it like this: "There is no liberation on earth like knowing that one is of no consequence. It sets the heart suddenly free from a thousand shackles."[16]

Needless to say, I don't think Stieglitz got it.

⌒

It wasn't merely Stieglitz's power and prestige that attracted O'Keeffe. He—and his 291 gallery—also represented artistic and intellectual freedom. Indeed, the idea of freedom was supremely important to Stieglitz. He made extravagant use of the word *free*. It anchors almost every idea, every thought he had: *free* to work, *free* to be himself, *free* to live without selling his soul ... For a woman tasting financial and social freedom, who spoke repeatedly of her love of spatial freedom, the promise of artistic, intellectual, and temporal liberty was alluring.

Little did she know just how much of her hard-earned freedom was about to be forfeited. In the meantime, Stieglitz was reborn: O'Keeffe rejuvenated him, breathing fresh life into the man who had called himself "ready for the scrap-heap—old junk."[17]

Since her late teens O'Keeffe had been migratory, spending her summers in one place and her winters in another. After Stieglitz enticed her to New York, this pattern continued: winters in New York and summers at the Stieglitz family summer house on Lake George, two hundred miles north of New York City. She fluttered between the two—although both quickly became a form of cage.

Even as she fluttered, she had to contend with regular periods of immobile restriction as Stieglitz's muse and model. For over a decade she was both an artist and the object of her husband's relentless gaze. Stieglitz photographed her hundreds of times, often alongside her own work, so that she appears confusingly as both artist and muse, subject and object. Often she's positioned so that her art seems to burst and flow provocatively from her body, giving voice to Stieglitz's Freudian, psychosexual views of woman as recipient of "the world through her womb ... the seat of her deepest feeling," etc., etc.

His three hundred photographs of her include nudes, portraits in which she is either mysteriously androgynous or blatantly sexual, and shots of cropped body parts—hands, torso, feet, neck. Many involved four-minute exposures, during which time O'Keeffe—who appears to have been posed wholly by Stieglitz—had to sit stock-still. As biographer Roxana Robinson notes, "Stieglitz took command of Georgia's time, her body, and her privacy." Or as O'Keeffe herself put it, "He photographed me until I was crazy."[18]

After he first photographed her, in 1917, she wrote to him saying she loved the pictures, but added, tellingly, "It makes me laugh that I like myself so much—like myself as you make me." Her enthusiasm didn't last: "It was something *he* wanted to do," she said later, with weary resignation. Fifty years on, she looked back over his photographs and wondered "who that person is."

The more I look at them, the more I ask myself the same question. Who is this woman? She bears no resemblance to the vivacious O'Keeffe conjured from her Texas letters, or the proudly wrinkled icon of later years. Eventually, after hours of staring at Stieglitz's portraits of her, my question shifts. I want to know not *who* she is but *where* she is. Her expression—blank, bemused, vacant—suggests neither collaborator nor "wounded bird," neither lively child nor radical artist. It's as if she's removed herself entirely. She's checked out.

~

I keep returning to Stieglitz's photographs of O'Keeffe, remembering some words from Susan Sontag on how photographing people violates them, "by seeing them as they never see themselves, by having knowledge of them they can never have; it turns people into objects that can be symbolically possessed."[19]

It is not O'Keeffe in these portraits, I realise. It is Stieglitz.

O'Keeffe was of the same mind, saying much later that he was really photographing himself. But it took distance to recognise that. We don't always see the very thing beneath our nose, it's just too close.

⌁

Years ago, I modelled for an artist. The agony began as soon as I had to choose clothes that represented *me*, a decision that prompted a deluge of existential and unanswerable questions. The angst proliferated when the clothes I'd chosen were too thin for an icy studio. For hours I stood, neck craned, feet frozen, staring at the rain on the window. My muscles seized up. My stomach rumbled with hunger. My bladder threatened to burst. One day the artist put a heater on. Immediately I began to perspire. Under strict instructions not to move, I discreetly blew mortified breaths up towards my glistening brow, mussing my fringe in the process. The artist became irritated, stamping his foot, huffing and puffing, making me acutely aware that he was the artist and I the mere model, less competent than a bowl of fruit.

Eventually he showed me his painting. I stared at it like an idiot. Who the hell was that? How had he not seen the skinniest slither of me in all that time? Worst of all, he'd given me strangely rolling eyes, like a panicked horse.

It took me months to realise that he'd painted me looking doggedly out of the window, a checked-out view of myself that was utterly unfamiliar. I only knew myself anxiously scrutinised in a mirror or caught grinning into a lens. Regardless, when we're posed by someone else, it's their interpretation of us that remains. Later he sent me the portrait, presumably having tired of looking at it himself. I couldn't bear the sight of it. I hid it in the back of a cupboard and later threw it on a bonfire. To see yourself not as *you* but as *other* is deeply unsettling.

The story of O'Keeffe and Stieglitz is well-known. He generously offered her a year of funding and a space in his New York gallery so that she could give up teaching and focus on painting. Shortly afterwards, he left his wife. His daughter, Kitty, subsequently had a breakdown and was confined to an asylum. Doctors suggested that if Stieglitz and O'Keeffe married, Kitty might better adjust to the idea of her parents' separation. So they married, although it had no effect on Kitty, who remained institutionalised all her life.

During the early years of their relationship, O'Keeffe and Stieglitz were besotted with each other. She quickly became absorbed into his lively extended family and his circle of friends. By the time they married, the passion of their early days was waning and the relationship was rapidly becoming transactional. O'Keeffe had always wanted a baby. Stieglitz refused, explaining to his niece that O'Keeffe was "herself such a kid."[20] She was thirty-three.

As O'Keeffe became more and more successful—thanks in part to Stieglitz's careful and manipulative marketing of her and her body—the relationship shifted. O'Keeffe was less inclined to spend hours posing. She disliked the sexual, gendered way in which her husband was marketing her as "the American woman." She needed more time alone. She was chafing beneath the demands of Stieglitz and his busy, boisterous family.

But her later comments suggest something deeper was festering. Ask yourself this: How does it feel to be surrounded by a world seen through the lens of another person, composed and choreographed by someone who is not you, who is nothing like you? Surrounded by the photographs, friends, family, chosen landscapes (all in photographic duplicate) of another person? Who and how do you *become* when engulfed by another, when that other is also telling you who to *be*?

O'Keeffe began disappearing alone, often to Maine, where she walked beside the emptiness of the ocean, collected seashells, and painted spacious pictures of waves and sky. Her sudden disappearances coincided with the periods when Stieglitz began photographing other women in the nude, including his fifteen-year-old niece and Rebecca Strand, the wife of his friend, Paul.[21] O'Keeffe already suspected him of infidelity, and less than four years after their wedding, Stieglitz began an affair with a wealthy married woman called Dorothy Norman, eighteen years younger than O'Keeffe and forty years younger than Stieglitz.

O'Keeffe began reassessing her priorities: she wanted more freedom, time, and space "for my way of life." She had lost her way, hijacked by Stieglitz: "I knew I must get back to some of my own ways or quit—it was mostly all dead for me," she wrote. For several years she had surrendered her own needs to her husband's, but as Stieglitz and Norman's liaison become both stronger and more public, O'Keeffe's mood changed.

When she was invited to the New Mexico home of heiress and patron Mabel Dodge Luhan, she accepted with alacrity.

As soon as she arrived in wild, open space, her mood improved. "I never feel at home in the East like I do out here," she wrote to a friend. "And finally feeling in the right place again—I feel like myself—and I like it."²² She began painting again, making preparatory sketches just as she had in Texas.

She learnt to drive, she smoked, danced, and drank wine with her dinner. "Can you imagine Georgia's emancipation?" gushed a friend in a letter home. Free from the controlling Stieglitz, O'Keeffe was tasting the liberty of her Texas days again. After four months, her unfettered *self* had returned, along with "a fresh inner strength."²³

⌒

It wasn't O'Keeffe's first time in New Mexico. She'd discovered its austere beauty quite by accident twelve years earlier when she and her sister were on their way to the Rocky Mountains for a month's holiday. A flood had washed away two bridges, forcing them to take a new route. O'Keeffe was instantly smitten: "The nothing ness [sic] is several times larger than in Texas," she wrote, delightedly.²⁴

The sisters stopped off in Santa Fe, where they walked in the Sangre de Cristo foothills. "There is so much more space between the ground and the sky out here. . . . I want to stay," wrote O'Keeffe, adding that it made her feel "like a sky rocket."²⁵

Returning twelve years later, she was elated and inspired all over again by a landscape "that stretches very far—far into me—touches things in me way beyond what I knew I was before—it is as tho I thought I was one thing and find I am something else."

But don't we all feel different, beyond ourselves, in the places that speak to our souls? The idea of a single intractable self has now been officially dismantled—it was ripped apart long ago by writers and philosophers, including the diarist Anaïs Nin, who declined to be profiled in *Harper's Magazine* because "I change every day, change my patterns, my concepts, my interpretations. I am a series of moods and sensations. I play a thousand roles."[26] Nin didn't mention the role of place in her constantly shifting self. But she didn't need to. If a landscape changes our moods, sensations, patterns, we are inevitably altered.

O'Keeffe was unutterably altered by New Mexico. In 1930, she claimed to love it so much she ached. Like Shepherd, she had fallen "into the mountain" and found herself in a "faraway state" that she could barely articulate in words. She had fallen in love. Not with a person, but with a place.

⌒

With O'Keeffe away, Dorothy Norman and Stieglitz became closer than ever. O'Keeffe's response was to disappear again, first to the ocean in Maine and later back to New Mexico. Both trips provided her with long walks and sufficient inspiration to bury herself in work. On her second trip to New Mexico, O'Keeffe found inspiration in every meander. She returned with twenty-two landscape paintings and more than a dozen paintings of churches, crosses, and flowers. Her sketchbooks were crammed with drawings of irises, lilies of the valley, callas, roses, hollyhocks, and freesias.

Returning to New York, she threw herself manically into her work, writing to a friend, "The vision ahead may seem a bit bleak but my feeling about life is a curious kind of triumphant feeling about—seeing it bleak—knowing it so—and walking into it fearlessly because one has no choice—enjoying one's consciousness." Work, she added, was all that mattered.[27]

She wasn't being entirely honest. Place mattered as much as work. For O'Keeffe, open landscape was inextricably bound up with her art, and with who she was. Every turning point in her life involved turning—in space. Preferably gargantuan, empty, and airy space. It is, after all, easier to turn when we're not constricted by walls, furniture, people, *stuff*.

In the process of turning, she wrote a heart-wrenching letter to Stieglitz desperately trying to explain why she had to spend time alone in New Mexico: "There is much life in me. . . . I realized it would die if it could not move toward something. . . . I chose coming away because here at least I feel good—and it makes me feel I am growing very tall and straight inside."[28]

Where we are is *who* we are. And while most of us do not have the luxury of swapping one place for another, O'Keeffe shows us how to wriggle through this conundrum, how to grow "tall and straight."

For the next few months, this line—*I am growing very tall and straight inside*—haunts me. Written when O'Keeffe was forty-one, it suggests she was finally growing into the woman she wanted to be, the woman she'd been on the verge of becoming fifteen years earlier. It reminds me that *growing* is never a linear process, that space is as crucial as time, that we bump and jolt our way to being *tall and straight inside*. Most of all, it's a reminder that we must boldly venture out if we are to change within.

During her decade in New York, O'Keeffe had veered from one illness to another, spending long periods in bed. Biographers blame her emotional anxieties for the endless physical ailments: unnamed illnesses, vicious colds, swollen legs, arthritis, periods of unexplained fatigue, headaches. In New Mexico she began her recovery, walking for miles and miles every day, bathing in streams, breathing in clean air and sunlight. "I've always liked to walk," she wrote. "I think I've taken a bath in every brook from Abiquiu to Española. Irrigation ditches are fine . . . just wide enough to lie down in."[29]

In 1931, O'Keeffe left New York two months earlier than usual for her summer stay, this time renting her own cottage in Alcade, a lean, spartan landscape of sandy soil and sagebrush. She converted her Model A Ford into an easel on wheels by removing the passenger seat and swivelling the driver's seat. Now she could paint *en plein air* in ever remoter and more isolated spots. Vivified by the landscape, she began painting in watercolour again, something she hadn't done since leaving Texas, something Stieglitz had discouraged. Once again New

Mexico took hold of her imagination: "I never had a better time painting," she wrote. "And never worked more steadily and never loved the country more."[30]

⌒

But while O'Keeffe began the slow process of reconstructing herself, Stieglitz had decided to do the same. On February 15, 1932, he held a forty-year retrospective of his photography. Among his photographs of a younger O'Keeffe, he hung photographs of twenty-six-year-old Dorothy Norman, in bed, nude, her puppy eyes wide and docile. "There is something about it all that makes me very sad," O'Keeffe wrote in a letter to her friend Dorothy Brett as the show opened. A few months later Stieglitz made Norman the manager of his New York gallery.

O'Keeffe immersed herself in work, but on this occasion work became the final straw, shaking her to the foundations of her existence. A few months after Stieglitz's show, the years of repressed anguish came to a head, spurred by her sudden desire to "paint something for a particular place—and paint it *big*."

Invited to paint a mural on the walls of the ladies' powder room in John D. Rockefeller's Radio City Music Hall, she accepted. The fee was a pittance. Stieglitz flew into a tantrum, claiming that O'Keeffe was a child, not responsible for her actions. It was too late—O'Keeffe had signed a contract and was determined to do it.

Sometimes I wonder if her need for "*big*" was really a displaced longing for open space, for an escape from the stifling air of New York City and her constrained life there. Her paintings of looming skyscrapers had always struck me as chokingly oppressive, almost claustrophobic in their lack of light or space. Perhaps it wasn't a mural she needed but air, space to breathe.

The walls of the powder room weren't ready for her to start painting until six weeks before the official opening date. As she began her preparations, she noticed that the canvas on which she was to paint her mural had started to pull away from the wall. Her usual reserve and calm fled. She became distraught, running out in tears. The following day Stieglitz explained that O'Keeffe couldn't complete the project because she'd had a nervous breakdown and was confined in a sanatorium. O'Keeffe was suffering from difficulty breathing and chest pains. Stieglitz's brother (a doctor) diagnosed her first with shock and then with early menopause. Neither diagnosis was correct. O'Keeffe improved enough to leave the sanatorium but promptly suffered a new set of symptoms: persistent weeping, insomnia, lack of appetite, headaches. Two months later she was admitted to another hospital, where she was diagnosed with psychoneurosis. For two months she was kept confined in a little room. Stieglitz was forbidden from visiting.

How ironic that the woman who lived for long, wind-scoured tramps in wild, open spaces was sequestered, in her ultimate moment of need, in a small room on East Eighty-Fifth Street, in the concrete bowels of New York City.

⁓

White lies . . . whitewash . . . white elephants . . . What is it about the colour white? I've never felt comfortable with the cleanliness of white, its bland conformity, its lurking treachery, its hidden aggression. And that's before we even start on lead white, the foundation that paled the faces of women and poisoned their bodies, killing them slowly in the name of beauty.

⌒

It seems to me that O'Keeffe's need for empty space is strikingly apparent in the white paintings she made before her breakdown. As she lay in the hospital, Stieglitz hung her new show: paintings of white bars, white shells, white weeds, white lilies, white roses, white-on-white abstractions. Why had O'Keeffe—who once said "color is one of the great things in the world that makes life worth living to me"[31]—painted so obsessively in shades of white?

There's something disturbingly prescient about O'Keeffe's white paintings. As if all that white foretells the clinical interior of a sanatorium, the drum-tight sheets of a hospital bed, the white of a doctor's coat. There are so many ways to read these paintings. Was she exploring the white of her own purity in contrast to the treacherous adultery of her husband? Was she using the key of white to symbolically cleanse herself? Or was this a coded cry for help, buried deep in the waxy white of death?

All that white. It reminds me so acutely of my own days of hankering for desert, for emptiness. As if the mind knows what it needs: the solace of space and silence and solitude. A desaturated, amnesiac world of nothingness.

Not one of her paintings sold. Not even her iconic white *Jimson Weed/White Flower No. 1*, which was bought in 2014 for

$44.4 million, the most expensive painting by a female artist ever sold at auction.

⁓

As O'Keeffe lay in the hospital, Stieglitz self-published a volume of Dorothy Norman's poetry interspersed with his own photographs, seemingly oblivious to his wife's prolonged, agonising pain. Meanwhile, in another New York gallery, two of O'Keeffe's sisters exhibited paintings threateningly similar to hers, prompting newspaper headlines suggesting a genetic talent. O'Keeffe—"thin, frightened, weeping, and unstable"[32]—was furious, writing to her sister, Catherine, and threatening to tear her paintings to pieces. The two sisters didn't communicate for another four years. And Catherine, devastated, never painted again.

On the day of her release from the hospital, O'Keeffe was collected by a friend and taken to Bermuda. Here she began her recovery in the way she knew best—by taking long, breezy walks beside the sea. Her friend returned to New York, but O'Keeffe stayed another two months, walking, cycling, and climbing rocks until she was so exhausted she needed bed rest to recover.

O'Keeffe didn't paint or draw for eighteen months. "She is not painting," Stieglitz wrote to Ansel Adams. "May never paint again."

"I just sit in my effortless soup . . . barely able to get out of bed," said O'Keeffe, whose doctor had forbidden her from going west.[33] Stieglitz busied himself organising another show of her paintings, regardless of her lack of new work.

In January 1934, an exhibition of forty-four of O'Keeffe's earlier paintings went on show: birch trees, clamshells, flowers. O'Keeffe complained that the show "makes me tired of myself." But Zelda Fitzgerald, also recovering from a nervous breakdown, disagreed. She was allowed out of the mental institution—where she lived permanently[34]—to see the O'Keeffe exhibition. Deeply moved, she described the paintings as "so lonely and magnificent and heartbreaking." On her way home, Zelda became so overwrought she had to be sedated by her nurse.

I walk through the desert thinking of all these women in their twilight universes, hungry for creative freedom and desperate for mobility, but still shouldering the conventions and expectations of the nineteenth century . . . O'Keeffe, Fitzgerald, Lucia Joyce, Janet Frame, Vivienne Eliot, Virginia Woolf, Sylvia Plath, Katharine Trevelyan, Charlotte Wilder, Edna St. Vincent Millay. In and out of small beds in small hospital rooms. Barred windows. Locked doors. Confinement.

O'Keeffe and her fellow female artists of the early twentieth century had a longing for freedom that conflicted with their presumed destiny as homebound women. In the writings of Nan Shepherd, in the suffering of Frieda Lawrence, in the paintings of Gwen John and O'Keeffe, it is this yearning for liberty, this endless chafing, that sings out.

In order to create, they had to whittle spaces and places of freedom in which to think and work. This *whittling* was achieved at a huge cost to their mental and physical health. Being continuously torn between home and away, constraint and autonomy, duty and freedom, subject and object took an enormous emotional toll.

For years O'Keeffe had found, within these tensions and complications, a slender vein of inspiration. Once the whole edifice came toppling down, what had once aided her art became unendurable. She saw that, despite breaking free of the expectations of conventional society, of family ties, of the ghosts of her past, of an artistic aesthetic dominated by Europe and by men, she remained bound—by the suffocating will of her husband. *A wounded bird. A child.*

Something happens when we live according to the vision, values, and needs of another person: we surrender our own liberty. And when we hand over our liberty, a part of us dies. No wonder O'Keeffe began picking up bones on her long walks into the desert, painting them compulsively. Skulls, femurs, pelvic bones.

"Bones were easy to find so I began collecting bones," she said, refusing any suggestion that her bone paintings might contain narrative, connotation, or symbolism. She shipped barrels of bones back to New York. Still Stieglitz did not change his ways.

She collected other things too—fossilised shells, feathers, rocks. When we collect things, aren't we really collecting the scattered pieces of ourselves?

⌣

O'Keeffe had no intention of returning control to her husband. Nor of remaining *his* version of herself. She had learnt plenty from her time with Stieglitz, but most of all she had learnt the art and craft of control. If you control what people see, you control how they think. She had learnt about the uncompromising power of the image. This time she would create the image of herself *she* wanted: solitary, strong, free.

But first she needed to fall in love with life all over again. And for this she needed distance and emptiness.

⌣

There's a particularly poignant line in one of O'Keeffe's letters to Stieglitz in which she explains how shedding her regrets has enabled her to "feel the stars touch the center of me . . . out there on the hills at night." As if night-walking and the process of reasserting herself were woven together in her tapestry of recovery.

I, too, start creeping out for starlit walks. Beneath a titanic lid of darkness stippled by stars and lit by a pale sickle moon, I roam around the plains. Drained of colour and light, the emptiness feels emptier, more expansive. O'Keeffe revelled in it. After one of her regular nocturnal walks, she wrote effusively,

"I loved the starlight—the dark—the wind"—a combination that made her feel "tremendously free."[35]

"I want to be out under the stars—out where there is lots of room," she said to her friend, the photographer Paul Strand, at a time of particular turmoil and after she'd been confined with illness.[36] Again and again she wrote about "the emptiness of the night," the "big quiet moonlight," the "wonderful big starlight," the night wind that stung her face.

O'Keeffe responded to landscape and nature with great intensity. Darkness was no different. She found it "curious," the way it sometimes accompanied her and sometimes left her alone. Out on the plains, she often felt it chasing her, "an enormous—intangible—awful thing."[37]

She had started taking midnight walks when she was twenty-four and newly arrived in Texas. They were as terrifying as they were exhilarating. After walking with her sister beneath a large white moon, she wrote in a letter, "I was afraid—didn't say so—but I was. . . . I was terribly afraid—but it was worth it."

Looking west, towards Amarillo and beyond, I see a hovering glare of amber haze. But looking east, I see nothing but stars and darkness. The air is charged with ice and frost, the wind chivvies at my hair and slaps at my face. And when I stop walking to gaze at the Milky Way, I feel a giddying sensation of movement, as if I am falling upwards into the air. As if the darkness is exerting some sort of gravitational force on me.

We need darkness in our lives. And starlight, and moonbeams. O'Keeffe recognised this: the first thing she did when she arrived in New York was to position her bed beneath a skylight so that she could watch the stars.

A decade on, in New Mexico, she yearned to go camping on her own, to spend entire nights beneath the stars. She was too fearful, and her fear was a source of great irritation. Eventually she found a companion happy to accompany her. Together the two women trekked miles into the mountains, setting up camp in the darkest and remotest of terrains, where night storms pummelled their tent, where their days started at the earliest, faintest light.

For O'Keeffe, conquering her fear was a lifetime's work. She used the full force of her inner reserves to transform her fear into a source of creative energy. Many years later, she bought a bronze hand sculpted into the Buddhist gesture of *abhaya mudra*, meaning *fear not*. She mounted it on the wall at the end of her bed—so that it was the last thing she saw at night and the first thing she saw in the morning. She fought her fear, then learnt to live alongside its dregs. In an interview recorded in her eighties, she spoke of her refusal to let her many fears stop her doing what she wanted. Her voice crackles with pride.

Female fear of (and desire for) the night endures. In a recent Twitter debate where women fantasised about what they'd most like to do if men disappeared for twenty-four hours, walking at night—freely, alone, and without fear—was cited most frequently. Sylvia Plath voiced the same desire, writing in her journal, "I want to be able to sleep in an open field, to travel west, to walk freely at night."

As I researched this book, I read hundreds of accounts of female walks. Night fear cropped up repeatedly. When I asked male friends if they ever walked with fear, they looked at me with incomprehension. I tried to imagine how it must feel to walk in quiet, dark places without fear. I looked at the nocturnally inspired art of writers and artists—Charles Dickens, Baudelaire, Van Gogh, Whistler—and found a space closed to women.

So. How are we to understand the beauty and simplicity of wild night if we cannot move beyond dread?

Of all the accounts I scrutinised, it was Katharine Trevelyan's riveting journal of her three-month walk from Montreal to Vancouver in 1930, aged twenty-two and alone, that most struck me. "There is only one way I have found of staving off that unreasoning fear of darkness," she wrote from her hand-stitched tent in an isolated Canadian forest. "It is by becoming a part of the night and the earth and the surroundings." By reconnecting with the night and the land, she overcame her fear. As the embers of her campfire died, she imagined herself as "part of the wood folk who are moving about all night and are part of the ground I am sleeping on. Then, since I know that the forest and the earth know no fear, I lose my fear also."[38]

This ability to feel utterly embodied within nature—rather than disconnected from it—was exactly what inspired and emboldened O'Keeffe, Beauvoir, and Shepherd, enabling them to either rise above, or live alongside, their innate fears. It's what Shepherd meant when she wrote of walking "out of the body and into the mountain." It's what O'Keeffe meant when she spoke of loving the earth "with my skin," and when she said that while painting a tree, she *became* a tree. It's what Beauvoir meant when she wrote, "I was as vapour in the blue airs of summer and knew no bounds."[39]

Which is not to say there aren't practical ways of reducing our fears. Trevelyan found her fear magnified when she was hungry or cold. After a meal and in the warmth of her sleeping bag, the night seemed to hold fewer fears and she found it easier to become part of the wilderness in which she slept.

⌒

My experience of walking through French woodland at twilight has rubbed away the edges of my fear. But I know the plains at night will be different. The emptiness feels vaster, lonelier. And yet I like it. I like the way everything changes when veiled by darkness. As my sight struggles, my other senses expand. My hearing seems more acute. My sense of smell is keener. I'm more aware of the wind on my skin, the dust in my mouth, the soft, pithy grass beneath my feet.

I like the way my ear adjusts to the silence, which isn't really silence at all. I hear my breath, notice the different timbre when I breathe through my mouth, or my nose. I hear the soft thud of boot-on-earth, notice how the placing of my heel has a different tone to that of the ball of my foot. A chocolate wrapper rustles in my pocket. A coyote wails. The low whine of a far-off plane comes and goes, echoing into the horizon. And then the strange bird-noise I hear every night, a single wistful note, drifting through the blackness. I call her my wind bird, and wonder where she's hiding in this endless stretch of grass, sky, darkness.

One of O'Keeffe's earliest and most beautiful abstract paintings was inspired at night, as she camped in the Blue Ridge Mountains of Virginia. Peering through the triangular entrance of her unlit tent, up to an indigo sky spiked with stars, she felt an isolation mirrored in her surroundings. Electrified by this experience, she produced a drawing, two watercolours, and an oil painting using the tent opening as a framing device.[40] From then on, whenever she felt in a state of transition, images of doors appeared in her work.

As I return to the cabin, I notice its porch, the line of its roof, the scrappy locust tree that grows beside it. In the darkness I see them entirely differently—as geometrical shapes and lines, plucked into abstraction.

Night-walking on the plains is a revelation that intensifies with each walk. As I shed layer after layer of fear, my experience of darkness changes. And I change too. Slowly. Bit by bit. Crystallising on the inside. Softening on the outside. Feeling the black earth tilt beneath my feet.

⁓

One of the most pernicious aspects of fear is what it does to our sense of curiosity, to our capacity for inventiveness, to our ability to remain *open*. A frightened mind is a stifled, less open mind. And openness—as numerous studies attest—is a prerequisite for creativity.

"Fear is the most evil and dark and paralysing of all sensations," wrote Trevelyan from her tent in the forested voids of Canada. "Fear is so cramping, so belittling . . . with fear gone [we] would blossom forth like flowers in the sun."[41]

⌒

O'Keeffe never left Stieglitz, despite becoming financially independent. Nor did she ever discuss her husband's infidelity except—briefly and after his death—to make known her revulsion for Dorothy Norman. And yet Norman provided O'Keeffe with a lifeline. As Stieglitz became older, needier, more infirm, Norman's presence enabled O'Keeffe to continue her lengthy, solitary trips to New Mexico knowing he was cared for. After a decade in which O'Keeffe was confined to places and a life not of her choosing, it was—perversely—Dorothy Norman who freed her from the humdrum obligations of looking after a difficult and sickly old man. O'Keeffe began spending more and more time in New Mexico, explaining that she needed "a dry, open space all by myself," writing of how she was moving "more and more toward a kind of aloneness, not because I wish it so but because there seems no other way."[42]

For the next decade she divided her time between winters in New York looking after Stieglitz and summers alone in New Mexico, where she eventually bought two houses, both of which became an integral part of the new identity she set about constructing. Here she began habits that were to last most of her life—rising at dawn with the sun, walking great distances to hunt for rocks, bones, and new vistas, and to paint *en plein air.* Here, for the first time, she had somewhere "with a kind of freedom" that she could call home.

When Stieglitz died, she moved permanently to her desert ranch, writing to a friend, "I cannot tell you how pleased I am to be back in this world again—what a feeling of relief it is to me. . . . With the dawn my first morning here I had to laugh to myself—it seemed as if all the trees and wide flat stretch in front of them—all warm with the autumnal grass—and the unchanging mountain behind the valley all moved into my room with me."[43]

For the first time in decades, O'Keeffe included a living creature in a painting—a bird in flight.[44] Some art historians think the bird symbolises the recently dead Stieglitz. I think it's O'Keeffe. Finally free.

⁓

Something else happened after Stieglitz died. O'Keeffe began revisiting the themes that had preoccupied her during her formative years in Texas, even repainting those immense empty plains all over again. A curator called Daniel Catton Rich was the first to notice this, saying of her new works, "Their shapes and rhythms go back to some of [her] basic drawings of 1915–1916."[45]

But O'Keeffe also recognised something in her early drawings and watercolours that urged her back, as if they represented a version of herself that she wanted to reclaim, a more truthful version. While reviewing them in preparation for her fifth retrospective in 1970, she suddenly turned to her agent and said,

"We don't really need to have the show, I never did any better."[46]
A few years later she repeated this sentiment, describing the
Texas period of her charcoals and watercolours as "one of the
best times in my life.... I was alone and singularly free, working
into my own, unknown—no one to satisfy but myself."

⌒

Matthew flies home and I make my way to the Greyhound bus
station. No knife. No gun. Big-heeled Bob's words about the
dangers of taking the bus have been repeated by several Texans,
most of whom fell into stunned silence when I told them I was
neither flying nor driving to New Mexico.

The waiting room is crushed with people and luggage:
holdalls, suitcases, plastic bags. The place simmers with anxiety.
People are confused. Buses come and go. Journeys are split. Buses
are late. Drivers shout. Tempers flare. Bags are pushed and shoved
and squeezed into corners. Cases burst open, zips rip, bags tear,
spilling their contents—soft toys, clothes, chocolate bars, cans of
Coke. People curse into their phones. Queues form and un-form.
A lady with pink hair shrieks at a driver refusing to take her to
Saint Louis. The air is close, breath-warm, with an undertow of
sweat and body and unwashed bedding. I look out for guns.

On the bus, the driver cracks jokes over the intercom and
invites us into his life, offering snippets of information on what
he ate for breakfast, what he's watching on TV tonight, where
he gets his hair cut. I chat to a Mexican mother travelling with
her little girl to Albuquerque, to visit her newly married sister.
For five hours the little girl darts shy smiles at me from behind

her hand. We make a pit stop at McDonald's and everyone clambers out and lights up. A pale-faced man with a scrawny ponytail tells me he once rode a motorbike across Scotland, it took him six months and it didn't rain once. Best time of his life, he says. We climb back onto the coach, which now reeks of french fries and cigarette smoke.

I stare out at the miles and miles of flat, arid plains, reflecting on the unpredictable joys of chance encounters. Why is it that the unexpected brings greater pleasure than the planned-for? Why do chance meetings—be it human, heron, mountain, mushroom—linger so much longer in the memory?

It seems to me that joy is often bound up with surprise. Perhaps this is why I like to travel on foot and on public transport, rather than in a car. But it's not just joy. Chance encounters shift the lens through which we see the world. They jolt us into looking at things differently. They free us from the burden of expectation.

⌇

While I'm wandering around New Mexico—Ghost Ranch, the O'Keeffe Museum, the places O'Keeffe painted and walked—I think about something an O'Keeffe scholar had told me, about her inventiveness, about how she forced herself to constantly innovate, to see things differently. It's true. Over and over, she shows us how to look at things with fresh eyes, from her early abstractions, through her huge cropped flowers, to her radical use of bones and her cloud compositions. In a career spanning almost seventy years, she never became stale. How did she do this? Had the landscape been a catalyst? Had her walking played a part?

Researchers have studied the impact of walking in nature on our inventiveness, on our ability to make connections and foster new ideas. They believe our ability to think more fluidly surges not only when we walk but when we walk through wild landscapes.[47] Is it the blood flooding freshly through our brains? The combination of phytoncides and nitric oxide? The endorphins? No one knows. But it's hardly a new idea. Wordsworth famously said he could compose poems only as he walked in the countryside. Both Rousseau and Nietzsche claimed to have their best thoughts while walking. O'Keeffe also knew that a long wild walk could break through periods of stagnation, writing in 1915, "I never felt such a vacancy in my life. . . . I'll be better for . . . a long walk . . . in the woods . . . maybe I'll have something to say then."[48]

Walking appears to encourage the brain to ramble, to make connections, to dip in and out of memories, to slip from one idea to another. In what Clara Vyvyan called the strange "blend of monotony and variety . . . routine . . . novelty, change and surprises"[49] something in us is released, freed. It's a cliché, but when we wander, we wonder.

I have my own little (unproven) theory. Out in the wilds, our bodies respond instantaneously—cool dew brushing our ankles, sun-baked thyme filling our nostrils, the sad, insistent call of a wood pigeon in our ears—long before our intellect can draw any rational conclusions. And in that tiny, temporal space ideas can germinate, incubate, collide, bloom, become.

One day I head to the Sangre de Cristo Mountains for a meandering, idea-inducing amble. O'Keeffe first experienced the New Mexico landscape here, in 1917, and I like the idea of following in her footsteps, imagining her first glimpse of the place that was to have such a profound effect on her.

I walk beneath a cold blue sky, traffic on one side and snow-spiked scrub on the other. Naturally, I get lost, but it's early and the sun is a lavish gold and the snow is spangled with diamonds and the sky is higher and bluer than I've ever seen. Besides, I'm reading Rebecca Solnit's book *A Field Guide to Getting Lost*, and her words are ringing in my ears: "Never to get lost is not to live." O'Keeffe had the same adventurous spirit, often heading off "without knowing where or why."⁵⁰ And why not? Who wants to live in perpetual geographic certainty?

When I can't find a trail sign, I decide that geographic certainty might be preferable to wandering around in suburbia. I ask a man arranging his outsized bin to point me in the right direction. He looks at my map, then shakes his head. "That's a very long way," he says dubiously. "My wife and I usually turn off here." He points at a red mark which is a fraction of my planned distance. "There's a lot of snow," he adds. "Mud too. I wouldn't risk it."

He points me to the path, but the track I eventually take isn't right. I'm scrubbing around in the juniper bushes when I look up and see a line of black-robed men with sleek black hair and beautiful black eyes walking barefoot along a frosted path.

"Hello," I shout, mesmerised by their beauty, the snaking line of their black kimonos, their long, pale feet. They're walking, very lightly and gracefully, towards a low building. I squint at a sign on the wall: "Zen Buddhist Center." "I'm looking for the trail," I add, pathetically.

A monk steps forward and indicates to the right. "Five minutes that way," he says, fluttering an elegant arm and smiling at me. His eyes are like bottomless pools. Light falls on his shining hair. Even his voice is music. He turns back and I watch their kimonoed bodies float into the building.

O'Keeffe developed a fondness for black kimonos after a mastectomy when she was sixty-eight. She didn't want anyone to know she'd lost a breast and she refused to wear a bra with a prosthetic bosom. Instead she wore kimonos to disguise her lopsided body. She had lots of them, all made from her favourite 100 percent cotton.

With a head full of monks and kimonos, I find the trail and follow a single pair of boot marks beside four paw prints. I walk for miles, pressing juniper berries and pine needles between my fingers and breathing in their scent. I lose the dog-walker prints and follow the tiny claw-scratchings of a bird. And when these end I press on, crunching into snow, slopping through thick red mud. My boots grow heavy with earth, two clotted weights dragging in and out of the snow. The wind blows in my face, cold and clean. Birds sing from the pine trees and the sun beats down hot on my back.

I find a new set of boot prints, just visible beneath last night's snow. Yesterday's prints. Or perhaps last week's prints. They take me upwards and westwards, weaving a soft path that edges the boggy sections. I feel oddly accompanied, as if a friend is walking in front of me. Eventually we—I and my fellow footprints—come to a sandy, snowless track heading south, downhill. I lose the boot prints but take the track, a dry riverbed, strewn with rocks and pebbles. Sunlight flashes from grains of silver mica embedded in black rock. Rust-red rocks, striated with grey and palest pink, soak up the warmth. I poke around, finding stones in green and ochre, and tiny shards of crystal. I put them in my pocket, just as O'Keeffe did. She loved pebbles and kept arrangements of them all over her house, along with bones and shards of Pueblo pottery that she found on her walks. "My treasures," she called them. Apparently she once so coveted a smooth black pebble that she stole it from a friend, slipping it silently into her pocket. The woman who died with an estate valued at $70 million wanted nothing more than a perfect pebble.

When I get home, I am utterly windswept. The wind has tugged my hair into tangled spires, twisted my scarf into knots, blown pine needles and debris into my pockets, into the lining of my coat. I feel piercingly alive but also suctioned clean. As if the wind has scoured me from the inside out. O'Keeffe adored the wind. Knowing how much she loved it has made me more receptive to it, helping me throw off a terrible memory of a clifftop walk when great gusts of raging wind forced me and the children to crawl across the turf on our stomachs.

The Dutch have a word for wild, windy walks: *uitwaaien.* O'Keeffe would have understood entirely.

I'm sitting in the Santa Fe Public Library, reading about the four million miles of US land that are now motorway, when I hear a woman's voice. Raised. It's coming from between the bookshelves, just behind the table where I'm working.

"All you English whores, just get out of here . . . get out of here. You fucking English whores . . . !"

I look sideways at the other people in the study room. They're all staring fixedly at their screens, but they're all men. She must have heard me talking to the librarian, recognised my English accent. I stare grimly at my screen. I've never been called an English whore before.

"You fucking English whores . . ." Her voice is receding. She's moving back through the stacks. Away.

I tap out a few words but they're clumsy and awkward. I feel too unsettled to work, so I pack away my things and go in search of a grocery shop. There aren't any so I walk two miles to an edge-of-town supermarket. It's dark, and snow is blowing. As usual the streets are empty except for a few dispossessed who, like me, are on foot: an old woman shuffling a shopping cart spewing with rags and rubbish, a man clutching at his trousers, which are stiff and blackened with dirt.

It strikes me that walking is almost a source of shame here, bound up with poverty and deprivation. Frieda and Lawrence walked everywhere with pride: walking was a bold assertion of their status as rebellious outsiders. O'Keeffe walked with pride too. She knew people thought her odd, dragging bones around the desert, walking for miles across the plains. But she made her love of walking a part of her identity, gloating over her ability to outwalk younger men.

I hurry on, six lanes of traffic thrumming beside me. Twice I have to sprint from oncoming cars that appear suddenly from side roads. There are no streetlights and the snow is thickening and swirling.

I buy some bread, lettuce, and cheese, then decide to check Google Maps for the quickest way back to my room. When I take out my phone it's dead, but I'm fairly sure I can find my way, in spite of the darkness and the gusting snow. I walk fast, fearful in these unlit, unpeopled streets. All the houses are similar in Santa Fe—city policy apparently—and I become disoriented. After twenty minutes I'm utterly lost. I appear to be outside of the city, on the edge of a vast black highway. Trucks and cars spin past me, their red tail lights disappearing into an ocean of darkness. The sidewalk tapers perilously to a kerb the width of my foot. I take a side road that feels to be in the right direction. The snow is melting into my jeans, settling into the creases of my coat, and I just want to get back to my warm little room with its crooked lamp, its cheerful cushions, its miniature kettle. The road is lined on one side with trees, which doesn't feel right. Surely if I were heading towards the city, there would be more concrete and fewer trees?

The emptiness of this side road frightens me—not only are there no pedestrians or streetlights, but there are no passing cars, no houses. No lights of any sort. Tears prickle at my eyes. I'm lost and cold, without a working phone, without anyone to ask. I start running back down to the highway, but I keep stumbling and tripping because the unrepaired sidewalks undulate and veer—they're designed for trucks emerging from parking lots rather than walkers. Suddenly I'm running and tumbling and sobbing all at once. In my mania I walk into a massive plastic garbage bin and send it rattling down the road.

When I get back to the highway, I notice a man ahead of me. He's the first pedestrian I've clocked in an hour of frantic, discombobulated walking. I'm so startled I stop sobbing and run towards him, in a great rush of relief. "Excuse me, where's Santa Fe?" I gasp. He looks at me wide-eyed, as stunned to see another walker as I am. Or perhaps he's only stunned by the red-eyed wildness of my appearance. He points up the road and says if I walk for half an hour I'll reach the city.

I start the trek back, slaloming between huge plastic bins and cursing the endlessly buckling sidewalk, the snow, the inky sky, myself for having such a hopeless sense of direction. Most of all, I curse America for its callous disregard for sidewalks and its monotonous, unbending miles of motorway.

At the next corner I see the neon flash of a drive-thru McDonald's and the lights of Santa Fe in the distance. Relief sweeps over me, and my angry fear turns to a mood of wistful longing. For the next mile I think, nostalgically, of home. Europe. The tightly tucked-up towns and villages of Bavaria, of Lake Garda and the Dolomites, of Scotland and Wales, of England. Their narrow, winding roads and twisting, curving streets, their secret squares and hidden gardens, their well-lit sidewalks, their dawdling cars, their cyclists and dog walkers, their corner shops and cafes blazing with light.

I think of the greenness, the lush, verdant foliage, the soft murmur of grass. O'Keeffe's voice creeps into my ear, complaining about the "heavy dark green" of Lake George. "The green is all so very clean—but I hate it," she wrote from the Stieglitz summer home. "Here I feel smothered with green.... Everything is soft here. I walk much and endure the green.... Give my love to the wind and the big spaces."

Beside her immense bleached landscapes of desert, canyon, cliffs, and sky, the Welsh valley of my soul seems bland, flavourless. And small. Terribly small. And yet I love the bright, thick-leaved green of home. When I was in India, I became so homesick I dreamt in shades of moss and leaf, yearning for the cool, sappy greenness of Wales.

I'm also missing the encompassed spaces—the furrowed fields, the sloping meadows of grazing sheep, the hedgerows, the little copses, the tangled banks, the dips and hills. Katharine Trevelyan experienced similar longings as she traversed the brutal, merciless miles of "bleak bare dusty" prairie on her cross-Canada hike, suddenly longing for "wealds and woods, meadows and streams . . . cottages and church towers."[51]

My thoughts swim back to home, my nostalgia blooming as traffic thunders past. I think of the hemmed-in, ramshackle buildings with toppling chimneys and small-paned windows. I think of zebra crossings and bicycle racks and trees. I think of the intimacy and smallness of it all. But most of all I think of walkers: people pulling dogs, and pushing prams, and carrying shopping. I see them hurrying to the post box, the pub, the corner shop. The hikers and strollers and joggers. I feel an ache under my ribs. For home. For the continent where I belong. I want to live where people walk, where sidewalks are repaired, where you can nip out (on foot) to buy a packet of tea or visit a friend. Where walkers are considered not dispossessed but perfectly normal.

The land of the car is a lonely place.

⌒

Funny how fear and uncertainty breed nostalgia. The next morning I open my curtains to another day of languid blue sky, unrolling red earth, the glint of snow. It's so quiet I can hear the grass sigh, and the beating of my own heart. For a mad, contrary moment I imagine myself living here. Could I?

With my head full of conflicting thoughts about home, I make a pilgrimage to the log cabin where Frieda and Lawrence lived, and where Frieda returned after Lawrence died. Frieda loved New Mexico and felt "very American," writing, "This country suits my very soul." Like O'Keeffe—who became her friend—Frieda chose to make her final home in an isolated and remote corner of New Mexico. The Kiowa Ranch clings to a mountain, eight thousand feet above sea level, five miles from the nearest village, looking out across "the vast wonderful desert . . . with its clear pure air."[52]

Here, Frieda held ceremonial burnings of Lawrence biographies she disliked, marking the ashy spot with a candle in a pickle jar. She also wrote her own memoir, while rats scuttled beneath the floorboards. Wealthy from Lawrence's royalties, she embarked on modernising the cabin, adding running water, an indoor toilet, and a Bavarian-style guest room for friends and family. When two of her long-lost children came to stay, her cabin finally became the home she'd dreamt of for so long. Frieda eventually died here, on the morning of her seventy-seventh birthday, having spent the night with her window open, looking at the stars.

Apparently her ghost visited the cabin for several weeks after she died, floating around in a nightie. There's no sign of it on my visit. But as I poke around, listening to the wind soughing in the pine trees, I ponder the notion of home, its significance, its complicated role in female identity. For centuries, mobility was the preserve of men. Women were restricted, immobile, homebound. Home—we were told—was a place of safety. And yet for many, home was infinitely more dangerous than wilderness.

As I ambled in and out of the lives and steps of Frieda Lawrence, Gwen John, Clara Vyvyan, Daphne du Maurier, Nan Shepherd, Simone de Beauvoir, and Georgia O'Keeffe, I was struck by something else they had in common. While they relished regular tramps in the wilds, they also had very particular attachments to their homes, either to the buildings or to the localities, and often to both. Many designed homes or gardens renowned for their stylishness and beauty: O'Keeffe's curated "treasures" and Beauvoir's wall-mounted statues, dolls, and textiles—miniature landscapes in their own right—were commented on in every biography; Gwen John spent hours tidying and painting her Paris room; Clara Vyvyan lovingly created a garden of rare trees and plants. Daphne du Maurier's deep attachment to Cornwall—like Shepherd's devotion to her corner of Scotland and Beauvoir's to Paris—is well-documented.

I wondered if their courage was partly fostered by this deep sense of home, of belonging to a specific place. Their ability to accommodate uncertainty in their lives—a necessity for women who walked alone or in little-known places without the safety nets we enjoy today—was impressive. But was it eased by their profound sense of home, and the certainty that brings? I groped along this thin thread of thought, looking for a pattern, questioning the unsteady attachment I had to my own home of thirty years, trying to fathom whether a feeling of belonging emboldens or impedes us. My questions felt fraughtly gendered. I couldn't shrug off the image of Gwen John desperately making herself a home, while Rodin "knew that his house was nothing to him. . . . Deep in himself he bore the darkness, shelter, and peace of a house, and he himself had become sky above it, and wood around it."[53]

Above all, I kept coming back to Emma Gatewood, who, in 1955, told her children she was going for a walk. She was sixty-seven, a mother of eleven children, a grandmother of twenty-three, and a great-grandmother of two. Instead of the afternoon stroll her children envisaged, Gatewood began walking the 2,050-mile Appalachian Trail, alone.[54]

Gatewood had no history of sporting prowess. In fact she had barely hiked before, as demonstrated in her footwear and perfunctory "gear." She wore dungarees and a pair of tennis shoes, which she cut open at the sides to relieve her bunions, later adding the rubber heel of a man's discarded shoe to support her arches. She carried a sack she'd sewn herself, containing a gingham dress, a penknife, Band-Aids, and a shower curtain to keep the rain off. No food but for the stock cubes, peanuts, and raisins stuffed into her pockets. No sleeping bag. No tent. At night she slept on leaves, in barns, on lawns, and—when offered—in the homes she passed.

So what drove her into the mountains at a time when most grandmothers were clicking knitting needles and baking biscuits? Gatewood was famously reticent. But her backstory is one of horrific and sustained abuse.

At eighteen she married a man with a violent temper, who raped her repeatedly, sometimes several times in a single day. The physical violence he inflicted on her was unimaginably cruel, from brutal beatings to attempted stranglings. She tried to escape, but her failed attempts made her husband more vigilant than ever, and he began letting her out only to take their daughters to the woods. The woods became a place of safety, a wild sanctuary. She tried to escape a second time, but couldn't bear being apart from her children. She returned home again. Incensed, her husband became more savage in his beatings: her teeth were broken, a rib smashed, and her face split and bloodied. Finally, she filed for divorce and he was gone.

Eight years on, in 1949, Gatewood read an article about the recently opened Appalachian Trail in *National Geographic* magazine. Something about the trail took hold of her imagination. She began walking ten miles a day to develop her leg muscles, although a lifetime of farm work and chasing children had left her fitter than she knew. By 1955, she was ready. She became the first woman to solo-hike the full length of the trail. She then walked it twice more—she was seventy-five when she completed it for the third time—becoming a legend among American thru-hikers. Which rather puts Beauvoir—who felt too old to distance-hike at the age of thirty-eight—to shame.

Home. That domestic space to which women have been confined for generations. That place of alleged safety in which it has been our duty to exist. When the German pastor Friedrich Evertsbusch wrote in 1867, "The house is the woman's proper home. . . . Miserable is the young woman who seeks her greatest joy outside the house,"[55] he merely voiced what society believed, and what Rousseau had asserted almost a century before.

While Gatewood was remaking herself and her home in the forests and mountains of the Appalachian Trail, O'Keeffe was erecting "No Trespassing" signs round her home, fulminating because the owners of the land surrounding her Ghost Ranch home had sold it to the Presbyterian Church—and not to her.

In the same year, Beauvoir was carefully dressing her first flat, arranging Mexican folk art on the walls, hanging her Picasso drawing and her Léger print, framing photographs of her friends, and having shelves specially built for her books and records. But if there's anyone who understands the ambiguities of our relationship with home, it's Beauvoir. "Woman," she wrote in *The Second Sex*, " . . . has to change this prison into a kingdom." She recognised that home, for most women, had become "the expression of her social worth, and her intimate truth."[56]

The violence inflicted within Emma Gatewood's home not only removed any semblance of safety, it destroyed her *social worth*, her *truth*—all that she was. It's too glib to say wild hiking returned Gatewood's worth and truth. She did that herself with her formidable courage and exceptional resilience. But my point is this: we mustn't be duped by age-old notions of home, notions readily perpetuated by an industry determined to sell us more and more home trappings (what a choice word that is—*trappings*). It seems to me that we should think of home not as a castle but as a *nest*, a place for walking to and from, for rebuilding and relocating when necessary. A place that is simultaneously safe *and* open. Open to change, to chance, to escape, to return.

O'Keeffe's perfect home included an inner nest which she called her "roofless room," with its fretted open ceiling of willow branches to keep away the scorching sun.[57] And yet walking outdoors continued to captivate her. At the age of ninety-six she walked circuits of her house, picking up a stone for each lap so that she was sure to complete an equal number each day. When her feet became too swollen, she walked indoors. When she could no longer walk indoors, she talked, with nostalgia and longing, of the glorious hikes she'd taken in the hills and arroyos around Ghost Ranch, and of the "beautiful yellow trees of Amarillo, Texas." Her memories had become spots of time on which she could feast, emotional impressions that sustained her spirit as her body floundered. I often think back over our family walks in the same way—they seem to exist beyond memory, as if stamped indelibly on my soul.

After O'Keeffe died, aged ninety-eight, her ashes were tossed into the winds whisking round the Cerro Pedernal, the blue table-topped ridge that had proved the most steadfast, loyal, and inspirational love of her life.

O'Keeffe's landscape paintings are so beguiling, so assured, the very rocks, trees, mesas seem alive, urging me to step outside and walk. But now it's my turn to go home, to a home that has changed irrevocably . . . I take the O'Keeffe images from the walls of my rented room and close my books. I pack my toiletry bag, my single change of clothes, my pyjamas, my maps.

As I walk to the bus stop, something catches my eye. Rays of sunlight flood through a leafless hedge, catching on a perfect circle slung between two spiked branches. It looks like a child's ball, so I ease my hand into the thicket. But it's not a ball. It's a bird's nest, and it comes away in my fingers as neatly as if it had been waiting for me. I hold it in my palm and look at its softly mossy interior, still carrying last spring's green. There's no trace of ice or snow in its frame of woven grass and twigs. Nor any hint of dampness in its mossy bowl. It's as if the mother bird knew her young would be completely unassailable, sheltered in this twiggy weft of hedge. I look up at the sky, half expecting a bird to be hovering above me, waiting to come home. And all of a sudden tears are tipping down my face. And I know I'm not ready for the empty, childless home awaiting me.

8

Home

I accept the peril.
I choose to walk high with sublimer dread
Rather than crawl in safety.

—GEORGE ELIOT, *Armgart*, 1870

For months I'd been mulling the stories of numerous women walkers, trying to understand why they took such risks with their safety and reputation, and what emboldened them to transgress with such determination. I came to the conclusion they were *compelled* to walk, compelled by emotional tumult that had nowhere to go. Their stories were of overcoming loss and confusion by outwalking it.

And yet it had taken me three years to see that I, too, was outwalking my own loss and confusion.

The women in this book were doing more than outpacing their inner pain. They were simultaneously and deliberately preparing themselves for a new path in life. They were testing their nerve, their resolve, their ability to be alone.

Without realising it, I was doing exactly the same: ending one life and preparing for another.

⌒

Each woman was also teaching herself how to live with fewer *trappings*. Minimally. To walk long-distance with a backpack reminds us of how little we need. It teaches us how to swap our fixation with appearance for an inner appreciation of how we *feel*. It shows us how to be self-reliant.

I needed to learn this too. For motherhood often seemed an endless accumulation of *stuff*. Our house had become awash in outgrown toys and clothes, unclaimed slippers, broken computers, sandwich toasters, smoothie makers, ice-cube trays in animal shapes, jigsaws missing half their pieces, single socks. Stuff, stuff, stuff . . .

In the process of walking, each woman discovered a new mode of being, a way of existing that was embodied, physical, sensuous. This sense of bodily reconnection, voiced most eloquently by Shepherd and Beauvoir, radiates from all their art and writings. Remote walking returned them to a more coherent self, in which movement and thought existed in tandem. But it also allowed them to confront an earthier version of themselves—dirtier, less fragrant. Wilder.

I too had needed this, obliquely sensing that the end of motherhood meant relinquishing an oozingly physical life. Pregnancy, birth, breastfeeding, the bathing, bed sharing, carrying, hugging, lifting, touching of motherhood. It was an embodied life—*sticky and rich*—that was slipping away from me.

I suspect all this was unfolding below the threshold of consciousness. As if we know instinctively how to mend, shift, alter, *become*.

Our home emptied in the flicker of an eyelid. The house that had once hummed with children, dogs, and all the comings and goings of a busy family fell silent overnight. No more slamming doors, thudding feet, blasting music, ringing phones, tuneless piano playing. No more laughter, sobs, raised voices, lowered voices, shouts for help or food or clean pants.

Every bedroom door stood open, glacial brightness streaming from the windows, beds made, floors cleared of clothes and clutter. Ghost rooms. The funny thing was, I'd waited so long for this moment, chafing beneath the constraints of it all, squeezing work into those cracks of time when I wasn't manoeuvring a shopping cart, walking a child to school, or taking the dog to the vet. I'd spent years railing at the never-endingness of it. And suddenly it was gone.

I needed to submit to the passing of time. More importantly, I needed to recalibrate so that I could embrace the life ahead of me, find its path, its kernel of sweetness. Now that I no longer had to balance in that angle of tension between longed-for liberty and maternal responsibility, I foresaw a life of splendour and marvels. I just wasn't sure how to reach for it.

Our dog of fifteen years had died a year earlier and I hadn't adjusted to walking without her at my side. She seemed to have taken a little part of me when she went, a fragment of myself that I hadn't recovered, that was adrift somewhere. I wasn't sure if I could get it back. Or if I wanted it back. Sometimes I imagined it was a part of me that I had gifted to her, in gratitude for all that she had given. In which case, why was I looking for it?

I had no answers, but I knew my life had turned full circle. And that I had changed beyond recognition. I wanted to understand who and what I was now. And I needed to move on, to *walk* on. Even then, as I plotted routes and read biographies, I imagined that walking could form a sort of ellipsis between chapters in my life. I hoped that in the wilds, and in the footsteps of these remarkable walkers, I could refind my own place in the world.

I suppose you could call it a pilgrimage, for I was honouring the audacity of those—infinitely braver than I—who had walked before. Those women who had walked not back to nature but forward *into* nature, forward into their future selves.

Not all becomings are of our own choosing. But often it's the unelected becomings—where we are thrust beyond our expectations and desires—that spark the highest flame, taking us to the very edge of our capabilities.

O'Keeffe never wanted Stieglitz to behave as he did. Frieda never wanted to lose her children. Shepherd never expected to be unmarried and without a family of her own. Beauvoir didn't ask for a life spiked with jealousy. And yet it was at these teetering, testing times that the call of the wild came loudest, most insistently. In moments of despair, confusion, grief, we have less to lose. As if there is less of ourselves worth preserving. A courage tinged with recklessness takes over, propelling us to the rim of the unknown.

But thank goodness! As Virginia Woolf wrote in her diary, "If we didn't live venturously, plucking the wild goat by the beard, and trembling over precipices, we . . . should be faded, fatalistic and aged."

And who wants that?

One morning, a few weeks after I returned from America, I pack a rucksack with a single change of clothes, a water bottle, a map, a sketchbook, Band-Aids, and a penknife. I walk out of the house, down to the River Thames. The sun is coming up, dappling the surface of the river with pale pools of liquid gold. I cross Putney Bridge and begin walking west, towards the source of the Thames, 180 miles away.

The exhilaration of escape, the sheer delight of being unshackled, of being free. I know this joy derives from my newly excavated confidence. Walking hundreds of miles has given me that confidence, but so has reading about those who went before me.

I think of all the women I've discovered over the past few years, the unread letters, the unpublished manuscripts, the out-of-print books, the overlooked accounts. I think of all the women who have walked and left no trace: the geese girls, the pedlars and gypsies, the servants and midwives, the foragers and firewood collectors, the washerwomen and water carriers. All of them navigating not only geographical routes but the complexities of being female, often alone, often in the wilds. In the dawn silence I seem to feel them collecting around me, clasping me in a gauzy mist of company. At one moment I turn, sure I can hear the sudden swishing of a skirt, the clatter of a milk pail, a stifled giggle. But there's nothing. I am alone. And yet I'm not alone. Because this river-hugging path belonged to all these women, for millennia. Like them, I am merely passing through, adding my steps to theirs.

⁓

On and on I walk. The sun rises, flushing the sky a pearly pink, its reflection shimmering from the pewter-grey river so that I am swimming in light. I think of O'Keeffe's paintings and Shepherd's poems—and all the other art I've encountered. Art helps us see the landscape differently, with refreshed eyes. It helps us fall in love, over and over, with the trees, clouds, grasses that we see every day, that we might otherwise take for granted.

My thoughts flow, meander, drift, dipping in and out of memories . . . Sprinting through a Bavarian thunderstorm as lightning crackled at our heels. Clambering over jaw-broken fields of boulders between the lighthouses strung along the Spanish coast. Eating greasy bowls of fried rabbit and chips with our fingers while sharp-winged vultures coiled overhead. The flaming forests of Provence. Mountain hail like grains of sharpened glass. Weightless drifts of Scottish snow. The sharp tang of a silver dawn. Light scattering over Lake Garda. Texas skies of scarlet, magenta, gold. Tiptoeing through frosted fields beneath a filigree moon. The velvet emptiness of night. The persistent, pleasurable ordinariness of walking, of exhaustion.

And finally, I think about the home I've left behind. The empty bedrooms with their neatly made beds, the eerie quietness, the end of motherhood. But in the crease of every ending lies the seed of a new beginning. In the process of casting off, we find a new fortitude, a tentative courage, a renewed curiosity.

I'm ready to stop outwalking. I'm ready to walk *in*. I'm ready "to discover most nearly what it is to be," as Nan Shepherd said. *To walk out of the body and into the mountain.* I have no mountain. But we all have something, somewhere. And I have a river—a glistening, serpentine stretch of water that promises to lead me, slowly, surely, to . . .

My phone bleeps. It's a message from my daughter.

"Hi Mum, weekend plans cancelled, so I'm free!! Wait for me in Kingston. I'll need a big breakfast obvs!! Love you!"

The phone bleeps again. It's a text from Matthew.

"Guess what—I've reserved two dogs for you?! Ready to collect right now!"

I turn my phone off and push it to the bottom of my backpack. As I sling the pack onto my shoulders I hear the heavy beat of wing-on-air. Ahead of me a heron has unfolded her enormous, violet wings and is skimming the surface of the Thames. My eye follows her, along the wide wash of water and into the butterfly-yellow horizon. And I walk.

Epilogue

Our Wild Walking Selves

In order to speak with the earth . . . to partake of the sanctity of a landscape we must appreciate the journey and put the destination aside and we must walk.

—SHIRLEY TOULSON, *The Moors of the Southwest*, 1983

In 1923 the Spanish writer and feminist Margarita Nelken identified *walking* as the single defining symbol separating twentieth-century women from previous generations. "This *footing*, this morning walk—elastic step, rhythmic body in loose, comfortable clothing—of the girls that walk for hygiene in these clear and warm days of early spring . . . they have opened the windows of the sad room in which their grandmothers sat," she wrote in a magazine called *La Moda Elegante*.[1] The freedom to walk, she said, was a greater emancipation than the freedom to work.

Beauvoir disagreed. She believed freedom began in the purse. And yet both are right: the early twentieth-century liberation of women was about infinitely more than winning the vote. It was about a change of mindset, a new awareness of sexuality, a fresh audacity, a new willingness and desire to explore the outside world, whether through working or walking. In their altered consciousness, women began viewing themselves differently within the landscape. They began reclaiming it.

When I think of Nelken's grandmothers in their sad rooms, I think of the women of Gwen John's paintings, peering anxiously through windows. Watching. Waiting.

But I also think of my own grandmother, who lost her walking self, who spent decades in her "sad" care home. Her walking life had dwindled from a stick when she was sixty to a wheelchair when she was seventy, to a life devoid of movement by the time she was eighty. It was a choice of her own making: she simply decided not to walk any more.

⌣

Somehow, we've allowed our bodies to be severed from the soil. Somewhere—after the Industrial Revolution that swept millions from the land and into factories, and more recently along the digital superhighway—we've forgotten the deep physiological need of our bodies to be in nature. We've forgotten that our genes were encoded for a life of walking, bending, stretching, lifting, twisting, and climbing.

It took us seven million years to evolve into the human beings we are today. We've spent a paltry fraction of that (0.01 percent as it happens) living as we do now—hunched in concrete jungles of alien complexity. For most of our evolutionary life we lived among the elements, within the sight and sound of water, wind, trees. Between the earth and the sky. Moving, always moving.

⌣

As hunter-gatherers women walked for miles, babies and toddlers bound to their bodies, arms weighed down with firewood, water, carcasses. Anthropologists estimate that we walked between four and ten miles every day, roaming as widely as men. The hunter-gatherer mother carried her child until the age of four, covering more than three thousand miles during this time.

According to historian Yuval Noah Harari, we lived like this for "tens of thousands of years" in a golden age of foraging—moving camp every month, every week, every day. As foragers, we were "the most knowledgeable and skilful people in history." We carried detailed mental maps in our head. We knew the habits of each plant and animal. We understood the progress of the seasons and the intricacies of the weather. We "studied every stream, every walnut tree, every bear cave and every flint stone." Our acute observational skills and our finely honed senses of smell and hearing let us catch the slightest slither of a snake. Our bodies, he claims, were "as fit as [those of] marathon runners."[2]

⌒

We know how the story goes from here: along came the agricultural revolution. We began confining ourselves, putting up enclosures to keep people and animals either safely in or safely out, farming rather than foraging.

Harari calls this "history's biggest fraud." Women bore the brunt of this "fraud." Shackled by endless pregnancies, restricted to an increasingly clipped and compressed space, we lost the physical strength of our forebears. Our muscles slackened and our bones weakened. We became vulnerable and fearful. Eventually we took refuge in *sad rooms*, looking longingly out of windows.

But here's the catch: despite the paucity of first-hand accounts, women have always walked in wild places. Not for pleasure, perhaps. And probably not for emotional restitution. But they routinely walked long distances to collect water, firewood, and food, to deliver animals or produce to market, to visit friends and family. It was perfectly common to see women carrying bundles of firewood, baskets of farm produce, and buckets of water for miles every day. Until the early twentieth century, when most houses finally had running water, the sight of women (and it was always women: men fetched water only if they were paid) walking up and down hills, through valleys and woods, on their own and lugging heavy buckets, was quite normal.[3]

Even the simplest things often involved lengthy excursions on foot: women walked their bread dough to the local bakehouse; they walked to buy eggs and milk. In Flora Thompson's home, milk "had to be fetched a mile and a half from the farmhouse." Even going to the lavatory often involved a walk to "a corner of the wood."[4]

I don't want to labour the point, but walking in wild places is deep in our molecular memories. It's embedded in our muscle memories. It's carved indelibly into our DNA. It may be vestigial, but it's there. Our heartland.

Epilogue

⌒

And yet at some point in this potted history, the wilds ceased to be a place in which women ventured freely and fearlessly. We were encouraged to make our outdoor home in the security of a garden or to take exercise by strolling in the peopled safety of an urban park. The wilds became an outlet for male adventure, courage, conquest. A space where men could exert their physicality and prowess. Whether they were climbing mountains, laying snares, stalking stags, shooting hares, poaching deer, fishing, measuring, surveying, axing trees, or merely strolling in the manner of Rousseau et al., the landscape beyond the garden was male.

But dig a bit, and up pop hundreds of women who refused to be sundered from their heartland, who refused to be intimidated by the newly emptied countryside or the threat of male violence or the fear of falling or the loss of reputation.

All of these profoundly modern women are exemplars. By living and walking with audacity, they give us licence to do the same. By their example they give us permission, inspiration, and the confidence to do as they did. To climb mountains. To backpack for days on end. To stroll solo. To sleep beneath the stars. To walk at night. To embrace wind, rain, heat, cold. To live alongside uncertainty, fear, and the additional complications of the female body. To find the wildness buried in the hinterland of ourselves.

Their gifts to us were not only their writings and their art but their lives. They are the mothers of us all.

Acknowledgments

I'd like to thank the following: the Estate of Nan Shepherd for permission to quote from Shepherd's unpublished letters and notebook, and *The Living Mountain*; the British Library for permission to quote from the unpublished memoir of Mathilde Blind; the National Library of Wales for permission to quote from the unpublished notebooks and letters of Gwen John.

This book was built with the expertise and help of numerous institutions. I'd like to thank the following for their unstinting help: the London Library, the National Library of Wales, the National Library of Scotland, the British Library, the University of East Anglia Library, the University of Nottingham Library, Gladstone's Library, the Library and Archive Reading Rooms at Tate Britain, the Georgia O'Keeffe Research Center and Archives, the Amarillo Museum of Art, and the Panhandle-Plains Historical Museum.

I'd like to thank the Dora Maar House and the Nancy B. Negley Artists Residency Program for its generous fellowship which allowed me to work intensively on the "French" sections of this book while also exploring the walks of Simone de Beauvoir, with extended thanks to Gwen Strauss for her support.

I am also indebted to the many individuals who gave so generously of their time and expertise. In particular I'd like to thank Charlotte Peacock, Erlend Clouston, Professor Amy Von Lintel, Alex Gregory, Professor Maggie Humm, Charlotte Batson, Simon Greaves, Margaret Fuller, Carol Purkiss, Meredith McKinney, Sharon Galant, and Thomasin Chinnery. For their extraordinary faith in this book (among other things), I wish to thank my agents: Rachel Mills and Alexandra Cliff in London; Stuart Krichevsky and Laura Usselman in New York. And of course, my publishers for their unstinting support: Lisa Highton and her team at Two Roads and Craig Popelars and Masie Cochran at Tin House.

As ever, I owe a debt of gratitude to the meticulous research of numerous scholars, in particular the biographers of Frieda Lawrence, Gwen John, Daphne du Maurier, Nan Shepherd, Simone de Beauvoir, Georgia O'Keeffe, and Emma Gatewood. Without their diligence and vim, this book would not exist. I would also like to thank Ann Prideaux for her blogs on Clara Vyvyan.

I'd like to thank the friends who walked and talked with me throughout the gestation and duration of this book: Philippa Aylmer, Alice Burnett, Clare Pooley, Annie Harris, Caroline Graham, Camille Bann, Susan Saunders, Mandy Durham, Nina Oden, Kate Lowe, Amy Robson, Duncan Minshull, Emma Robertshaw, and Rhiannon Jones.

A special mention must go to my father, who kindled my love of walking, and who died, suddenly and unexpectedly, just before the publication of this book. I miss him every day. A second special mention goes to my mother, who showed me how to confront an emptying house: when I left home aged eighteen, she took off in her battered car—having just learnt to drive—crossing Europe in search of forgotten and abandoned gardens for her own debut book.

Finally, my family—Matthew, Imogen, Bryony, Saskia, and Hugo. Thank you for being such splendid adventurers and walking companions, now and always.

Three days into my River Thames walk, COVID-19 struck and the world reeled, lurched, paused, shifted. As I write this, much of the world is in lockdown, with many of us confined to our homes. Women have always been disproportionately susceptible to many of the *causes* of poor mental health, from domestic violence to the burden of caring for others—many of which came to the fore during the pandemic. Unsurprisingly, women typically suffer more anxiety and depression, and early studies suggest that the collateral damage of COVID-19 on female mental health could be formidable.

A research report[1] recently landed on my desk showing that walking in rural or remote locations for either full or multiple days frequently enables women to go through processes of "psychological transformation" and "emotional rescue and restoration." Just as it did for the women in this book.

I hope you too feel sufficiently emboldened and inspired to find a route of your own.

Bibliography

Bair, Deirdre. *Parisian Lives: Samuel Beckett, Simone de Beauvoir, and Me: A Memoir*. London: Atlantic, 2020.

———. *Simone de Beauvoir: A Biography*. New York: Touchstone, 1990.

Barson, Tanya, ed. *Georgia O'Keeffe*. London: Tate, 2016.

Beauvoir, Simone de. *Force of Circumstance*. Translated by Richard Howard. London: Penguin, 1965.

———. *Letters to Sartre*. Translated and edited by Quintin Hoare. New York: Arcade, 2012.

———. *Memoirs of a Dutiful Daughter*. Translated by James Kirkup. London: Penguin, 1963.

———. *The Prime of Life*. Translated by Peter Green. London: Penguin, 1973.

———. *The Second Sex*. Translated by Constance Borde and Sheila Malovany-Chevallier. London: Vintage, 2011.

———. *She Came to Stay*. Translated from the French *L'Invitée*, by Yvonne Moyse and Roger Senhouse. London: Harper Perennial, 2006.

Benke, Britta. *O'Keeffe*. Cologne, Germany: Taschen, 1995.

Birkett, Dea. *Off the Beaten Track: Three Centuries of Women Travellers*. London: National Portrait Gallery, 2004.

Borzello, Frances. *A World of Our Own: Women as Artists*. London: Thames & Hudson, 2000.

Byrne, Janet. *A Genius for Living: A Biography of Frieda Lawrence*. New York: HarperCollins, 1995.

Bibliography

Carlson, Paul H., and John T. Becker. *Georgia O'Keeffe in Texas: A Guide.* College Station, TX: State House Press, 2012.

Chitty, Susan. *Gwen John 1876–1939.* London: Hodder & Stoughton, 1981.

Christy, Bayard H. *Going Afoot: A Book on Walking.* South Yarra, Australia: Leopold Classic Library, 2015.

Damrosch, Leo. *Jean-Jacques Rousseau: Restless Genius.* New York: Mariner, 2007.

Drohojowska-Philp, Hunter. *Full Bloom: The Art and Life of Georgia O'Keeffe.* New York: W. W. Norton, 2004.

Du Maurier, Daphne. *The Birds and Other Stories.* London: Virago, 2004.

Forster, Margaret. *Daphne du Maurier.* London: Arrow, 1994

Foster, Alicia. *Gwen John.* London: Tate, 2015.

Glendon, Mary Ann. "Les lettres inedites de Marie-Thérèse Le Vasseur." *Columbia: A Journal of Literature and Art* 18/19 (1993): 165–72.

Godwin, Fay, and Shirley Toulson. *The Drovers' Roads of Wales.* London: Wildwood House, 1977.

Götsch-Trevelyan, Katharine. *Unharboured Heaths: Reminiscences of Canada.* London: Selwyn & Blount, 1934.

Green, Martin. *The Von Richthofen Sisters: The Triumphant and the Tragic Modes of Love.* Albuquerque: University of New Mexico Press, 1974.

Greenough, Sarah, ed. *My Faraway One: Selected Letters of Georgia O'Keeffe and Alfred Stieglitz,* Vol. 1. New Haven, CT: Yale University Press, 2011.

Grunfeld, Frederic V. *Rodin: A Biography.* New York: Da Capo, 1998.

Hesp, Anneke. *Walking with Simone de Beauvoir.* Privately published, 2015.

Holroyd, Michael. *Augustus John: The New Biography.* London: Vintage, 1997.

Humble, Kate. *Thinking on My Feet: The Small Joy of Putting One Foot in Front of Another.* London: Octopus, 2018.

Jebb, Miles. *Walkers.* London: Constable, 1985.

John, Augustus. *Chiaroscuro: Fragments of Autobiography.* London: Jonathan Cape, 1952.

John, Rebecca, and Michael Holroyd, eds. *The Good Bohemian: The Letters of Ida John.* London: Bloomsbury, 2017.

Kirkpatrick, Kate. *Becoming Beauvoir: A Life.* London: Bloomsbury, 2019.

Langdale, Cecily, and David Fraser Jenkins. *Gwen John: An Interior Life.* New York: Rizzoli, 1986.

Lanzmann, Claude. *The Patagonian Hare: A Memoir.* New York: Farrar, Straus and Giroux, 2012.

Lawrence, D. H. *Sons and Lovers.* London: Penguin, 1948. First published 1913.

———. *The Rainbow.* London, Penguin, 2007. First published 1915.

———. *Twilight in Italy.* New York: B. W. Huebsch, 1916.

———. *Women in Love.* London: Penguin, 1960. First published 1921.

Lawrence, Frieda. *And the Fullness Thereof.* Included in Tedlock's *The Memoirs and Correspondence* (see below)

———. *The Memoirs and Correspondence.* Edited by E. W. Tedlock Jr. New York: Knopf, 1964.

———. *"Not I, but the Wind."* London: Granada Publishing, 1983.

Laws, Bill. *Byways, Boots & Blisters: A History of Walkers & Walking.* Stroud, England: The History Press, 2009.

Leng, Flavia. *Daphne du Maurier: A Daughter's Memoir.* Edinburgh: Mainstream Publishing, 1995.

Lisle, Laurie. *Portrait of an Artist: A Biography of Georgia O'Keeffe.* New York: Washington Square Press, 1997.

Lloyd-Morgan, Ceridwen, ed. *Gwen John: Letters and Notebooks.* London: Tate, 2004.

Lucas, Robert. *Frieda Lawrence: A Biography.* London: Secker & Warburg, 1973.

Maathai, Wangari. *Unbowed: My Autobiography.* London: Arrow, 2008.

Malchik, Antonia. *A Walking Life: Reclaiming Our Health and Our Freedom One Step at a Time.* New York: Da Capo, 2019.

Marples, Morris. *Shanks's Pony: A Study of Walking.* London: J. M. Dent, 1959.

McKinney, Meredith. *Travels with a Writing Brush: Classical Japanese Travel Writing from the Manyōshū to Bashō.* London: Penguin, 2019.

Messinger, Lisa Mintz. *Georgia O'Keeffe.* London: Thames & Hudson, 2001.

Minshull, Duncan. *Beneath My Feet: Writers on Walking.* London: Notting Hill Editions, 2019.

———. *While Wandering: A Walking Companion.* London: Vintage, 2014.

Bibliography

Montgomery, Ben. *Grandma Gatewood's Walk: The Inspiring Story of the Woman Who Saved the Appalachian Trail.* Chicago: Chicago Review Press, 2016.

Morris, Mary, with Larry O'Connor, eds. *The Virago Book of Women Travellers.* London: Virago, 1996.

Nichols, Wallace J. *Blue Mind: How Water Makes You Happier, More Connected and Better at What You Do.* London: Abacus, 2014.

O'Mara, Shane. *In Praise of Walking: The New Science of How We Walk and Why It's Good for Us.* London: Penguin, 2019.

Peacock, Charlotte. *Into the Mountain: A Life of Nan Shepherd.* Cambridge: Galileo, 2017.

Peters, Sarah Whitaker. *Becoming O'Keeffe: The Early Years.* New York: Abbeville Press, 1991.

Roe, Sue. *Gwen John: A Life.* London: Vintage, 2001.

Robinson, Roxana. *Georgia O'Keeffe: A Life.* London: Bloomsbury, 1991.

Rosnay, Tatiana de. *Manderley Forever: The Life of Daphne du Maurier.* London: Allen and Unwin, 2017.

Rousseau, Jean-Jacques. *Confessions.* Translated by Peter France. Cambridge: Cambridge University Press, 1987. First published 1782.

———. *Emile, or Education.* Translated by Barbara Foxley. London: Penguin, 1991. First published 1763.

Sagner, Karin. *Women Walking: Freedom, Adventure, Independence.* New York: Abbeville Press, 2017.

Sarton, May. *Journal of a Solitude.* New York: W. W. Norton, 1993.

Selhub, Eva M., and Alan C. Logan. *Your Brain on Nature: The Science of Nature's Influence on Your Health, Happiness, and Vitality.* London: Collins, 2014.

Seymour-Jones, Carole. *A Dangerous Liaison.* London: Century, 2008.

Shepherd, Nan, *The Grampian Quartet: The Quarry Wood, The Weatherhouse, A Pass in the Grampians, The Living Mountain.* Edinburgh: Canongate, 1996.

———. *In the Cairngorms.* Cambridge: Galileo, 2018.

———. *The Living Mountain.* Edinburgh: Canongate, 2011.

———. *Wild Geese.* Edited by Charlotte Peacock. Cambridge: Galileo, 2018.

Solnit, Rebecca. *Wanderlust: A History of Walking.* London: Granta, 2014.

Squires, Michael. *D. H. Lawrence and Frieda: A Portrait of Love and Loyalty.* London: Andre Deutsch, 2008.

Bibliography

Squires, Michael, and Lynn K. Talbot. *Living at the Edge: A Biography of D. H. Lawrence & Frieda von Richthofen*. London: Robert Hale, 2002.

Storr, Anthony. *Solitude*. London: HarperCollins, 1997.

Strayed, Cheryl. *Wild: A Journey from Lost to Found*. London: Atlantic, 2013.

Tamboukou, Maria. *Nomadic Narratives, Visual Forces: Gwen John's Letters and Paintings*. New York: Peter Lang Publishing, 2010.

Taubman, Mary. *Gwen John*. London: Scolar Press, 1985.

Thomas, Alison. *Portraits of Women: Gwen John and Her Forgotten Contemporaries*. Cambridge: Polity Press, 1994.

Toulson, Shirley, *The Country of Old Age: A Personal Adventure in Time*. London: Hodder & Stoughton, 1998.

———. *East Anglia: Walking the Ley Lines and Ancient Tracks*. London: Wildwood House, 1979.

Trevelyan, Katharine. *Fool in Love*. London: Gollancz, 1962.

———. *Through Mine Own Eyes: The Autobiography of a Natural Mystic*. Whitefish, MT: Kessinger, 2010.

———. *See also* Götsch-Trevelyan, Katharine.

Van der Kolk, Bessel. *The Body Keeps the Score: Mind, Brain and Body in the Transformation of Trauma*. New York: Penguin, 2015.

Von Lintel, Amy. *Georgia O'Keeffe: Watercolors 1916–1918*. Santa Fe, NM: Radius Books and Georgia O'Keeffe Museum, 2016.

———. *Georgia O'Keeffe's Wartime Texas Letters*. College Station: Texas A&M University Press, 2020.

Vyvyan, C. C. *Arctic Adventure*. London: Transatlantic Books, 1961. Republished as *The Ladies, the Gwich'in, and the Rat: Travels on the Athabasca, Mackenzie, Rat, Porcupine, and Yukon Rivers in 1926*. Edited by I. S. MacLaren and Lisa N. LaFramboise. Edmonton: University of Alberta Press, 1998.

———. *Down the Rhône on Foot*. London: Peter Owen, 1955.

———. *Journey up the Years*. London: Peter Owen, 1966.

———. *On Timeless Shores: Journeys in Ireland*. London: Peter Owen, 1957.

———. *Roots and Stars*. London: Peter Owen, 1962.

———. *Temples and Flowers: A Journey to Greece*. London: Peter Owen, 1955.

Williams, Florence. *The Nature Fix: Why Nature Makes Us Happier, Healthier, and More Creative*. New York: W. W. Norton, 2017.

———. *The 3-Day Effect*. Read by the author. Audible Original, 2019.

Winn, Raynor. *The Salt Path*. London: Michael Joseph, 2018.

Wohlleben, Peter. *The Hidden Life of Trees: What They Feel, How They Communicate: Discoveries from a Secret World*. Translated by Jane Billinghurst. London: William Collins, 2017.

———. *Walks in the Wild: A Guide through the Forest*. Translated by Ruth Ahmedzai Kemp. London: Rider, 2017.

Wright, Susan. *Georgia O'Keeffe: An Eternal Spirit*. New York: Todtri, 1996.

Notes

Introduction

1. Rebecca Solnit, *Wanderlust: A History of Walking* (London: Granta, 2014), 233.

In the Beginning

2. All quotations from Jean-Jacques Rousseau, *Emile, or Education*, trans. Barbara Foxley (London: Penguin, 1991), with the exception of "Everything is good as it leaves etc" which my father knew from the original, "Tout est bien sortant les mains de l'Auteur des choses, tout dégénère entre les mains de l'homme."

3. Jean-Jacques Rousseau, *The Confessions*, trans. J. M. Cohen (London: Penguin, 1953), 157.

4. Mary Ann Glendon, "Les lettres inedites de Marie-Thérèse Le Vasseur," *Columbia: A Journal of Literature and Art* 18/19 (1993): 165–72.

In Search of Freedom: Frieda von Richthofen

Quotes attributed to Frieda Lawrence but not footnoted are taken from her own writings: "Not I, but the Wind" *and* Frieda Lawrence: The Memoirs and Correspondence, *ed. E. W. Tedlock (see bibliography).*

1. D. H. Lawrence, "The Crucifix across the Mountains," in *Twilight in Italy* (New York: B. W. Huebsch, 1916), 3–4.

2. Frieda Lawrence, *"Not I, but the Wind,"* (London: Granada Publishing, 1983), 31.

339

3. Frieda Lawrence, *"Not I, but the Wind,"* 42.

4. Clemens G. Arvay, *The Biophilia Effect: A Scientific and Spiritual Exploration of the Healing Bond Between Humans and Nature* (Boulder, CO: Sounds True, 2018).

5. Frieda Lawrence, *"Not I, but the Wind,"* 31.

6. D. H. Lawrence, "Pan in America," in *Phoenix: The Posthumous Papers of D. H. Lawrence*, ed. Edward D. McDonald (London: Heinemann, 1936), 25.

7. D. H. Lawrence, "Whistling of Birds," in *Phoenix: The Posthumous Papers of D. H. Lawrence*, ed. Edward D. McDonald (London: Heinemann, 1936), 6.

8. D. H. Lawrence, *The Rainbow* (London: Penguin, 1915), 287.

9. "Leg Exercise Is Critical to Brain and Nervous System Health," *Neuroscience News*, May 23, 2018, https://neurosciencenews.com/leg -exercise-brain-health-9118.

10. Friedrich Nietzsche, *Twilight of the Idols*, trans. Duncan Large (Oxford: Oxford Classics, 2009), 9.

11. D. H. Lawrence to Edward Garnett, April 8, 1912, in *The Collected Letters of D. H. Lawrence*, vol. 1, ed. Harry T. Moore (London: Heinemann, 1962), 137.

12. Frieda Lawrence, *"Not I, but the Wind,"* 53.

13. For more on awe, see Florence Williams, *The Nature Fix: Why Nature Makes Us Happier, Healthier, and More Creative* (New York: W. W. Norton, 2017), 187–201.

14. Frieda Lawrence, *"Not I, but the Wind,"* 48.

15. All quotations from D. H. Lawrence, "Hymns in a Man's Life," in *A Selection from Phoenix*, ed. A. A. H. Inglis (London, Penguin, 1971), 19–24.

16. Frieda Lawrence, *"Not I, but the Wind,"* 48.

17. Barbara Weekley Barr, *Memoir of D. H. Lawrence*, from *D. H. Lawrence: Novelist, Poet, Prophet*, ed. Stephen Spender (London: Weidenfeld and Nicolson, 1973), 8–36.

18. D. H. Lawrence, "Whistling of Birds," in *Reflections on the Death of a Porcupine and Other Essays* (Cambridge: Cambridge University Press, 1988), 24.

19. Frieda Lawrence, *"Not I, but the Wind,"* 98.

20. Shirley Toulson, *The Country of Old Age: A Personal Adventure in Time* (London: Hodder & Stoughton, 1998).

In Search of Self and Solitude: Gwen John

Quotes attributed to Gwen John but not footnoted are taken from her letters and notebooks (archived at the National Library of Wales) or from the two biographies of her (Chitty and Roe, see bibliography).

1. Quoted in Michael Holroyd, *Augustus John: The New Biography* (London: Vintage, 1997), 49.

2. Gwen John to Ursula Tyrwhitt, in Sue Roe, *Gwen John: A Life*, (London: Vintage, 2002), 118.

3. Quoted in Susan Chitty, *Gwen John 1876–1939* (London: Hodder & Stoughton, 1981), 56.

4. Mrs. Aubrey Le Blond, *Day In, Day Out* (London: John Lane, the Bodley Head, 1928), 90.

5. Bessel van der Kolk, *The Body Keeps the Score: Mind, Brain and Body in the Transformation of Trauma* (New York: Penguin, 2015), 2.

6. Karlen Lyons-Ruth and Deborah Jacobvitz, "Attachment Disorganization: Unresolved Loss, Relational Violence, and Lapses in Behavioral and Attentional Strategies," in *Handbook of Attachment: Theory, Research, and Clinical Applications*, ed. Jude Cassidy and Phillip R. Shaver (New York: Guilford Press, 1999), 520–54, https://psycnet.apa.org/record/1999-02469-023.

7. Ida John to her mother, 1898, quoted in *The Good Bohemian: The Letters of Ida John*, ed. Rebecca John and Michael Holroyd (London: Bloomsbury, 2017), 69.

8. Gwen John to John Quinn, quoted in Maria Tamboukou, "Farewell to the Self: Between the Letter and the Self-Portrait," *Life Writing* 12, no. 1 (June 25, 2013): 75–91.

9. Augustus John, quoted in Tamboukou, "Farewell to the Self."

10. One example of a study that finds daughters are twice as likely as sons to care for ageing parents: Angelina Grigoryeva, presentation to the American Sociological Association, August 2014, https://www.asanet.org/press-center/press-releases/daughters-provide-much-elderly-parent-care-they-can-sons-do-little-possible.

11. All quotations in this passage from Gwen's letters in the Gwen John Collection at the National Library of Wales, or reproduced in Chitty, *Gwen John 1876–1939.*

12. Flora Thompson, *Lark Rise to Candleford* (London: Oxford University Press, 1939), 8.

13. Frieda Weekley to Otto Gross, reproduced in John Turner, et al. "The Otto Gross—Frieda Weekley Correspondence: Transcribed, Translated, and Annotated," *The D. H. Lawrence Review* 22, no. 2 (Summer 1990): 137–227.

14. Mathilde Blind (unpublished manuscript, 1862), British Library.

15. Mary Eyre, *Over the Pyrenees into Spain* (London: Bentley, 1865).

16. Odette Keun, *I Discover the English* (London: John Lane, the Bodley Head, 1934), 192.

17. All quotes from Tove Jansson, *Letters from Tove*, ed. Boel Westin and Helen Svensson (Sort of Books, 2020), 84–85.

18. We may feel safer in the city but the statistics suggest we're actually safer in the country. In the UK the rate of sexual offences in predominantly rural areas was 2.3 per 1,000 population, compared with 2.7 per 1,000 population in predominantly urban areas (2019/20 stats).

19. Simone de Beauvoir, *The Prime of Life*, trans. Peter Green (London: Penguin, 1973), 93.

20. Mary Lee Settle, *Turkish Reflections: A Biography of a Place* (New York: Touchstone, 1992), 212.

21. Sue Roe, *Gwen John: A Life* (London: Vintage, 2001), 14. Attributed to Augustus John.

22. Jeanne Foster to John Quinn, quoted in Roe, *Gwen John: A Life*, 219.

23. Antony Gormley, quoted in Sarah Lea, "Antony Gormley: Body and Soul," *Royal Academy Magazine*, September 2019, 46.

24. Jean-Jacques Rousseau, *The Confessions*, trans. J. Cohen (London: Penguin 1973, first published 1782), 167.

25. Gwen John to Ursula Tyrwhitt, 1904, quoted in Roe, *Gwen John: A Life*, 43.

26. Ida John to Gwen John, quoted in *The Good Bohemian: The Letters of Ida John*, ed. Rebecca John and Michael Holroyd (London: Bloomsbury, 2017).

27. Chitty, *Gwen John 1876–1939*, 152.

28. Roe, *Gwen John*, 181–90.

29. Roe, *Gwen John*, 300.

30. Chitty, *Gwen John: 1876–1939*, 197.

31. Mireia Gascon et al., "Outdoor Blue Spaces, Human Health and Well-Being: A Systematic Review of Quantitative Studies," *International Journal of Hygiene and Environmental Health* 220, no. 8 (November 2017): 1207–21.

32. Wallace J. Nichols, *Blue Mind: How Water Makes You Happier, More Connected and Better at What You Do* (London: Abacus, 2014), 155.

33. Willa Cather, *Willa Cather in Europe: Her Own Story of the First Journey* (Lincoln: University of Nebraska Press, 1956), 159.

34. Cecily Langdale and David Fraser Jenkins, *Gwen John: An Interior Life* (New York: Rizzoli, 1986), 36.

The Weight of Complexity: Clara Vyvyan and Daphne du Maurier

Quotes attributed to Clara Vyvyan but not footnoted are taken from her own writings, with most from Down the Rhône on Foot, Journey up the Years, Arctic Adventure, *and* Temples and Flowers *(see bibliography).*

1. Karin Arndt, "The Fear of Being Alone," *Psychology Today*, April 8, 2018, https://www.psychologytoday.com/gb/blog/hut-her-own/201804/the-fear-being-alone.

2. Interview from A. A. Prideaux, www.aaprideaux.com/general/lady-clara-coltman-vyvyan-1885-1976-aka-c-c-rogers.

3. Daphne du Maurier to Oriel Malet, in *Letters from Menabilly: Portrait of a Friendship*, ed. Oriel Malet (Lanham, MD: M. Evans, 1992), 29.

4. Thomas L. Friedman, "Cellphones, Maxi-Pads and Other Life-Changing Tools," *New York Times*, April 6, 2007, https://www.nytimes.com/2007/04/06/opinion/06friedman.html.

5. Letter from Daphne du Maurier to Sheila Hodges, in Sheila Hodges, "Editing Daphne du Maurier," *Women's History Review* 11, no. 2 (2002): 293–308.

6. Frieda Lawrence, *"Not I, but the Wind"* (London: Granada Publishing, 1983), 131.

7. C. C. Vyvyan, *Journey up the Years* (London: Peter Owen, 1966), 153–54.

8. C. C. Vyvyan, *On Timeless Shores: Journeys in Ireland* (London: Peter Owen, 1957), 11; and *Down the Rhône on Foot* (London: Peter Owen, 1955), 177.

9. All quotations in this passage from C. C. Vyvyan, *Arctic Adventure* (London: Transatlantic Books, 1961), and Clara C. Rogers, "The Rat River," *Geographical Journal* 73, no. 5 (May 1929), 447–52.

10. Lionel Trilling, "The Situation of the American Intellectual at the Present Time," in *A Gathering of Fugitives* (Boston: Beacon Press, 1956), 60.

11. Werner Herzog, *Of Walking in Ice* (London: Vintage, 2014), 5.

12. All quotations in this passage from Nan Shepherd, *The Living Mountain* (Edinburgh: Canongate, 2011), 14.

13. Tohoku University, "Walking Together: Personal Traits and First Impressions Affects Step Synchronization," *ScienceDaily*, February 21, 2020, www.sciencedaily.com/releases/2020/02/200221160737.htm.

14. C. C. Vyvyan, *Temples and Flowers: A Journey to Greece* (London: Peter Owen, 1955).

In Search of Being and Meaning: Nan Shepherd

*Quotes attributed to Nan Shepherd but not endnoted are from her biography (*Into the Mountain, *Charlotte Peacock) or—more often—from Shepherd's own work: namely her letters and notebooks (those archived at the National Library of Scotland),* The Grampian Quartet, The Living Mountain, Wild Geese, *and* In the Cairngorms *(see bibliography).*

1. Nan Shepherd, *The Living Mountain* (Edinburgh:Canongate, 2011), 7.

2. Shepherd's words are: "Suddenly the work is there, bursting out of its own ripeness . . . life has exploded, sticky and rich and smelling oh so good." Letter to Barbara Balmer, January 15, 1981, quoted in Charlotte Peacock, *Into the Mountain: A Life of Nan Shepherd* (Cambridge: Galileo, 2017), 258.

3. Virginia Nicholson, *Singled Out: How Two Million Women Survived without Men after the First World War* (London: Penguin, 2008), 177.

4. Nicholson, *Singled Out.*

5. Nicholson, *Singled Out*, 70.

6. Simone de Beauvoir, *The Second Sex*, trans. Constance Borde and Sheila Malovany-Chevallier (London: Vintage, 2011), 155.

7. Quoted in Peacock, *Into the Mountain*, 128.

8. Several of Lawrence's novels were found in Shepherd's library, carefully inscribed with her name. Georgia O'Keeffe had a full collection of Lawrence's works; Gwen John was sent his novels by her friends; and Simone de Beauvoir wrote a stinging chapter of *The Second Sex* on Lawrence and his phallocentric worldview.

9. Robert Macfarlane, introduction to *The Living Mountain*, by Shepherd, xiv.

10. The themes of motherhood and children run like glittering threads throughout Shepherd's notebook, letters, and novels. Among her remaining possessions are several notebooks in which she handwrote notes on the development of a neighbour's child, Sheila, and then Sheila's own children, to whom she became a very close friend, a sort of semi-adopted grandmother. (Erlend Clouston—semi-adopted grandson of Shepherd and now executor of her estate—and Charlotte Peacock, interviews with author, December 18, 2019, and May 3, 2019.)

11. Anne Brontë, "Dreams," *Brontë Poems*, ed. Arthur C. Benson (London: Smith, Elder, 1915), 290–91. All poems are in Shepherd's unpublished notebook, "Gleanings," National Library of Scotland.

12. Peacock, *Into the Mountain*, 103.

13. Erlend Clouston, interview with author, December 18, 2019.

14. Nan Shepherd to Jessie Kesson, quoted in Peacock, *Into the Mountain*, 141.

15. Nan Shepherd, *The Burning Glass*, 1921, reproduced in *Wild Geese*, ed. Charlotte Peacock (Cambridge: Galileo, 2018), 78.

16. Nan Shepherd to Lyn Irvine, June 25, 1957, St. John's Library/GB275/NewmanL/ShepherdN/3. This was the view from the house where her family took their holidays, just outside Kingussie.

17. Robert Macfarlane, foreword to *In the Cairngorms*, by Nan Shepherd (Cambridge: Galileo, 2018), xv.

18. John E. Costello, *John Macmurray: A Biography* (Edinburgh: Floris, 2002), 217–18.

19. Costello, *John Macmurray*, 214.

20. Betty Macmurray, "Now and Then" (unpublished manuscript, quoted in Peacock, ibid., and discussed during interviews and correspondence with Peacock).

21. Shepherd to Neil Gunn, April 2, 1931, National Library of Scotland.

22. Shepherd, *The Weatherhouse*, in *The Grampian Quartet* (Edinburgh: Canongate, 1996), 10.

23. Gina Rippon, *The Gendered Brain: The New Neuroscience That Shatters the Myth of the Female Brain* (London: Bodley Head, 2019), includes an excellent summary of how the myth of women's inferior navigational abilities has come about, why it's inaccurate, and how it can be remedied.

24. Lewis Grassic Gibbon, review of *A Pass in the Grampians*, by Nan Shepherd, 1933, quoted in Peacock, *Into the Mountain*, 195.

25. Peacock, *Into the Mountain*, 198.

26. Kathryn Aalto, *Writing Wild: Women Poets, Ramblers, and Mavericks Who Shape How We See the Natural World* (Portland, OR: Timber Press, 2020), 76.

27. Adam Watson, *Essays on Lone Trips, Mountain-Craft, and Other Hill Topics* (Rothershorpe, England: Paragon Publishing, 2016), 15.

28. Peacock, *Into the Mountain*.

29. Shepherd to Neil Gunn, quoted in Peacock, *Into the Mountain*, 97.

30. J. P. Watson, R. Gaind, and I. M. Marks, "Prolonged Exposure: A Rapid Treatment for Phobias," *British Medical Journal* 1, no. 5739 (January 1971): 13–15, and examined in more recent studies, i.e., P. Frankland et al., "Facing Your Fears," *Science*, June 15, 2018, https://www.ncbi.nlm.nih.gov/pmc/articles/PMC1794779.

31. Shepherd, *The Living Mountain*, 90.

32. David A. Sinclair, *Lifespan: Why We Age—and Why We Don't Have To* (London: Thorsons, 2019).

33. "Writer of Genius Gave Up," *Aberdeen Evening Express*, December 15, 1976.

34. *The Living Mountain* was included with Shepherd's three novels in a combined reprint titled *The Grampian Quartet* in 1984 (see bibliography).

35. Jim Perrin, "Pennant Melangell, Powys," Country Diary, *Guardian*, October 20, 2007, https://www.theguardian.com/uk/2007/oct /20/ ruralaffairs.comment; quoted on the cover of *The Living Mountain* (Edinbugh: Canongate, 2011).

36. Sarah Stoddart Hazlitt and William Hazlitt, *The Journals of Sarah and William Hazlitt 1822–1831*, ed. William Hallam Bonner (Buffalo, NY: University of Buffalo Press, 1959), 208–51.

37. Professor Stephen Stanfeld, quoted in Harry Wallop, "How Noise Pollution Affects Your Health—It Takes Years Off Your Life," *Times*, June 18, 2019, https://www.thetimes.co.uk/article/noise-pollution-isnt-just-annoying-it-affects-your-health-and-takes-years-off-your-life-q36rn2bvr.

38. Nan Shepherd, "Above Loch Avon," *In the Cairngorms* (Cambridge: Galileo, 2018), 2.

39. Aaron Baggish, quoted in Chrissy Sexton, "The Human Heart Evolved for Endurance, Not for a Sedentary Lifestyle," Earth.com, October 22, 2019, https://www.earth.com/news/human-heart-evolved. Study can be accessed at Robert E. Shave et al., "Selection of Endurance Capabilities and the Trade-Off between Pressure and Volume in the Evolution of the Human Heart," *Proceedings of the National Academy of Sciences of the United States of America* 116, no. 40 (October 1, 2019): 19905–10, https://www.pnas.org/content /116/40/19905/ tab-article-info.

40. Shepherd to Kesson, June 29, 1980, quoted in Peacock, *Into the Mountain*, 255.

In Search of the Body: Simone de Beauvoir

Quotes attributed to Simone de Beauvoir but not footnoted are taken from her own writings, with most from her memoirs (in particular Memoirs of a Dutiful Daughter, The Prime of Life, *and* Force of Circumstance*), her first novel* L'Invitée *(translated into English as* She Came to Stay*), The Second Sex, and her letters, or from Deirdre Bair's biography (see bibliography).*

1. Simone de Beauvoir, *The Prime of Life*, trans. Peter Green (London: Penguin, 1973), 97, 100.

2. Frédéric Gros, *A Philosophy of Walking*, trans. John Howe (London: Verso, 2014)—a book that barely mentions a woman.

3. Beauvoir, *The Prime of Life*, 80.

4. Simone de Beauvoir, quoted in Deirdre Bair, *Simone de Beauvoir: A Biography* (New York: Touchstone, 1990), 171.

5. Beauvoir, *The Prime of Life*, 90.

6. The basket was replaced by a rucksack, which in those days was made of weighty canvas and leather with solid brass buckles.

7. Simone de Beauvoir, *Memoirs of a Dutiful Daughter*, trans. James Kirkup (London: Penguin, 1963), 124–5.

8. A few years later Beauvoir abandoned God and every shred of religious faith, but she never lost her sense of spiritual unity with nature.

9. Bair, *Simone de Beauvoir*, 61.

10. Beauvoir, *Memoirs of a Dutiful Daughter*, 152.

11. Deirdre Bair, *Parisian Lives: Samuel Beckett, Simone de Beauvoir, and Me: A Memoir* (London: Atlantic, 2020), 261.

12. Bair, *Simone de Beauvoir*, 163–64.

13. Beauvoir, *The Prime of Life*, 100.

14. The Sartre-Beauvoir relationship was complicated. There are three theories currently in circulation: that Beauvoir was devoted to Sartre, heterosexual, and rarely strayed; that Beauvoir was as sexually rapacious and salacious as Sartre, preying on her pupils for her own needs; and that Beauvoir's indiscretions were an attempt to curry favour with Sartre in a curiously incestuous, girl-grooming "family" in which she—like everyone else—danced involuntarily to Sartre's tune. Read the biographies and come to your own conclusion.

15. Beauvoir, *Memoirs of a Dutiful Daughter*, 127.

16. Beauvoir, *Memoirs of a Dutiful Daughter*, 162.

17. René Maheu, quoted in Carole Seymour-Jones, *A Dangerous Liaison* (London: Century, 2008), 61.

18. Simone de Beauvoir, *She Came to Stay* (London: Harper Perennial, 2006), 326.

19. Beauvoir, *The Prime of Life*, 100.

20. Bair, *Simone de Beauvoir*, 180.

21. Beauvoir, *The Prime of Life*, 88.

22. Bair, *Simone de Beauvoir*, 180.

23. Beauvoir, *Memoirs of a Dutiful Daughter*, 237.

24. Beauvoir, *The Prime of Life*, 327.

25. Beauvoir, *Memoirs of a Dutiful Daughter*, 307.

26. Simone de Beauvoir, *The Second Sex*, trans. Constance Borde and Sheila Malovany-Chevallier (London: Vintage, 2011), 311, 353–93.

27. Seymour-Jones, *A Dangerous Liaison*, 169.

28. Simone de Beauvoir, *Force of Circumstance*, trans. Richard Howard (London: Penguin, 1965), 134.

29. Seymour-Jones, *A Dangerous Liaison*, 331.

30. Beauvoir, *Force of Circumstance*, 113.

31. Beauvoir, *She Came to Stay*, 143.

32. All quotations in this passage from Claude Lanzmann, *The Patagonian Hare: A Memoir* (New York: Farrar, Straus and Giroux, 2012).

33. Anneke Hesp, *Walking with Simone de Beauvoir* (privately published, 2015, see www.walkingwithhesp.wordpress.com).

34. Bair, *Parisian Lives*, 216.

35. From Elizabeth Austen, "The Girl Who Goes Alone," *The Girl Who Goes Alone* (Seattle, WA: Floating Bridge Press, 2010). "The girl / who goes alone / is always afraid, always negotiating to keep the voices / in her head at a manageable pitch of hysteria."

36. Charlotte Peacock, interview with author, May 3, 2019.

37. Mark Leary, *Understanding the Mysteries of Human Behaviour, The Great Courses*, read by the author, Audible Original, 2013, 12:11.

38. Peter Wohlleben, *Walks in the Wild: A Guide through the Forest*, trans. Ruth Ahmedzai Kemp (London: Rider, 2017), 118.

39. Wohlleben, *Walks in the Wild*, 119.

40. "A History of the Waldensians," Musée Protestant (website), accessed December 19, 2020, https://www.museeprotestant.org/en/notice/a-history-of-the-waldensians.

41. All quotes in this passage from Beauvoir, *The Second Sex*, 377–89.

42. V. Bala Chaudhary et al., "MycoDB, a Global Database of Plant Response to Mycorrhizal Fungi," *Scientific Data* 3, no. 160028 (May 2016), https://doi.org/10.1038/sdata.2016.28.

43. Nguyen Thi Hoai et al., Selectivity of Pinus sylvestris extract and essential oil to estrogen-insensitive breast cancer cells Pinus sylvestris against cancer cells, *Pharmacognosy Magazine* 11, no. 44 (2015): 290–95.

44. Peter Wohlleben, *The Hidden Life of Trees: What They Feel, How They Communicate: Discoveries from a Secret World*, trans. Jane Billinghurst (London: William Collins, 2017), 31–36.

45. Edmund Burke, *A Philosophical Enquiry into the Origin of Our Ideas of the Sublime and Beautiful* (London: F. & C. Rivington, 1803).

46. Jennifer E. Stellar et al., "Positive Affect and Markers of Inflammation: Discrete Positive Emotions Predict Lower Levels of Inflammatory Cytokines," *Emotion* 15, no. 2 (April 2015): 129–33, https://doi.org/10.1037/emo0000033.

47. Rosie Swale, *Winter Wales* (Carmarthen, Wales: Golden Grove, 1989), 41.

48. In fairness, contemporary male walkers write with refreshing honesty about their fears.

49. Beauvoir, *Memoirs of a Dutiful Daughter*, 291.

50. Beauvoir, *The Second Sex*, 355.

51. Beauvoir, *Force of Circumstance*, 674.

52. Nan Shepherd, "Descent from the Cross," *Wild Geese*, ed. Charlotte Peacock (Cambridge: Galileo, 2018), 37.

53. Nan Shepherd to Barbara Balmer, quoted in Charlotte Peacock, *Into the Mountain: A Life of Nan Shepherd* (Cambridge:Galileo, 2017), 258.

In Search of Space: Georgia O'Keeffe

Quotes attributed to Georgia O'Keeffe but not footnoted are taken either from her collected letters or from the many biographies of her (see bibliography), although I relied most heavily on the newest biography, Full Bloom: The Art and Life of Georgia O'Keeffe *by Hunter Drohojowska-Philp, and on the work of Amy Von Lintel (see bibliography).*

1. Etty Hillesum, *Etty: The Letters and Diaries of Etty Hillesum, 1941–1943*, ed. Klaas A. D. Smelik, trans. Arnold J. Pomerans (Cambridge, England: Eerdmans, 2002), 55–56.

2. Quoted in Paul H. Carlson and John T. Becker, *Georgia O'Keeffe in Texas: A Guide* (College Station, TX: State House Press, 2012), 31.

3. Amy Von Lintel, *Georgia O'Keeffe: Watercolors 1916–1918* (Santa Fe, NM: Radius Books and Georgia O'Keeffe Museum, 2016), 132–35.

4. Calvin Tomkins, "Georgia O'Keeffe's Vision: The Painter Considers Her Life and Work," *New Yorker*, March 4, 1974, https://www.newyorker.com/magazine/1974/03/04/the-rose-in-the-eye-looked-pretty-fine.

5. John Matthews, "The Influence of the Texas Panhandle on Georgia O'Keeffe," *Panhandle-Plains Historical Review* 57 (1984): 107–36.

6. Tomkins, "Georgia O'Keeffe's Vision," *New Yorker*.

7. See, for instance, her *Pelvis* series, in which the sky is viewed through the holes in a pelvic bone.

8. See, for example, *From the Plains II* (1954) at the Thyssen-Bornemisza Museum, Madrid.

9. O'Keeffe to Anita Pollitzer, 1916, quoted in *Lovingly, Georgia: The Complete Correspondence of Georgia O'Keeffe and Anita Pollitzer*, ed. Clive Giboire (New York: Touchstone, 1990), 187.

10. O'Keeffe to Alfred Stieglitz, January 5, 1918, in *My Faraway One: Selected Letters of Georgia O'Keeffe and Alfred Stieglitz*, vol. 1, ed. Sarah Greenough (New Haven, CT: Yale University Press, 2011).

11. O'Keeffe to Stieglitz, October 22, 1916, quoted in Von Lintel, *Georgia O'Keeffe's Wartime Texas Letters* (College Station: Texas A&M University Press, 2020), 54.

12. Simone de Beauvoir, *The Second Sex*, trans. Constance Borde and Sheila Malovany-Chevallier (London: Vintage, 2015), 167. Beauvoir writes extensively on male fear of "Mother Earth" after "the coming of patriarchy" and the male need to exploit and control nature.

13. Nan Shepherd, *The Living Mountain* (Edinburgh: Canongate, 2011), 60.

14. King's College London News Centre, "Exposure to Trees, the Sky and Birdsong in Cities Beneficial for Mental Wellbeing," January 16, 2018, https://www.kcl.ac.uk/news/spotlight/exposure-to-trees-the-sky-and-birdsong-in-cities-beneficial-for-mental-wellbeing.

15. Before she died, O'Keeffe left five thousand of their letters to the Beinecke Library at Yale, on condition they remained sealed for twenty years (until 2006). They've since been edited by Sarah Greenough as *My Faraway One: Selected Letters of Georgia O'Keeffe and Alfred Stieglitz*, vol. 1. (New Haven, CT: Yale University Press, 2011).

16. Katharine Trevelyan, *Fool in Love* (London: Gollancz, 1962), 203.

17. Stieglitz to O'Keeffe, August 22, 1917, in Greenough, *My Faraway One*, 183.

18. *Georgia O'Keeffe*, directed by Perry Miller Adato, documentary film in which O'Keeffe is interviewed (PBS, 1977), 55 min.

19. Susan Sontag, "In Plato's Cave," in *On Photography* (New York: Farrar, Straus and Giroux, 1977), 14.

20. Quoted in Roxana Robinson, *Georgia O'Keeffe: A Life* (London: Bloomsbury, 1991), 235, 8.

21. He famously said that when he photographed, he "made love."

22. Quoted in Hunter Drohojowska-Philp, *Full Bloom: The Art and Life of Georgia O'Keeffe* (New York: W. W. Norton, 2004), 297.

23. Drohojowska-Philp, *Full Bloom*, 311.

24. O'Keeffe to Paul Strand, quoted in Drohojowska-Philp, *Full Bloom*, 140.

25. Greenough, *My Faraway One*, 181.

26. Maria Popova, "In Defense of the Fluid Self: Why Anaïs Nin Turned Down a *Harper's Bazaar* Profile," *Brain Pickings*, December 19, 2012, https://www.brainpickings.org/2012/12/19/anais-nin-leo -lerman.

27. O'Keeffe to Dorothy Brett, quoted in Drohojowska-Philp, *Full Bloom*, 326.

28. Greenough, *My Faraway One*, 469.

29. Quoted in Drohojowska-Philp, *Full Bloom*, 329.

30. Quoted in Drohojowska-Philp, *Full Bloom*, 330.

31. O'Keeffe to William Milliken, November 1, 1930, quoted in Britta Benke, *O'Keeffe* (Cologne, Germany: Taschen, 1995), 32.

32. The episode is recounted in all O'Keeffe biographies listed here, including in Drohojowska-Philp, *Full Bloom*, 353.

33. O'Keeffe to Beck Strand, August 1933, quoted in Sharyn R. Udall, "Georgia O'Keeffe and Emily Carr: Health, Nature and the Creative Process" *Woman's Art Journal* 27, no. 1 (2006): 17–25. www.jstor.org/stable/20358067.

34. And, bizarrely, the same sanatorium that had treated Stieglitz's own daughter, Kitty, who—like Zelda—was never to live freely again.

Notes

35. O'Keeffe to Stieglitz, October 31, 1916, quoted in Von Lintel, *Georgia O'Keeffe's Wartime Texas Letters*, 55.

36. O'Keeffe to Paul Strand, 1917, quoted in Drohojowska-Philp, *Full Bloom*, 138.

37. O'Keeffe to Stieglitz, September 26, 1916, quoted in Greenough, *My Faraway One*.

38. Katharine Götsch-Trevelyan, *Unharboured Heaths: Reminiscences of Canada* (London: Selwyn & Blount, 1934), 109.

39. Simone de Beauvoir, *Memoirs of a Dutiful Daughter*, trans. James Kirkup (London: Penguin, 1963), 125.

40. See also *Starlight Night* and *Light Coming on the Plains*, both 1917.

41. Götsch-Trevelyan, *Unharboured Heaths*, 113, 132.

42. O'Keeffe to Jean Toomer, quoted in Drohojowska-Philp, *Full Bloom*, 354.

43. Jack Cowart, *Georgia O'Keeffe: Art and Letters* (National Gallery of Art, 1987), 105.

44. The painting is *A Black Bird with Snow-Covered Red Hills*, 1946.

45. Daniel Catton Rich, *Georgia O'Keeffe: Forty Years of Her Art* (Worcester, MA: Worcester Art Museum, 1960), exhibition catalogue.

46. Ralph Looney, "Georgia O'Keeffe," *Atlantic Monthly*, April 1965, quoted in Drohojowska-Philp, *Full Bloom*, 504.

47. For instance, see Shane O'Mara, *In Praise of Walking: The New Science of How We Walk and Why It's Good for Us* (London: Penguin, 2019); Florence Williams, *The Nature Fix: Why Nature Makes Us Happier, Healthier, and More Creative* (New York: W. W. Norton, 2017); and Eva Selhub and Alan C. Logan, *Your Brain on Nature: The Science of Nature's Influence on Your Health, Happiness, and Vitality* (London: Collins, 2014).

48. O'Keeffe to Anita Pollitzer, September 1915, quoted in Sarah Whitaker Peters, *Becoming O'Keeffe: The Early Years* (New York: Abbeville Press, 1991), 31.

49. C. C. Vyvyan, *Down the Rhône on Foot* (London: Peter Owen, 1955), 177.

50. O'Keeffe to Stieglitz, October 26, 1916, quoted in Von Lintel, *Georgia O'Keeffe's Wartime Texas Letters*, 55.

51. Götsch-Trevelyan, *Unharboured Heaths*, 66, 122.

52. Frieda Lawrence, *"Not I, but the Wind"* (London: Granada Publishing, 1983), 119.

53. The poet Rainer Maria Rilke worked for Rodin at the time when Gwen and Rodin were lovers. This is Rilke's description of Rodin, quoted in David Kleinbard, *The Beginning of Terror: A Psychological Study of Rainer Maria Rilke's Life and Work* (New York: NYU Press, 1995), 166.

54. The full story of Emma Gatewood can be read in Ben Montgomery, *Grandma Gatewood's Walk: The Inspiring Story of the Woman Who Saved the Appalachian Trail* (Chicago: Chicago Review Press, 2016).

55. Friedrich Evertsbusch, quoted in Karin Sagner, *Women Walking: Freedom, Adventure, Independence* (New York: Abbeville Press, 2017), 107.

56. Beauvoir, *The Second Sex*, 483.

57. Drohojowska-Philp, *Full Bloom*, 432.

Epilogue

1. Margarita Nelken, quoted in Elizabeth Munson, "Walking on the Periphery: Gender and the Discourse of Modernization," *Journal of Social History* 36, no. 1 (Autumn 2002): 63–75, http://www.jstor.org / stable/3790566.

2. Yuval Noah Harari, *Sapiens: A Brief History of Humankind* (London: Vintage, 2011), 55.

3. Caroline Davidson, *A Woman's Work Is Never Done: A History of Housework in the British Isles 1650–1950* (London: Chatto & Windus, 1982), 8–18.

4. Flora Thompson, *Lark Rise to Candleford* (London: Oxford University Press, 1939), 8.

Acknowledgements

1. Ralf Buckley and Diane Westaway, "Mental health rescue effects of women's outdoor tourism: A role in COVID-19 recovery," *Annals of Tourism Research*, vol. 85 (2020), https://covid19.elsevierpure.com/en/ publications/mental-health-rescue-effects-of-womens-outdoor-tourism-a-role-in-.

Annabel Abbs-Streets

is an award-winning author and journalist. She writes regularly for a wide range of newspapers and magazines and lives in London, with her husband and four children.